Digital Wellbeing

Dana Rad / Valentina E. Balas /
Vasile Marineanu / Roxana Maier (eds.)

Digital Wellbeing

Implications for Psychological Research

PETER LANG

Bibliographic Information published by the Deutsche Nationalbibliothek
The Deutsche Nationalbibliothek lists this publication in the Deutsche Nationalbibliografie; detailed bibliographic data is available online at http://dnb.d-nb.de.

Library of Congress Cataloging-in-Publication Data
A CIP catalog record for this book has been applied for at the Library of Congress.

ISBN 978-3-631-85278-1 (Print)
E-ISBN 978-3-631-85633-8 (E-PDF)
E-ISBN 978-3-631-85634-5 (EPUB)
E-ISBN 978-3-631-85635-2 (MOBI)
DOI 10.3726/b18489

Peter Lang – Berlin · Bern · Bruxelles · New York · Oxford · Warszawa · Wien

This publication has been peer reviewed.

www.peterlang.com

Table of Contents

List of Contributors

Cornelia Evelina BALAŞ
Aurel Vlaicu University of Arad, Romania, evelinabalas@yahoo.com

Assoc. Prof. Delia BÎRLE, Ph.D.
University of Oradea, Romania, delia.birle@gmail.com

Florinda GOLU
Department of Psychology, University of Bucharest, Romania, florindagolu@yahoo.com

Assist. Prof. Bulbul GUPTA, Researcher
Jamia Hamdard, New Delhi Jamia Hamdard, New Delhi, India, bulbulgup17@gmail.com

Smaranda M. GUŢU
Department of Psychology, University of Bucharest, Romania, smaranda.gutu@drd.unibuc.ro

Torkos HENRIETTA
Faculty of Educational Science, Psychology and Social Sciences, Aurel Vlaicu University of Arad, Romania, torkos_henriette@yahoo.com

Ramona HENTER
Transilvania University of Brasov, Romania, ramona.henter@unitbv.ro

Sonia IGNAT, Ph.D.
Faculty of Educational Sciences, Psychology and Social Sciences, Aurel Vlaicu University of Arad, Romania, soniabudean@yahoo.com

Assist. Prof. Sapna JAIN, Researcher
Jamia Hamdard, New Delhi Jamia Hamdard, New Delhi, India, drsapnajain@jamiahamdard.ac.in

Prof. Gabriela KELEMEN, Ph.D.
Faculty of Educational Science, Psychology and Social Sciences, Aurel Vlaicu University of Arad, Romania, gabriela.kelemen@uav.ro

Assoc. Prof. Roxana MAIER, Ph.D.
Aurel Vlaicu University of Arad, Romania, roxanamaierpsiho@gmail.com

Egerău Anca MANUELA
Faculty of Educational Science, Psychology and Social Sciences, Aurel Vlaicu University of Arad, Romania, anca_petroi@yahoo.com

Coşarbă Editha MARGARETA
Faculty of Educational Science, Psychology and Social Sciences, Aurel Vlaicu University of Arad, Romania, ecoşarbă@yahoo.com

Assist. Prof. Swati MAURYA, Researcher
Jamia Hamdard, New Delhi Jamia Hamdard, New Delhi, India, maurya2026@gmail.com

Alina MICLĂUŞ, Psychologist, MD
Faculty of Educational Sciences, Psychology and Social Sciences, Aurel Vlaicu University of Arad, Romania, alina.miclaus@gmail.com

Assist. Prof. Preeti Sharma NAIR
Bansal College of Engineering, Bhopal, India, preetirajitnair@gmail.com

Assist. Prof. Rajit NAIR
Jagran Lakecity University, Bhopal, India, rajit.nair@jlu.edu.in

Assoc. Prof. Laura Elena NĂSTASĂ, Psychotherapist, Ph.D.
Faculty of Psychology and Education Sciences, Transilvania University of Brasov, Romania, nastasalaura@yahoo.com

Daniela NEAŢA, MD alumni
Aurel Vlaicu University of Arad, Romania, neatadana@yahoo.com

Gabriel-Constantin NICOLA, School Counselor, Ph.D. Student
University of Oradea, Romania, gabi.nicola@yahoo.com

Cristina NICOLAU
Transilvania University of Brasov, Romania, cristina.nicolau@@unitbv.ro

Oana POPA
Faculty of Psychology and Education Sciences, Transilvania University of Brasov, Romania, oana.popa.07.07@gmail.com

Assoc. Prof. Dana RAD, Ph.D.
Faculty of Educational Sciences, Psychology and Social Sciences, Aurel Vlaicu University of Arad, Romania, dana@xhouse.ro

Gavril RAD, Ph.D. Candidate
Faculty of Educational Sciences, Psychology and Social Sciences, Aurel Vlaicu University of Arad, Romania, radgavrilarad@gmail.com

Prof. Alina ROMAN, Ph.D.
Aurel Vlaicu University of Arad, Romania, romanalinafelicia@yahoo.com

Lect. Univ. Dr. Ionel Nicu SAVA, Ph.D.
Universitatea "Andrei Şaguna", Constanţa, Romania, nicusava2004@yahoo.com

Aurelian STOICA, Ph.D.
National Institute for Research and Development in Informatics - ICI Bucharest, Romania, aurelian.stoica@ici.ro

Raluca ZARO, MA Students
University of Oradea, Romania, zaro.raluca@gmail.com

Preface

In today's society, where the development of digital technologies is emerging, it is important to take into consideration the development of the individual well-being when it comes to the engagement with the digital environment. This book represents one of the first scientific attempts to understand how the rapid deployment of digital technologies and their uptake by society has modified our relationships to ourselves, each other, and our environment. As a result, our individual and social well-being is now intimately connected with the state of our information environment and the digital technologies that mediate our interaction with it, which poses pressing ethical questions concerning the impact of digital technologies on our well-being that need to be addressed.

Technology has changed the way people perceive well-being. What is the impact of digital technology on our health, relationships, and society? How do we ensure our own digital well-being? Readers will learn new and established technologies and their impact on society, looking at the positives and negatives of engaging with technology. The book will guide the reader into introduction to the digital society and well-being, considering new and established digital technologies; modern culture and trends; exploration of digital identity; the balance of online and offline activities; consideration of negative behaviors online; strategies and approaches for managing them; and positive uses of technology for health, society, and education.

Digital well-being is a concept used to represent the effect of digital technology and programs on people's mental, physical, social, and emotional health. It is an emerging construct that can be viewed from a multidisciplinary perspective and in various circumstances and scenarios:

- Individual perspective (personal, learning, and job contexts): this includes recognizing and knowing the positive benefits and possible negative aspects of participating in digital practices and being mindful of ways to handle and monitor them to increase well-being.
- Societal or corporate perspective: suppliers of digital platforms, programs, and information have a duty to ensure that they are properly regulated, funded, open, and equal. They will need to motivate and develop capacity among consumers so that anyone who interacts with them is prepared to do so in a way that encourages and/or enhances their well-being.

The online environment allows the individual to create and manage a digital identity; therefore, actively managing one's digital identity and reputation can represent an essential element for a positive digital well-being in today's digital society. Technology has entered in human life with fast speed, neglecting its impact over the mental health and well-being of people digitally connected. Well-being is more demanded whether it is education, marketing, finance, or information technology. This book will provide the effective platform for high quality submissions and stimulate the cutting-edge research discussions about latest trends in enhancing digital well-being.

Dana Rad
Valentina Emilia Balaş
Vasile Mărineanu
Roxana Maier

Dana RAD and Gavril RAD

1 Model of Emergent Digital Misbehavior (EDM) – a Novel Theoretical Framework under the Digital Behavior Change Interventions (DBCI) Paradigm

Abstract: Digital culture has deeply influenced our social, economic, political, and cultural system, characterized by fast and constant technological transition, as people are increasingly interconnected and compelled to reject the past paradigms. It has the potential to turn power relations and interactions from institutions of centralized and hierarchical control to systems of more flexible and independent power. Emergent behavior is the behavior of a system that does not depend on its components, but on its relationships with each other. Thus, the emergent behavior cannot be determined by the analysis of the individual parts of the system. It can only be anticipated, regulated, or operated by knowing the components and their relationship. The main argument for why the emergent behavior becomes difficult to predict resides in the fact that the interactional pattern between systems' elements increases exponentially along with the amount of new input, allowing for a myriad of novel and latent behavioral patterns to emerge. Emergence is considered often to be the outcome of specific interactional patterns. Validation of emergent behavior involves an analysis of behavioral information and the circumstances under which it occurs. Digital emergent behavior refers to the set of behaviors that are occurring under the direct interaction between people and technology. Commitment to health interventions is a requirement for efficiency; this is of vital importance to digital behavior change interventions (DBCIs), meaning interventions that utilize emerging internet technology, smart phones, and electronic sensors. Model of Emergent Digital Misbehavior (EDM) is not intended to offer a definitive meaning; instead, it is conceptualized in terms of a variety of emerging systems shared features. Implications for the new learning process, digital evidence-based interventions, are discussed.

Keywords: Emergent behavior, complex systems in applied psychology, digitalization, emergent digital behavior, and emergent digital misbehavior

1. Introduction

Digital culture has deeply influenced our social, economic, political, and cultural system, characterized by fast and constant technological transition, as people are increasingly interconnected and compelled to reject the past paradigms. It has the potential to turn power relations and interactions from institutions of centralized and hierarchical control to systems of more flexible and independent power. The radical influence of the digital environment not only promotes the globalization of everything but also encourages exponential engagement between people and, in addition, has the capacity to transform ways of acting, thinking, performing, relating to information, knowledge, and learning processes. The digital environment has the ability to expand the involvement of individuals and organizations. Therefore, it becomes more important not just the use of a specific digital environment, such as Twitter, Instagram, Tik Tok, or Facebook, when relating to social media, but rather the overarching concept or ideal of perfect openness, access to information and, in particular, sharing and overcoming the existing barriers.

The social influence of the digital world has an effect on our democracies: applications, networks, technologies, and online environments are "built" and thus create those types of social experiences. More interconnection can improve human behavior, from empathic to violent, by allowing the interactive participant to move from consumerism to engagement.

In addition to transforming the way, we collaborate and connect with each other, our new interfaces often change the way we are as human communicators. Along with the pervasive growth, greater freedom of expression through the anonymity of digital media also raises the exposure of intolerance, violence, and hate speech. Governments would not be able to monitor unrestricted global human activity, although there are major efforts to curb the detrimental side of hyper communication. Focus should therefore be put on educating people, creating positive attitudes toward peace, justice, equality, and the rule of law, and thereby reaffirming how modern systems can be made positive to the human destiny.

2. Digital Emergent Behavior versus Digital Emergent Misbehavior

Systems theory focuses on the components' design, relationship, and interdependence, whereas the complexity theory relates to the nature of the different subsystems and how the sub-level elements of the complex structure influence the system's emergent behavior and result (Amagoh, F., 2016).

Emergent behavior is the behavior of a system that does not depend on its components, but on its relationships with each other. Thus, the emergent behavior cannot be determined by the analysis of the individual parts of the system. It can only be anticipated, regulated, or operated by knowing the components and their relationship. Emergent behavior is also depicted in the scientific literature as emergence or emergent property or "the whole is greater than the sum of the parts".

All structures are made up of individual components. Something sorts all the pieces into a design, a structure. The configuration defines the behavior of the structure. Function analysis is thus a matter of defining the underlying structure of the system and its most critical components. The primary insight into the idea of emerging behavior is that it is the organization of the components, and not the components themselves that makes a major difference.

Examples of components are molecules, machine parts, humans, and territories. Each of them is a structure, and it's built up of several different smaller units. Each of these properties or behaviors is a part of a larger structure and emerge only as they engage in a broader environment. If we are to isolate them and measure the outcome, neither variable will create them by itself. In the theory of integrative mechanisms and complex structures, emergence plays a vital role. Life itself, human intelligence (Hillis, D. W., 1988), and aspects of sustainability in the digital well-being setting are considered as emergent behaviors.

The idea of emergent behavior is particularly important for addressing the sustainability dilemma, since it is the emergent behavior that is the challenge to solve. Currently researchers and policymakers are discussing the sustainability issue as a whole, not examining the underlying framework of the mechanism as a whole. Mostly, they research individual parts or subsystems that are not so essential to root causes. The essence of the philosophy of systems thinking is that the action of a system is an emergent product of its configuration, and not the parts. Problem symptoms are considered emergent behaviors; symptoms can be traced back to various elements of the system. If the nature of a complicated social system is not known, it is impossible to solve the problem, except by trial and error.

The main argument for why the emergent behavior becomes difficult to predict resides in the fact that the interactional pattern between systems' elements increases exponentially along with the amount of new input, allowing for a myriad of novel and latent behavioral patterns to emerge. Emergence is considered often to be the outcome of specific interactional patterns. Negative feedback creates constraints that are being utilized to regulate processes or actions. On the other hand, positive feedback enhances growth, permitting local differences to evolve into global trends.

Negative feedback or balancing feedback happens when a process, system, or procedure output operation is being fed back. This feed-back appears to eliminate output variability, whether induced by input changes or other disturbances.

Although positive feedback appears to lead to chaos by accelerated expansion, oscillation, or disorderly behavior, negative feedback usually encourages equilibrium. Negative feedback helps to facilitate a balance-setting mechanism and decreases the consequences of disturbance. Negative feedback loops can be very efficient and effective in applying the necessary amount of correction at the appropriate moment.

Negative feedback is commonly utilized in electronic and mechanical engineering, as well as in living organisms (Ross Ashby, W., 1957; Ricklefs, R. E., & Miller, G. L., 2000), and can be used in many other scientific domains. Control systems engineering is studying negative feedback systems. Another manner by which relationships contribute to emergent properties is by dual-phase development. The process happens in the case that associations are introduced intermittently, resulting in two phases: in the first step, patterns shape or evolve, and in the second, they are modified or withdrawn. Likewise, it is not possible to establish emergent behavior by providing a sufficient amount of interactions alone; certain interactions may be marginal or insignificant, or may be cancelled.

In certain situations, a large number of interactions may potentially impede the development of fascinating behavior by generating "noise" to abolish new "signals"; new emergent behavior has to be momentarily separated from any other interaction until it achieves sufficient momentum to sustain itself. Emergence is also triggered by the manner in which these associations are organized. Hierarchical structure may contribute to emergent behavior, and yet decentralized organizational systems can also trigger emergent behavior. In certain cases, the system must meet the cumulative degree of complexity, structure, and interaction before the development of emergent behavior.

Strongly related to the emergent properties are the unexpected results and side effects. The element has a specific functionality, but this is not recognized as a global interface sub-function, but instead incorporates an operation whose side effect is linked to global functionality.

The accumulation of side effects of each behavior offers functionality (Goldstein, J., 1999). Thus, the general functionality of a specific emergent design is given by the summing of all collateral effects of each emergent property and functionality.

Let free to govern themselves, groups of human beings seem to create natural order, rather than the chaotic anarchy that is often expected. Human beings are the fundamental elements of social structures that constantly communicate and establish, sustain or untangle reciprocal social ties. The relations in social networks are continually evolving in the light of the continuing reconfiguration of their existence (Luhmann, N., 1995). An order results from a disturbance as a multitude of persons interact: a trend, a decisional process, a procedure, or a shift in direction occurs (Miller, P., 2010).

Emergent norm theory suggests that nontraditional behavior like the collective action is arising in groups of people as an output of the appearance of novel behavioral norms as an output to an adverse situation (Arthur, M. M. L., 2013; Rad, D., & Demeter, E., 2020). In the light of this conceptualization, even mental disorders like PTSD, depressive symptomatology, or anxiety disorder are considered responses to adversity rather than chemical imbalances, seen as a way of working that has developed in an ancient world but does not fit the way people are living nowadays (Syme, K. L., & Hagen, E. H., 2020).

Validation of emergent behavior involves an analysis of behavioral information and the circumstances under which it occurs. Explanation Exploration (EE) was introduced by Gore, R., and Reynolds, P. F. (2008) using semiautomatic model adaptation to gain insight into emergent behaviors, later strengthened by iteratively using protocols for causal inference, exposing the relationships within the model of particular constructs that cause emergent behaviors (Gore, R., & Reynolds, P. F., 2008).

As related to software industry, systems are getting more dynamic, integrated, and globally dispersed, raising the possibility of unintended emergent behavior. Unpredictable systems are impossible to modify and difficult to handle. Artificial intelligence (AI) researchers need improved resources and approaches for predicting, identifying, diagnosing, and optimizing emerging misbehavior, approaches that include analysis into the causes and essence of emergent misbehavior in information systems (Mogul, J. C., 2006).

As for digital psychology domain, further it is designed as a theoretical framework of emergent digital misbehavior. What exactly is a digital behavior? In terms of marketing analysis, digital behavior basically refers to all the digital traces people live when going online, namely what computers they use, the places they visit, the ads they choose to see, the pages they switch to, in general the content they interact with, and in short, their digital behavior signature. Digital behavioral research is a collection of methods and techniques that will offer a detailed look into how users' digital activity is changing moment by moment. Predictive research is a powerful method that may also expose long-term behavioral patterns, allowing behavioral scientists to analyze digital behavior and misbehavior. Digital emergent misbehavior can be defined as an undesired emergent behavior.

Commitment to health interventions is a requirement for efficiency; this is of vital importance to digital behavior change interventions (DBCIs), meaning processes that utilize emerging internet technology, smart phones, and electronic sensors (Yardley, L. et al., 2016). DBCIs represent programs using digital technology for facilitating and sustaining behavioral change, encouraging and preserving well-being (Hekler, E. B. et al., 2016).

DBCIs promote the advancement of well-being by offering help in reality in order to modify particular behaviors under particular circumstances (Riley, W. T., 2011; Patrick, K., et al., 2008). Knowledge about an individual is constantly being used to tailor the care providing services to the particular and frequently evolving individual conditions. A particular DBCI form is "just-in-time" adaptive intervention (JITAI) (Intille, S. S., et al., 2003). JITAI offers assistance to people in just-in-time situations when they are driven to partake in healthier actions, or they are becoming vulnerable to negative behavior (misbehavior) and are responsive to guidance (Nahum-Shani, I., et al., 2016). More broadly, JITAI and DBCI need frameworks that take into account differences in human traits and circumstances and accept that these differences can evolve over time (Hekler, E. B., et al., 2016). Present behavioral theories offer little insight into this form of approach (Riley, W.T., 2011), but the underlying complexity of real behavioral change needs to be addressed (Cole-Lewis H., et al., 2019).

Digital behavior changes initiatives, especially those using pervasive computing technologies, are very promising to enable individuals to improve their behavior. However, most approaches do not take the usual behavior into account and restrict their possible effects. This deficiency is partially motivated by a proliferation of conflicting behavior change models and analytical approaches that do not take into consideration the function of habits. Pinder, C. (2018) underpinned the potential of Dual Process Theory, modern habit theory, and Goal Setting Theory, modeling the way in which people develop and dissolve conducts together to create efficient digital interventions (Pinder, C., et al., 2018), synthesizing them through the Habit Alteration Model, an explanatory structure (Pinder, C., et al., 2018).

Hedin, B., et al. (2019) has been shown that several studies fail to associate interventions with scientific principles or structures, such as the Behavior Change Wheel (Michie, S. et al., 2011; Michie, S. et al., 2014) and the Behavior Change Technique Taxonomy v1 (Michie, S., 2013). Because BCW and BCT are utilized in the domain of well-being enhancement processes, in particular, it becomes important to explore their acting to be able to design sustainable initiatives. One can notice a discrepancy between strategies for well-being and strategies for sustainable interventions. The second deals with consequences that also exist externally, rather than immediate impacts on individuals own well-being. Novel BCT approaches that are more applicable to these forms of behavioral change interventions will need to be added.

3. Model of Emergent Digital Misbehavior

Emergence continues to be a controversial term, being impossible to provide an agreed-by-all definition. Model of Emergent Digital Misbehavior (EDM) is not intended to offer a definitive meaning; instead, it is conceptualized in terms of a variety of emerging systems shared features, and however, the central viewpoint will remain on dynamic emergence and not on static emergence (Abbott, 2006, 2007).

Static emergence is exemplified by emergent properties, like a spider web's durability. Over time the dynamic emergent properties change. As "coming into being" they represent emergent behaviors (Groenewegen, P., Wagnenaar, P., 2006).

Dynamic emergent behavior can be engineered and planned (functionality) or non-designed and unanticipated. Although non-designed, unanticipated behavior can be both beneficial and undesirable, the designed emergent behavior is typically beneficial.

In Fig. 1, it is illustrated the theoretical classification of digital emergent behavioral characteristics, derived from Ferreira et al. (2013) and Iivari, J. (2017).

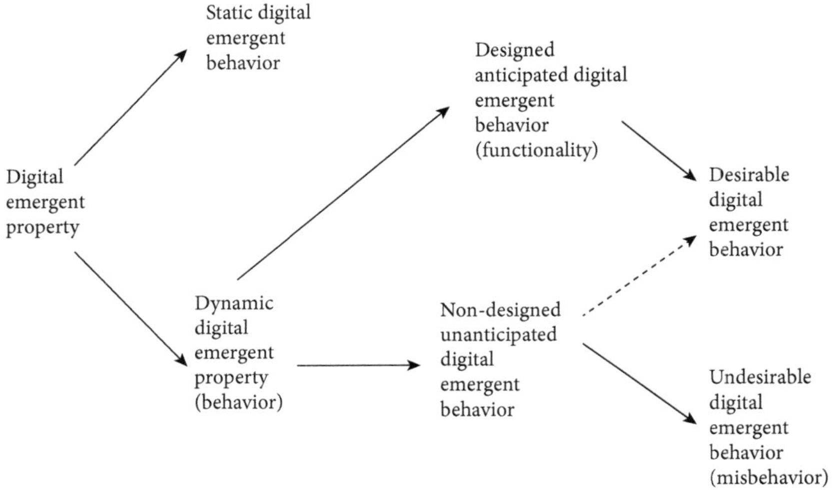

Fig. 1. Classification of digital emergent behavioral properties adapted from Ferreira et al. (2013) and Iivari, J. (2017)

One approach to handle the idea of emergence is to analyze at the features of variables perceived to be emerging: the system's sophistication, its adherence to the context, the learning and adaptation processes, lack of central regulation, and failure to anticipate. Emergency is also correlated with complex systems (Holland, 1999) and specifically complex dynamic systems (Bar-Yam, 1997) that demonstrate complex emergent behavior. In the case of the system interacting with multiple environmental objects at the same time, the behavioral complexity of the system significantly increases. It can therefore be inferred that not only the intrinsic level of complexity, in terms of total quantity of its components and their interdependencies, can lead to emergent behavior, but also the complexity of environmental influences.

Holland (1999) explains how emergent behavior can be shown by an adaptive system controlled by comparatively few and essential laws, indicating that learning should mainly be discussed by any significant emergence study. The author (Holland, 1999) is also associated with the absence of central regulation. The role of centralized control in the operating system may be explored where there is a mechanism that manages the entire system centrally, and the essence of centralized management of processes, particularly when the information system is installed into a decentralized framework. With regard to Stenholm and Nielsen (2019), it may be argued that the direction is toward institutions without coordinated regulation.

In particular, predictability was explored with respect to the reducibility of emergent processes, such as to what degree they can be described with references to low-level structures. The topic was of great concern to philosophers (Chalmers, D. J., 2006; Clayton, P., 2004; Kim, J., 2005, 2006). Chalmers (2006) distinguishes between a strong and a weak emergence: a strong emergence suggests that from a low-level domain an emergent concept emerges. Weak emergence implies that, given the rules governing the low-level system, the details about the phenomenon are unexpected.

When characterizing emergent phenomena, Kim (2005) distinguishes inductive predictability and analytical predictability. The author suggests that one should model new phenomena inductively. Noting that if a system that has a given low-level state L, the emerging phenomenon EM occurs, it can be concluded that a specific system can manifest an emergent phenomenon EM at a certain moment, provided that the low-level S at a specific moment in time is known. Inductive predictability would not mean theoretical predictability in such a way that even maximum knowledge on the low-level structure status does not enable anticipation of the emerging phenomena (Cockshott, P., Michaelson, G., 2007).

As Kim (2006) stated, inductive predictability represents the ability to predict the emergent entity the next period the base appears, after an emergent entity has been observed to appear at the same time as a specific base. Inductive predictability does not require a complete understanding of the structure or how the basis contributes to the emergent. In comparison, theoretical predictability is more rigorous. In the form of the emergence, that would mean that one had a hypothesis such that if one had an interaction between the base and the emergent element, one might foresee how the shift in the base would modulate the emergent element. In other words, it will require a model that could determine the specific emergent that will be around in any given base conditioning (Kirchhoff, M., 2014).

Complex software and information systems appear to arise very spontaneously, as their behavior is typically difficult to forecast because the system's state space is very wide, the system seldom returns to an already visited state, particularly in the case that the system can learn and adjust (Holland, J. H., 1999, Parnas, D. L., 1985).

As a conclusion, following the presented novel model of emergent digital misbehavior, researchers would be equipped with theoretical argumentation for the process of digital behavior change interventions.

4. Implications

We continue to see instructional, formal, and nonformal systems that do not implement emerging innovations into their teaching content subject or techniques in use. These emerging innovations pose an exponential step forward from our typical books, libraries, and educational settings, as well as from universities, colleges, and extracurricular programs. Looking ahead, we can see how unconventional knowledge sources will gradually be viewed as authoritative; as youth become deeper involved in self-drive and peer-based process learning, higher educational institutions can develop into other structures. From static presentation of concepts to dynamical presented information, links in blogs, hypertext, virtual meetings, high-speed video, our technological, and networking developments are shifting our connection to text and the modalities of exchanging knowledge. This rise has an immense effect on our relationship with literacy and language: languages such as tweeting, writing, and uploading are being developed that obey modern rules of expression; young people participate in inventive ways of language; and images increasingly overshadow text and developments of traditional literature.

The shift influences education in relation to utilizers' success and social success. Time when people were merely internet users is gone, and in the new paradigm we are all now social media content producers. Now is the time when someone who is connected to the Internet may impact facts, data, and opinions. For our educational systems, this has many implications, the most important being providing and maintaining student's interest in learning processes, redesigning attention span expectations, and much more.

Individuals experience the content they like to use, interpret it, internalize it, and then send it back to others as stories, enrich it with self-creativity and expertise, and they influence their perception and create meaning. Youth accept less the narratives of professors and are more likely to take lessons and insights on their own (Besso, B., Huber, J., Mompoint-Gaillard, P., & Rohman, S., 2014).

We assume that, from now on, there should be more background for modern methods. In other words, they must be based on a theory of behavior modification that would also decide what the desired action is as well as be properly assessed. It is time to turn from exploratory experiments to more rigorous studies on the possible contribution of interventions to behavioral improvements.

Many of these and other common misbehaviors in our experience were the result of not thoroughly knowing the origins of process problems and choosing the most readily available approach. Not often readily evident is the root cause of a problem and can include answering questions such as:

- *When did the challenge of this process start?*
- *Besides those that are apparent, what variables could have been involved?*
- *To help a positive outcome, should our environment be changed?*

The responses to these questions will contribute to deeper perspectives into the true root cause, providing people with better knowledge from which to generate behavioral resolutions.

References

Amagoh, F. (2016). Systems and Complexity Theories of Organizations. In: Farazmand, A. (eds.), Global Encyclopedia of Public Administration, Public Policy, and Governance. Cham: Springer. doi:10.1007/978-3-319-31816-5_73-1.

Arthur, M. M. L. (2013). Emergent Norm Theory. The Wiley-Blackwell Encyclopedia of Social and Political Movements. Hoboken, NJ: Blackwell Publishing Ltd.

Besso, B., Huber, J., Mompoint-Gaillard, P., & Rohman, S. (2014). Education for Change, Change for Education, A Teacher Manifesto for the 21st Century of the Conference "The professional image and ethos of teachers", April 2014, Council of Europe, Strasbourg http://www.coe.int/t/dg4/education/pestalozzi/Source/Documentation/T21/FinalManifesto_En.pdf

Chalmers, D. J. (2006). Strong and Weak Emergence. In P. Calyton & P. Davis (eds.), The Re-emergence of Emergence: The Emergentist Hypothesis from Science to Religion (pp. 244–256). Oxford: Oxford University Press.

Clayton, P. (2004). Mind and Emergence: From Quantum to Consciousness. Oxford: Oxford University Press.

Cockshott, P., & Michaelson, G. (2007). Are There New Models of Computation: A Reply to Wegner and Eberbach'. Computer Journal, 50(2), 232–247.

Cole-Lewis, H., Ezeanochie, N., & Turgiss, J. (2019). Understanding Health Behavior Technology Engagement: Pathway to Measuring Digital Behavior Change Interventions. JMIR Form Res, 3(4): e14052. doi:10.2196/14052.

Goldstein, J. (1999). Emergence as a Construct: History and Issues. Emergence, 1(1): 49–72. doi:10.1207/s15327000em0101_4.

Gore, R., & Reynolds, P. F. (2008). Applying Causal Inference to Understand Emergent Behavior, 2008 Winter Simulation Conference, Miami, FL, USA, 712–721, doi: 10.1109/WSC.2008.4736133.

Groenewegen, P., & Wagnenaar, P. (2006). Managing Emergent Information Systems: Towards Understanding How Public Information Systems Come into Being. Information Polity, 11: 135–148.

Hedin, B., Katzeff, C., Eriksson, E., & Pargman, D. A. (2019). Systematic Review of Digital Behaviour Change Interventions for More Sustainable Food Consumption. Sustainability, 11: 2638.

Hekler, E. B., Klasnja, P., & Riley, W. T., et al. (2016). Agile Science: Creating Useful Products for Behavior Change in the Real-World. Translat Behav Med., Feb 26; Online. doi: 10.1007/s13142-016-0395-7.

Hekler, E. B., Michie, S., Pavel, M., Rivera, D. E., Collins, L. M., Jimison, H. B., Garnett, C., Parral, S., & Spruijt-Metz, D. (2016). Advancing Models and Theories for Digital Behavior Change Interventions. American Journal of Preventive Medicine, 51(5), 825–832. doi: 10.1016/j.amepre.2016.06.013.

Hillis, D. W. (1988). Intelligence as an Emergent Behavior; or, The Songs of Eden, pp. 175–189, Dædalus, Journal of the American Academy of Arts and Sciences, Special Issue on Artificial Intelligence, Winter 1988.

Holland, J. H. (1999). Emergence: From Chaos to Order. Boston, US: Addison-Wesley.

Iivari, J. (2017). Endogenously Emergent Information Systems. In Gołuchowski, J., Pańkowska, M., Linger, H., Barry, C., Lang, M., & Schneider, C. (eds.), Complexity in Information Systems Development – Proceedings of the 25th International Conference on Information Systems Development, Lecture Notes in Information Systems and Organizations, 22, Springer.

Intille, S. S., Kukla, C., Farzanfar, R., & Bakr, W. (2003). AMIA Annual Symposium Proceedings. American Medical Informatics Association, Just-in-time technology to encourage incremental, dietary behavior change, 874.

Kim, J. (2005). Physicalism—or Something Near Enough. Cambridge: Princeton University Press.

Kim, J. (2006). Being Realistic about Emergence. In P. Clayton & P. Davis (eds.), The Re-emergence of Emergence: The Emergentist Hypothesis from Science to Religion (pp. 187–202). Oxford: Oxford University Press.

Kirchhoff, M. (2014). In Search of Ontological Emergence: Diachronic, But Non-supervenient. Axiomathes, 24: 89–116. doi: 10.1007/s10516-013-9214-7.

Luhmann, N. (1995). Social Systems. Stanford: Stanford University Press.

Michie, S., Atkins, L., & West, R. (2014). The Behaviour Change Wheel: A Guide to Designing Interventions. London, UK: Silverback.

Michie, S., Richardson, M., Johnston, M., Abraham, C., Francis, J., Hardeman, W., Eccles, M. P., Cane, J., & Wood, C. E. (2013). The Behavior Change Technique Taxonomy (v1) of 93 Hierarchically Clustered Techniques: Building an International Consensus for the Reporting of Behavior Change Interventions. Annals of Behavioral Medicine, 46: 81–95.

Michie, S., van Stralen, M. M., & West, R. (2011). The Behaviour Change Wheel: A New Method for Characterising and Designing Behaviour Change Interventions. Implementation Science, 6: 42.

Miller, P. (2010). The Smart Swarm: How Understanding Flocks, Schools, and Colonies Can Make Us Better at Communicating, Decision Making, and Getting Things Done. New York: Avery.

Mogul, J. C. (2006). Emergent (Mis)behavior vs. Complex Software Systems. Operating Systems Review, 40(4): 293–304. doi:10.1145/1218063.1217964.

Nahum-Shani, I., Hekler, E. B., & Spruijt-Metz, D. (2016). Building Health Behavior Models to Guide the Development of Just-in-Time Adaptive Interventions: A Pragmatic Framework. Health Psychology, 34(Suppl): 1209–1219. doi:http://dx.doi.org/10.1037/hea0000306.

Parnas, D. L. (1985). Software Aspects of Strategic Defense Systems. Communications of the ACM, 28(12): 1326–1335.

Patrick, K., Griswold, W. G., Raab, F., & Intille, S. S. (2008). Health and the Mobile Phone. The American Journal of Preventive Medicine, 35(2): 177–181. doi:10.1016/j.amepre.2008.05.001.

Pinder, C., Vermeulen, J., Cowan, B. R., & Beale, R. (2018). Digital Behaviour Change Interventions to Break and Form Habits. ACM Transactions on Computer-Human Interaction, 25(3), Article 15 (June 2018): 66. doi:10.1145/3196830.

Rad, D., & Demeter, E. (2020). A Moderated Mediation Effect of Online Time Spent on Internet Content Awareness, Perceived Online Hate Speech and Helping Attitudes Disposal of Bystanders. Postmodern Openings, 11(2Sup1): 107–124. doi:10.18662/po/11.2Sup1/182.

Ricklefs, R. E., & Miller, G. L. (2000). Homeostasis Depends upon Negative Feedback. Ecology. Macmillan.

Riley, W. T., Rivera, D. E., Atienza, A. A., Nilsen, W., Allison, S. M., & Mermelstein, R. (2011). Health Behavior Models in the Age of Mobile Interventions: Are Our Theories Up to the Task? Translational Behavioral Medicine, 1(1): 53–71. doi:10.1007/s13142-011-0021-7.

Ross Ashby, W. (1957). Chapter 12: The Error-Controlled Regulator. Introduction to Cybernetics. Chapman & Hall Ltd.; Internet (1999), pp. 219–243.

Stenholm, P., & Nielsen, M. S. (2019). Understanding the Emergence of Entrepreneurial Passion: The Influence of Perceived Emotional Support and Competences. International Journal of Entrepreneurial Behavior & Research, 25(6), 1368–1388. doi:10.1108/IJEBR-02-2018-0065.

Syme, K. L., & Hagen, E. H. (2020). Mental Health Is Biological Health: Why Tackling "diseases of the mind" Is an Imperative for Biological Anthropology in the 21st Century. American Journal of Physical Anthropology. 2020 May; 171(Suppl 70): 87–117. doi:10.1002/ajpa.23965.

Turner, R. H., & Killian, L. M. (1972). Collective Behavior, 2nd edn. Englewood Cliffs, NJ: Prentice-Hall.

Turner, R. H., & Killian, L. M. (1987). Collective Behavior, 3rd edn. Englewood Cliffs, NJ: Prentice-Hall.

Yardley, L., Choudhury, T., Patrick, K., & Michie, S. (2016). Current Issues and Future Directions for Research Into Digital Behavior Change Interventions. The American Journal of Preventive Medicine, 51(5): 814–815. doi:10.1016/j.amepre.2016.07.019.

Yardley, L., Spring, B. J., & Riper, H., et al. (2016). Understanding and Promoting Effective Engagement with Digital Behavior Change Interventions. American Journal of Preventive Medicine. Nov;51(5): 833–842. doi:10.1016/j.amepre.2016.06.015.

Florinda GOLU and Smaranda M. GUȚU

2 Bullying and Well-Being: An Intertwining Perspective

Abstract The detrimental but potentially protective role of well-being on bullying and its outcomes are discussed. This chapter describes and discusses some key points in the existing literature on bullying: (1) types of bullying, (2) bullying roles, (3) causes and determining factors; (4) consequences of bullying, (5) protective factors, and finally, (6) the relationship between bullying and well-being. Special attention is paid to developmental issues, antecedents, and how different bullying participant behaviors are related to psychosocial (self-esteem, depressive symptoms, and anxiety) and health (illness adaptation and coping) outcomes in nonclinical and clinical populations. Additionally, the chapter addresses some of the many implications that the conceptualization of well-being using a positive psychology framework holds for bullying intervention.

Keywords: Bullying, well-being, positive psychology, psychological distress, psychological well-being

Introduction

Bullying in schools is a significant problem occurring worldwide and can be harmful to well-being (Biswas et al., 2020). Bullying encompasses a series of intentional, aggressive, repeated, and unwanted behaviors by one or more individuals aimed toward those who can't easily defend themselves (Olweus, 1993). More specifically, Olweus (1994) describes bullying as a repeated aggressive behavior characterized by an imbalance of power and an intention to inflict injury, making victims feel threatened and powerless. The aggressive behavior can take numerous forms: threats, intimidation, harassment, abuse, physical form, coercion, provocation, and many others. Thus, this destructive and persistent phenomenon can subtly present itself making it difficult for teachers to recognize it correctly.

When dealing with bullying, a common mistake is confusing it with aggression. There are critical differences between them: aggression consists of a singular act, while bullying of recurring actions; power imbalances characterize bully-victim relationships, whereas aggression can occur between individuals of equal power; in the case of bullying, acts are intentional, unlike aggression, which can include acts of malice (Dooley, Pyżalski, & Cross, 2009). Therefore, to avoid this misunderstanding, Perron (2013) offers three criteria for identifying bullying: (1) unwarranted negative and aggressive behaviors; (2) a repetitive pattern of behavior; and (3) an imbalance of power.

Types of Bullying

Bullying can occur in various forms, such as physical, verbal, relational, and cyberbullying.

Physical bullying entails repeatedly hitting, pushing, shoving, beating, spitting, pinching, punching, biting, stealing, or intentionally damaging someone else's property, and other similar actions (Gordon, 2018).

Verbal bullying involves nicknames, name-calling, teasing with a negative comment, parroting, mimicking, and similar behaviors repeatedly (Gordon, 2018).

Social/Relational bullying includes either a form of direct or indirect exclusion from a group by intentionally ignoring, gossiping, or spreading rumors about someone else, stealing friends or romantic partners, and other similar actions. This type of bullying also includes sexual bullying that stands for repeated unwanted jokes, touching, teasing, eye-rolling, exclusion, or mistreatment of those with a different sexual orientation (Pepler, & Craig, 2016).

Cyberbullying consists of using electronic devices to insult, mimic, threaten, gossip, spread private information, or post embarrassing information about others repeatedly to cause harm (Kowalski, & Limber, 2013).

A particular form of bullying is *bullying by proxy* when bullies persuade others to harass victims (Perron, 2013).

Bullying Roles

Taking into account that bullying is a social phenomenon, some scholars propose other roles: assistants that join bullies in attacking victims; defenders that intervene in favor of the victim; outsiders who stay away from bullying (e.g., Salmivalli et al., 1997; Demaray et al., 2016) while others focus solely on the roles of aggressors, victims, and observers (e.g., Schaefer et al., 2005; Turns, & Sibley, 2018). Explicitly, the following roles are theorized: bully, victim, bully/victim, passive observer, and involved observer.

The individuals committing bullying are called *bullies*, and those repeatedly attacked are called *victims*. In case someone is both a victim and an aggressor, but in different moments in time, then the role *bully/victim* is used.

Observers can be either *passive* (outsider – doesn't get involved) or *active* (defender – actively trying to protect the victim; bully's assistant – supporting the bully and harassing the victim) (Demaray et al., 2016; Knauf et al., 2018).

Regardless of the roles mentioned above, peers' behaviors and reactions of peers have a significant positive or negative impact on bullying (Swearer et al., 2010).

Causes and Determining Factors

What makes bullies persecute others? At the moment, no straightforward answer is available. Still, there are a myriad of motivations for bullies, such as consolidating their social status, their need to feel superior, their belief that this behavior will make them more popular or help them fit in, uncertainty, their previous role as a victim, and even their need for control (Swearer, & Cary, 2003; Espelage, & Swearer, 2004). Various causes can be behind this phenomenon as any student can become a victim regardless of their gender, religion, ethnicity, and social-economic status.

Some bullies are students with low self-esteem, while others have high self-esteem. The latter lack empathy and compassion, and when they feel threatened, they answer in an aggressive manner. However, more frequently, preschool and school-aged bullies and victims have a lower self-esteem than peers who aren't involved in bullying (O'Moore, & Kirkham, 2001).

Another possible cause can be their need for attention. Aggressors could be from a dysfunctional family, where they might or might not have been victims of abuse or negligence, and aggressive behavior toward others can be fueled by desperation, anger, frustration, and jealousy (Graham, 2016).

Graham (2016) shows that even though bullying can happen from an early age (i.e., from preschool) the height of occurrence is during middle school and early adolescence when interacting with others becomes a vital part of life. However, recurring victimization can be a predictor for self-reported symptoms of anxiety and depression in early puberty for girls. This brings to attention the potential long-term mental health effects of bullying (Bond et al., 2001).

While at a first glance bullying might seem to involve solely a dyadic relationship, it is in fact a group phenomenon involving several students with roles of bully, victim, observer, accomplices, and defenders in at least 85 % of bullying instances (Pepler, Craig, & O'Connell, 2010).

Bully/victim are students that can simultaneously be both victims and bullies. They are labeled as provocative or aggressive victims (Schwartz, Proctor, & Chien, 2001). They can develop either internalizing tendencies and aim their negative feelings toward themselves or externalizing tendencies and focus their aggression toward their bullies. Typically, these students have attentional and emotional regulation difficulties. Their double role causes them to be rejected by their peers, so they can't enjoy any social benefits associated with either specific role (Unever, 2005; Graham, 2006).

Menesini and Salmivalli (2017) discuss a meta-analysis done by Cook and his collaborators in 2010 that identified general stability for the roles of victim and bully with a discrete increase in frequency of bullying behavior with age – the peak of occurrence between 12 and 15 years with a tendency to steadily decline until the end of high school. Concerning forms of bullying, aging goes hand in hand with the switch from physical to relational bullying. In accordance with other studies (e.g., Crick, & Grotpeter, 1995; Besag, 2006), there's a higher incidence of physical aggressive behaviors among boys, while girls focus on verbal or relational aggression.

Salmivalli, Huttunen, and Lagerspetz (1997) analyzed the association between social groups and bullying. They found that students are more likely to be in a group based on how similar they would respond, and that individual behavior was closely linked to how a network would react in bullying situations. Bullies, witnesses, and accomplices belong to more extensive networks than victims and defenders, while any students left out of systems are more likely to be victims.

As a whole, school climate can also play a determining role in bullying. Among risk factors, there are demographic attributes (class size and number by gender), peer group dynamic (popularity, power, and competition), and teacher characteristics (communication skills and teaching style) (Menesini, & Salmivalli, 2017). In addition, a low academic load was associated with disruptive behaviors in students, and students exposed to peers with deviant tendencies are at an increased risk for antisocial behaviors. But organizing study groups with pupils who suffer from bullying can help them become less exposed and less vulnerable (Juvonen, & Graham, 2014).

Baldry (2003) investigated the relationship between bullying and victimization in schools and exposure to interparental violence on a nonclinical sample of 1059 students using a cross-sectional design. Results indicated that almost half of them reported different types of bullying and victimization within the last three months with a higher prevalence in the case of male participants being aggressive toward others. Exposure to interparental physical violence was directly associated with bullying, especially for girls who witness acts of violence from their father toward their mother and vice versa, being more likely to harm others compared to girls who weren't exposed to violence. Baldry proposed Bandura's social learning theory as a possible explanation for this theory. Therefore, bullying and victimization can be predicted by exposure to interparental violence.

Bullying was also investigated from a developmental psychology point of view, specialists theorizing that there's a certain temporal stability to it. Thus, a series of studies explored the stability of bullying from early childhood to adolescence using a repeated measures design (Juvonen, & Graham, 2014). For example, when a study examined longitudinal data of over 5000 boys and girls from Canada, New Zealand, and the USA in order to identify the developmental trajectory of aggressive youth (Broidy et al., 2003), the following categories were identified: chronically aggressive youth (5–10 %), diminished aggressive tendencies, and increased aggressive tendencies. Consequently, according to some authors, this could suggest a mechanism discontinuity since only a small percentage (up to 10 %) of young people are chronically bullies. However, these results don't necessarily indicate that aggressive tendencies disappeared because they could've changed their expression form (Juvonen, & Graham, 2014).

Several meta-analyses and literature reviews investigated the relationship between gender and relational aggression (Archer, 2004; Archer, & Coyne, 2005; Card et al., 2008). Even though girls use more frequently relational aggression than physical bullying, no significant differences were found between boys and girls as both genders tend to initiate reputation-damaging behaviors to peers. Nonetheless, during middle adolescence, the most frequently used form of bullying is relational bullying (Juvonen, & Graham, 2014).

Juvonen and Graham (2014) suggest that a series of risk factors for victimization (e.g., internalizing problems and social relations) can be at the same time bullying consequences. Supporting evidence from the meta-analysis conducted by Reijntjes et al. (2010) shows the cyclic process of bullying and internalizing problems. Researchers analyzed two types of studies: (1) 11 studies in which internalizing disorders were considered victimization antecedents; (2) 15 studies in which changes to internalizing problems were considered victimization consequences. The subsequent effect size analysis indicated a slightly higher, but statistically insignificant result for the second set of data. Thus, if this cyclic process isn't broken, victims will suffer from psychosocial difficulties in later years as well (Juvonen, & Graham, 2014).

Examining psychiatric records ranging from preadolescence until adulthood, several authors (e.g., Copeland et al., 2013; Takizawa et al., 2014) have identified both in the case of bullies and victims a higher incidence of mental health problems during early adulthood. Even in instances where childhood psychiatric difficulties were treated, victims still had a higher prevalence rate of anxious and depressive disorder during adulthood (Winsper et al., 2012).

The ecological system theory postulates that children adapt to the environment in which they grow up as they develop cognitively, linguistically, socially, and physically. This environment can be mediated by a series of factors related to community and society. These act as an ecological system and abilities or vulnerabilities of children also reflect system proprieties, not only individual characteristics. By applying this theory on bullying, Swearer and Doll (2001) propose that bullying appears not only due to personal attributes, but also due to factors such as peer and teacher group actions, physical characteristics of the school environment, parental factors, cultural, and community factors. Citing Bronfenbrenner (1977), Swearer and Doll describe this process as a bullseye target with the child in the middle and environments in concentric circles from closest (family) to furthest (community). According to these authors, in order to better understand bullying, it is essential to understand how each participant interacts within its system.

From this perspective, aggressors are more prone to aggressive behavior because they're more inclined to be impulsive, lack empathy, and be dominant and aggressive in conflict management (Olweus, 1997). They're inflexible and easily discouraged (Scholte, 1992). However, all these are mediated by parental characteristics (Olweus, 1993, 1997; Smith & Myron-Wilson, 1998). Peer influence can be seen through social learning when respect for aggressive behaviors and victim devaluation is learned (Pellegrini et al., 1999). Furthermore, teachers and support staff can also facilitate bullying perpetration by inadequately supervising children and by not taking action when they witness bullying cases (Olweus, 1993; Craig, Pepler, & Atlas, 2000).

Given the ecological systems framework, when this ecosystem child-family-peers-school is in a community filled with violence, bullying results from a complex system interaction. Swearer and Doll (2001) highlight the following six essential assertions for understanding and dealing with bullying:

1. Bullying must be defined as a constellation of behavioral interactions;
2. Internalizing disorders contribute to bullying and victimization, but are often ignored;
3. Families must be active partners in anti-bullying interventions;
4. Anti-bullying interventions must interrupt and neutralize the peer support for bullying behavior;
5. Bullying interventions must alter the responses toward bullying of teachers and other adults;

6. Anti-bullying interventions require changes within those with decision-making power to have a lasting effect.

In order to create truly effective bullying intervention programs, it is vital to understand the ecological system complexities surrounding bullying to break the aggression cycle and help grow healthy behaviors.

Consequences of Bullying

Bullying has numerous and potentially debilitating consequences. Victims of bullying report adverse health, emotional, social, and academic outcomes. However, these effects aren't limited solely to victims, as perpetrators and observers suffer from similar long-term and short-term conditions (Jordan, & Austin, 2012). Consequently, bullying consequences can be organized in the following categories: effects on well-being, social adjustment, psychological distress, and physical illness (Rigby, 2003).

The increased prevalence of bullying is even more concerning considering its association to numerous negative mental health consequences (Lund, & Ross, 2017). For instance, low psychological well-being has been associated with bullying. It refers to unpleasant states of mind associated to bullying, for example, general unhappiness, low self-esteem, and feelings of anger (Rigby, 2003).

Typically, poor social adjustment refers to feelings of aversion toward one's social environment. Bullying has also been associated with a low ability to form long-lasting relationships (Wolke, & Lereya, 2015). Victimization has been found to negatively correlate with academic achievement (Graham, 2016). Bullying perpetration increases the risk of violence later in life by two thirds, while victimization by one third (Ttofi, Farrington, & Lösel, 2012). School bullying is also a specific and robust risk factor for subsequent felonies (Ttofi, Farrington, Lösel, & Loeber, 2011).

Psychological distress refers to chronic levels of anxiety, depression, and suicidal thinking. Stressful events can cause symptoms of depression and anxiety. As victimization is particularly stressful, it can lead to a higher risk of mental health disorders in adulthood (McDougall, & Vaillancourt, 2015). Self-reported victimization strongly correlates with high levels of depression, anxiety, and self-inconsideration (Hawker, & Boulton, 2000). Also, bullying leads to an increased suicidal risk for those involved in bullying (Klomek et al., 2010); bullying participation is associated with suicidal ideation and suicidal behavior (Holt et al., 2015). Victimization of peers is also linked to suicide attempts in children and teenagers (Van Geel et al., 2014). Furthermore, involvement in bullying activities online, as well as offline, positively correlates to suicidal behavior and thoughts (Katsaras et al., 2018). Moreover, there's tentative evidence suggesting that witnessing bullying activities can be a more reliable predictor for mental health risks than being a bully or victim (Rivers et al., 2009).

Bullying is a significant risk factor for physical health (Wolke, & Lereya, 2015). Frequently, psychosomatic symptoms (i.e., headaches, stomachaches, low appetite, and trouble sleeping) fall into this category (Gini, & Pozzoli, 2013). Victims, bullies, and bully/victim suffer from more psychosomatic problems than uninvolved colleagues (Gini, & Pozzoli, 2009, 2013). Furthermore, there are hints that bullying can alter adolescents' brain structures (González-Chica et al., 2019).

Given the many abovementioned short-term and long-term studies on the effects of being bullied by peers, bullying peers, and witnessing bullying, it is evident that bullying is a severe problem that requires swift action.

Protective Factors

Not all victims of bullying suffer from physical, mental health, or academic difficulties. Various adaptive patterns have been studied that allowed for the identification of some protective factors.

Friendships help victims deal better with bullying situations (Yeung & Leadbeater, 2012) because the emotional support of friends helps them feel more secure.

An external variable associated with ethnic diversity in schools was analyzed. Juvonen and collaborators (2006) examined vulnerable school experiences, including victimization, aggression, uncertainty, loneliness, and lack of confidence. They found that ethnic diversity was associated with a lower perceived vulnerability by students.

The Relationship between Bullying and Well-Being

Being a highly stressful experience, bullying can have a negative impact on children's well-being and development. Typically, psychological well-being can be defined using a combination of the hedonic (e.g., happiness) and eudaimonic (e.g., a balance between individual and social life) perspective (Deci & Ryan, 2008). But there are numerous theoretical drivers associated with well-being and ill-being (Huppert, 2009), which is why a conceptual framework is required to understand their potential implications better.

Given the numerous adverse outcomes associated with bullying, in research, well-being has been used as an umbrella term for a wide range of related concepts. For example, it has been posited that repeated exposure to school bullying can affect a student's level of well-being. This claim is supported by several studies linking a dropinstudent's self-esteem level with being bullied at school (Gendron, Williams, & Guerra, 2011; Robson & Witenberg, 2013; Fanti & Henrich, 2015; Tsaousis, 2016; Jones et al., 2017). Moreover, in a study conducted by Rigby (1997), it was found that adolescents with high levels of peer victimization in their first two years of high school reported low levels of well-being even three years later. Being bullied at school represents a critical source of psychosocial stress with adverse and long-lasting effects on students' well-being (Olweus, 1992; Rigby, 1997; Turner et al., 2014; Olweus & Breivik, 2014; Savahl et al., 2019).

However, the relationship between bullying and well-being is not entirely clear, because several well-being conceptualizations have been proposed as our understanding of the construct evolved. Psychological well-being is best described multidimensionally using a profile comprised of indicators spread through numerous dimensions, not through a solely unidimensional approach. Unidimensional measures, such as satisfaction with life, are susceptible to the current state of mind of the individual and may end up ignoring other key aspects of well-being. Hence, multidimensional measures allow for a more comprehensive assessment of well-being (Kern, Waters, Adler, & White, 2015). This is why we propose using Seligman's model (2011) to guide future interventions.

PERMA Theory of Well-Being

Seligman provides a groundbreaking conceptualization of subjective well-being through the lenses of positive psychology. Positive psychology aims to help people flourish by providing and encouraging long-lasting psychological well-being. Seligman recommends using the PERMA model in order to achieve individual and collective well-being (Seligman, 2011).

In 2011, Seligman described the PERMA model and its five pillars: positive emotions, engagement, relationships, meaning, and achievement. Thus, Seligman provides a framework, which analyzes, individualizes, and articulates aspects of well-being.

Positive emotions refer to hedonic emotions such as happiness, pleasure, and comfort (Khaw, & Kern, 2014). Traditionally, happiness was considered the unique component of well-being, which raised particular difficulties for individuals who are, by disposition, low in experiencing emotions (Huppert, 2009).

However, keep in mind that focusing on positive emotions means more than just smiling; it refers to the ability to be optimistic and to be able to see the past, present, and future in a positive light. These emotions are essential for one's mental well-being as they can increase positivity by linking memories and protecting against negative emotions and disorders (e.g., depression) in the future (Seligman et al., 2006). Evidence from neuroscience research also highlights the influence of positive emotions on thoughts about the past, future, and present as individuals are able to mental time travel using past experiences to simulate past and future events (Atance, & O'Neill, 2005; Schacter, & Addis, 2007; Eacott, & Easton, 2012).

Engagement represents a profound psychological state of connection (e.g., interest, involvement, and absorption) with a specific challenging task, activity, organization, or cause. Engagement has the following key dimensions: behavioral engagement (expressed through involvement, motivation, and school participation), cognitive engagement (self-regulation and learning goals), and emotional engagement (interest and positive attitudes toward school and learning). Engagement is strongly associated with a flow state (i.e., of deep concentration in activities). In other words, time stops during flow states. Flow is positively associated with optimal psychological functioning and well-being (Xanthopoulou et al., 2009; Schueller, & Seligman, 2010).

The pillar of **relationships** stands for the sense of belonging to a society in a group, being genuinely linked to others and feeling nurtured and satisfied within our social group. In other words, relationships can be described as the heart of person's life (Roffey, 2012). Positive relationships include feelings of social integration within a community and receiving nurture and support from others. Relationships are well established as contributors to well-being as individuals need supportive, positive relationships, and feelings of social belonging (Diener & Seligman, 2004; Butler & Kern, 2016).

Meaning refers to the presence of a life purpose, a sense of direction, and a connection to something bigger (Seligman, 2012). Meaning is a multidimensional construct, which includes: (1) presence of purpose, (2) sources of purpose, and (3) search for purpose.

Achievement can be defined both from an objective and from a subjective point of view (e.g., sense of accomplishment). Regardless of how one defines it, having ambition, setting and achieving goals contributes to general well-being (Seligman, 2012).

The PERMA model is an expression of flourish with all its elements are interconnected and interdependent, affecting each other both negatively and positively. However, each of these pillars can be pursued individually as they are defined and measured independently.

Numerous studies investigated the correlates of the PERMA model and found significant benefits of well-being when it comes to physical and mental health, academic and job performance (Chida & Steptoe, 2008; Huppert, 2009; Haar & Roche, 2010; Nes et al., 2011; Alarcon et al., 2013). For example, it can help improve the quality of life by lowering depressive symptoms (Gander, Proyer, & Ruch, 2016). Satisfaction with life correlates positively with positive emotions, relationships, and achievement. Positive emotions and achievement are strongly linked to good physical health and vitality. Achievement negatively correlates to stressful life events and depression, while conscientious individuals with a strong sense of purpose have a higher job performance (Barrick & Mount, 1991).

The unique contribution of the PERMA theory of well-being is that it provides at the same time a comprehensive conceptualization of well-being and valuable information and indicators on building blocks that require attention. For example, an underdeveloped pillar such as "relationship" could further harm a bullying victim because it would account for a smaller pool of potential defenders. Interestingly, there has been tentative evidence showing that the availability of social support may differ by gender, as girls will more frequently seek and receive emotional support from other girls (Rigby, 1997). Thus, it can be hypothesized that a boy could greatly benefit from an intervention aimed at helping him create and maintain meaningful connections. More precisely, PERMA informed interventions should focus on improving participants' means on well-being measures, as well as for each component to test whether it has a domino effect on reducing bullying rates and increasing the occurrence of participant defending behavior. Currently, numerous researchers (e.g., Bowes et al., 2009; Gendron, Williams, & Guerra, 2011) argue in favor of addressing both proximal and distal factors when dealing with bullying. Given this recommendation, PERMA theory of well-being represents a particularly promising framework for developing proper bullying interventions.

Conclusion

Our goal in this chapter has been to investigate the relationship between bullying and well-being. Then we attempted to explore how a novel framework for well-being from positive psychology could provide insights to practitioners, researchers, and other interested parties.

Well-being should be the central goal of every country for each of its citizens, but especially for adolescents, as it's a critical transitional period in human life. By taking into account several short-term and long-term studies, it is evident that bullying has a detrimental effect on well-being. An argument can even be made that it's the opposite of well-being. However, successful preventive measures and interventions must address both proximal and distal contextual aspects, and practices should be designed towards this goal. More precisely, the model proposed by Seligman could inform effective methods and techniques.

References

Alarcon, G. M., Bowling, N. A., & Khazon, S. (2013). Great expectations: A meta-analytic examination of optimism and hope. *Personality and Individual Differences*, *54*(7), 821–827.

Archer, J. (2004). Sex differences in aggression in real-world settings: A meta-analytic review. *Review of General Psychology*, *8*, 291–322.

Archer, J., & Coyne, S. M. (2005). An integrated review of indirect, relational, and social aggression. *Personality and Social Psychology Review*, *9*, 212–300.

Atance, C. M., & O'Neill, D. K. (2005). The emergence of episodic future thinking in humans. *Learning and motivation*, *36*(2), 126–144.

Baldry, A. C. (2003). Bullying in schools and exposure to domestic violence. *Child Abuse & Neglect*, *27*(7), 713–732.

Barrick, M. R., & Mount, M. K. (1991). The big five personality dimensions and job performance: A meta-analysis. *Personnel psychology*, *44*(1), 1–26.

Besag, V. E. (2006). Bullying among girls: Friends or foes?. *School psychology international*, *27*(5), 535–551.

Biswas, T., Scott, J. G., Munir, K., Thomas, H. J., Huda, M. M., Hasan, M. M., ... & Mamun, A. A. (2020). Global variation in the prevalence of bullying victimisation amongst adolescents: Role of peer and parental supports. *EClinicalMedicine*, 100276.

Bond, L., Carlin, J. B., Thomas, L., Rubin, K., & Patton, G. (2001). Does bullying cause emotional problems? A prospective study of young teenagers. *BMJ*, *323*(7311), 480–484.

Bowes, L., Arseneault, L., Maughan, B., Taylor, A., Caspi, A., & Moffitt, T. E. (2009). School, neighborhood, and family factors are associated with children's bullying involvement: A nationally representative longitudinal study. *Journal of the American Academy of Child & Adolescent Psychiatry*, *48*(5), 545–553.

Broidy, L. M., Nagin, D. S., Tremblay, R. E., Bates, J. E., Brame, B., Dodge, K. A., ... & Lynam, D. R. (2003). Developmental trajectories of childhood disruptive behaviors and adolescent delinquency: A six-site, cross-national study. *Developmental psychology*, 39(2), 222.

Bronfenbrenner, U. (1977). Toward an experimental ecology of human development. *American psychologist, 32*(7), 513.

Butler, J., & Kern, M. L. (2016). The PERMA-Profiler: A brief multidimensional measure of flourishing. *International Journal of Wellbeing, 6*(3), 1–48. doi:10.5502/ijw.v6i3.526.

Card, N. A., Stucky, B. D., Sawalani, G. M., & Little, T. D. (2008). Direct and indirect aggression during childhood and adolescence: A meta-analytic review of gender differences, intercorrelations, and relations to maladjustment. *Child Dev, 79*, 185–229.

Chida, Y., & Steptoe, A. (2008). Positive psychological well-being and mortality: A quantitative review of prospective observational studies. *Psychosomatic medicine, 70*(7), 741–756.

Cook, C., Williams, K. R., Guerra, N. G., Kim, T., & Sadek, S. (2010). Predictors of bullying and victimization in childhood and adolescence: A meta-analytic investigation. *School Psychology Quarterly, 25*, 65–83.

Copeland, W. E., Wolke, D., Angold, A., & Costello, E. J. (2013). Adult psychiatric outcomes of bullying and being bullied by peers in childhood and adolescence. *JAMA psychiatry, 70*(4), 419–426.

Craig, W. M., Pepler, D., & Atlas, R. (2000). Observations of bullying in the playground and in the classroom. *School Psychology International*, 21, 22–36.

Crick, N. R., & Grotpeter, J. K. (1995). Relational aggression, gender, and social-psychological adjustment. *Child development, 66*(3), 710–722.

Deci, E. L., & Ryan, R. M. (2008). Facilitating optimal motivation and psychological well-being across life's domains. *Canadian psychology/Psychologie canadienne, 49*(1), 14–23.

Demaray, M. K., Summers, K. H., Jenkins, L. N., & Becker, L. D. (2016). Bullying Participant Behaviors Questionnaire (BPBQ): Establishing a reliable and valid measure. *Journal of school violence, 15*(2), 158–188.

Diener, E., & Seligman, M. E. (2004). Beyond money: Toward an economy of wellbeing. *Psychological science in the public interest, 5*(1), 1–31.

Dooley, J. J., Pyżalski, J., & Cross, D. (2009). Cyberbullying versus face-to-face bullying: A theoretical and conceptual review. *Zeitschrift für Psychologie/Journal of Psychology, 217*(4), 182–188.

Eacott, M. J., & Easton, A. (2012). Remembering the past and thinking about the future: Is it really about time?. *Learning and Motivation, 43*(4), 200–208.

Espelage, D. L., & Swearer, S. M. (Eds.). (2004). *Bullying in American schools: A social-ecological perspective on prevention and intervention*. Oxfordshire, England, UK: Routledge.

Fanti, K. A., & Henrich, C. C. (2015). Effects of self-esteem and narcissism on bullying and victimization during early adolescence. *The Journal of Early Adolescence, 35*(1), 5–29.

Gander, F., Proyer, R. T., & Ruch, W. (2016). Positive psychology interventions addressing pleasure, engagement, meaning, positive relationships, and accomplishment increase well-being and ameliorate depressive symptoms: A randomized, placebo-controlled online study. *Frontiers in psychology, 7*, 686.

Gendron, B. P., Williams, K. R., & Guerra, N. G. (2011). An analysis of bullying among students within schools: Estimating the effects of individual normative beliefs, self-esteem, and school climate. *Journal of school violence, 10*(2), 150–164.

Gini, G., & Pozzoli, T. (2009). Association between bullying and psychosomatic problems: A meta-analysis. *Pediatrics, 123*(3), 1059–1065.

Gini, G., & Pozzoli, T. (2013). Bullied children and psychosomatic problems: A meta-analysis. *Pediatrics, 132*(4), 720–729.

Gordon, J. U. M. (Ed.). (2018). *Bullying Prevention and Intervention at School. Integrating Theory and Research into Best Practices*. Cham, Switzerland: Springer Nature.

Graham, S. (2016). Victims of bullying in schools. *Theory Into Practice, 55*(2), 136–144.

Graham, S., Bellmore, A., & Mize, J. (2006). Aggression, victimization, and their co-occurrence in middle school. *Journal of Abnormal Child Psychology, 34*, 363–378.

Haar, J. M., & Roche, M. A. (2010). Family supportive organization perceptions and employee outcomes: The mediating effects of life satisfaction. *The International Journal of Human Resource Management, 21*(7), 999–1014.

Holt-Lunstad, J., Smith, T. B., Baker, M., Harris, T., & Stephenson, D. (2015). Loneliness and social isolation as risk factors for mortality: A meta-analytic review. *Perspectives on psychological science, 10*(2), 227–237.

Huppert, F. A. (2009). Psychological well-being: Evidence regarding its causes and consequences. *Applied Psychology: Health and Well-Being, 1*(2), 137–164.

Jones, A., Robinson, E., Oginni, O., Rahman, Q., & Rimes, K. A. (2017). Anxiety disorders, gender nonconformity, bullying and self-esteem in sexual minority adolescents: Prospective birth cohort study. *Journal of Child Psychology and Psychiatry, 58*(11), 1201–1209.

Jordan, K., & Austin, J. (2012). A review of the literature on bullying in US schools and how a parent–educator partnership can be an effective way to handle bullying. *Journal of Aggression, Maltreatment & Trauma, 21*(4), 440–458.

Juvonen, J., & Graham, S. (2014). Bullying in schools: The power of bullies and the plight of victims. *Annual review of psychology, 65*, 159–185.

Juvonen, J., Nishina, A., & Graham, S. (2006). Ethnic diversity and perceptions of safety in urban middle schools. *Psychological Science, 17*(5), 393–400.

Katsaras, G. N., Vouloumanou, E. K., Kourlaba, G., Kyritsi, E., Evagelou, E., & Bakoula, C. (2018). Bullying and suicidality in children and adolescents without predisposing factors: A systematic review and meta-analysis. *Adolescent Research Review, 3*(2), 193–217.

Kern, M. L., Waters, L. E., Adler, A., & White, M. A. (2015). A multidimensional approach to measuring well-being in students: Application of the PERMA framework. *The journal of positive psychology, 10*(3), 262–271.

Khaw, D., & Kern, M. (2014). A cross-cultural comparison of the PERMA model of well-being. *Undergraduate Journal of Psychology at Berkeley, University of California, 8*(1), 10–23.

Klomek, A. B., Sourander, A., & Gould, M. (2010). The association of suicide and bullying in childhood to young adulthood: A review of cross-sectional and longitudinal research findings. *The Canadian Journal of Psychiatry, 55*(5), 282–288.

Knauf, R.-K., Eschenbeck, H., & Hock, M. (2018). Bystanders of bullying: Social-cognitive and affective reactions to school bullying and cyberbullying. *Cyberpsychology: Journal of Psychosocial Research on Cyberspace, 12*(4), Article 3. https://doi.org/10.5817/CP2018-4-3

Kowalski, R. M., & Limber, S. P. (2013). Psychological, physical, and academic correlates of cyberbullying and traditional bullying. *Journal of Adolescent Health, 53*(1), S13–S20.

Lund, E. M., & Ross, S. W. (2017). Bullying perpetration, victimization, and demographic differences in college students: A review of the literature. *Trauma, Violence, & Abuse, 18*(3), 348–360.

McDougall, P., & Vaillancourt, T. (2015). Long-term adult outcomes of peer victimization in childhood and adolescence: pathways to adjustment and maladjustment. *American Psychologist, 70*(4), 300.

Menesini, E., & Salmivalli, C. (2017). Bullying in schools: The state of knowledge and effective interventions. *Psychology, health & medicine, 22*(sup1), 240–253.

Nes, L. S., Carlson, C. R., Crofford, L. J., de Leeuw, R., & Segerstrom, S. C. (2011). Individual differences and self-regulatory fatigue: Optimism, conscientiousness, and self-consciousness. *Personality and individual differences*, *50*(4), 475–480.

O'Moore, M., & Kirkham, C. (2001). Self-esteem and its relationship to bullying behaviour. *Aggressive Behavior: Official Journal of the International Society for Research on Aggression*, *27*(4), 269–283.

Olweus, D. (1993). Bullying at school: What we know and what we can do. Cambridge, MA: Blackwell.

Olweus, D. (1994). Annotation: Bullying at school: Basic facts and effects of a school based intervention program. *Journal of Child Psychology and Psychiatry, 35*(7), 1171 – 1190.

Olweus, D. (1997). Bully/victim problems in school: Facts and intervention. *European journal of psychology of education*, *12*(4), 495.

Olweus, D., & Breivik, K. (2014). Plight of victims of school bullying: The opposite of well-being. *Handbook of child well-being*, 2593–2616.

Pepler, D., & Craig, W. (2016). *Bullying Prevention and Intervention in the School Environment: Factsheets and Tools*. Retrieved on 07.25, 2020, from PrevNet: https://www.prevnet.ca/research/fact-sheets

Pepler, D., Craig, W., & O'Connell, P. (2010). Peer processes in bullying: Informing prevention and intervention strategies. In S. R. Jimerson, S. M. Swearer, & D. L. Espelage (Eds.), *Handbook of bullying in schools: An international perspective* (pp. 469–479). Routledge/Taylor & Francis Group.Perron, T. (2013). Peer victimization: Strategies to decrease bullying in schools. *British Journal of School Nursing, 8*(1), 25–29.

Reijntjes, A., Kamphuis, J. H., Prinzie, P., & Telch, M. J. (2010). Peer victimization and internalizing problems in children: A meta-analysis of longitudinal studies. *Child abuse & neglect*, *34*(4), 244–252.

Rigby, K. (1997). What children tell us about bullying in schools. *Children Australia*, *22*(2), 28–34.

Rigby, K. (2003). Consequences of bullying in schools. *The Canadian journal of psychiatry*, *48*(9), 583–590.

Rivers, I., Poteat, V. P., Noret, N., & Ashurst, N. (2009). Observing bullying at school: The mental health implications of witness status. *School Psychology Quarterly*, *24*(4), 211.

Robson, C., & Witenberg, R. T. (2013). The influence of moral disengagement, morally based self-esteem, age, and gender on traditional bullying and cyberbullying. *Journal of school violence*, *12*(2), 211–231.

Roffey, S. (2012). Pupil wellbeing—Teacher wellbeing: Two sides of the same coin?. *Educational and Child Psychology*, *29*(4), 8.

Salmivalli, C., Huttunen, A., & Lagerspetz, K. M. J. (1997). Peer networks and bullying in schools. *Scandinavian Journal of Psychology, 38*(4), 305–312.

Savahl, S., Montserrat, C., Casas, F., Adams, S., Tiliouine, H., Benninger, E., & Jackson, K. (2019). Children's experiences of bullying victimization and the influence on their subjective wellbeing: A multinational comparison. *Child development, 90*(2), 414–431.

Schacter, D. L., & Addis, D. R. (2007). The cognitive neuroscience of constructive memory: Remembering the past and imagining the future. *Philosophical Transactions of the Royal Society B: Biological Sciences, 362* (1481), 773–786.

Schaefer, M., Korn, S., Brodbeck, F. F., Wolke, D., & Schulz, H. (2005). Bullying roles in changing contexts: The stability of bullying rolesc from primary to secondary school. (B. Laursen, Ed.) *International Journal of Behavioral Development, 29*(4), 323–335.

Scholte, E. M. (1992). Prevention and treatment of juvenile problem behavior: A proposal for a socio-ecological approach. *Journal of Abnormal Child Psychology, 20*(3), 247–262.

Schueller, S. M., & Seligman, M. E. (2010). Pursuit of pleasure, engagement, and meaning: Relationships to subjective and objective measures of well-being. *The Journal of Positive Psychology, 5*(4), 253–263.

Schwartz, D., Proctor, L. J., & Chien, D. H. (2001). The aggressive victim of bullying: Emotional and behavioral dysregulation as a pathway to victimization by peers. In J. Juvonen & S. Graham (Eds.), *Peer harassment in school: The plight of the vulnerable and victimized* (pp. 147–174). The Guilford Press.Seligman, M. (2018). PERMA and the building blocks of well-being. *The Journal of Positive Psychology, 13*(4), 333–335.

Seligman, M. E. (2012). *Flourish: A visionary new understanding of happiness and well-being.* New York, US: Simon and Schuster.

Seligman, M. E., Rashid, T., & Parks, A. C. (2006). Positive psychotherapy. *American psychologist, 61*(8), 774.

Smith, P. K., & Myron-Wilson, R. (1998). Parenting and school bullying. *Clinical Child Psychology and Psychiatry,* 3, 405–417.

Swearer, S. M., & Cary, P. T. (2003). Perceptions and attitudes toward bullying in middle school youth: A developmental examination across the bully/victim continuum. *Journal of Applied School Psychology, 19*(2), 63–79.

Swearer, S. M., & Doll, B. (2001). Bullying in schools: An ecological framework. *Journal of Emotional Abuse, 2*(2–3), 7–23.

Swearer, S. M., Espelage, D. L., Vaillancourt, T., & Hymel, S. (2010). What can be done about school bullying? Linking research to educational practice. *Educational researcher, 39*(1), 38–47.

Takizawa, R., Maughan, B., & Arseneault, L. (2014). Adult health outcomes of childhood bullying victimization: Evidence from a five-decade longitudinal British birth cohort. *American journal of psychiatry, 171*(7), 777–784.

Tsaousis, I. (2016). The relationship of self-esteem to bullying perpetration and peer victimization among schoolchildren and adolescents: A meta-analytic review. *Aggression and violent behavior, 31*, 186–199.

Ttofi, M. M., Farrington, D. P., & Lösel, F. (2012). School bullying as a predictor of violence later in life: A systematic review and meta-analysis of prospective longitudinal studies. *Aggression and Violent Behavior, 17*(5), 405–418.

Ttofi, M. M., Farrington, D. P., Lösel, F., & Loeber, R. (2011). Do the victims of school bullies tend to become depressed later in life? A systematic review and meta-analysis of longitudinal studies. *Journal of Aggression, Conflict and Peace Research.*

Turner, I., Reynolds, K. J., Lee, E., Subasic, E., & Bromhead, D. (2014). Well-being, school climate, and the social identity process: A latent growth model study of bullying perpetration and peer victimization. *School psychology quarterly, 29*(3), 320–335.

Turns, B. A., & Sibley, S. D. (2018). Does maternal spanking lead to bullying behaviors at school? A longitudinal study. *Journal of Child and Family Studies, 27*, 2824–283.

Unever, J. (2005). Bullies, aggressive victims, and victims: Are they distinct groups? *Aggressive Behavior*, 31, 153–171.

Van Geel, M., Vedder, P., & Tanilon, J. (2014). Relationship between peer victimization, cyberbullying, and suicide in children and adolescents: a meta-analysis. *JAMA pediatrics, 168*(5), 435–442.

Winsper, C., Lereya, T., Zanarini, M., & Wolke, D. (2012). Involvement in bullying and suicide-related behavior at 11 years: A prospective birth cohort study. *Journal of the American Academy of Child & Adolescent Psychiatry, 51*(3), 271–282.

Wolke, D., & Lereya, S. T. (2015). Long-term effects of bullying. *Archives of disease in childhood, 100*(9), 879–885.

Xanthopoulou, D., Bakker, A. B., Demerouti, E., & Schaufeli, W. B. (2009). Reciprocal relationships between job resources, personal resources, and work engagement. *Journal of Vocational behavior, 74*(3), 235–244.

Yeung Thompson, R. S., & Leadbeater, B. J. (2013). Peer victimization and internalizing symptoms from adolescence into young adulthood: Building strength through emotional support. *Journal of research on adolescence, 23*(2), 290–303.

Roxana MAIER

3 The Therapeutic Endeavour of Stress and Anxiety in Regaining the Quality of Life in a Pandemic

Abstract The study shows data regarding the way of offering therapeutic support during the pandemic to diminish the negative emotional states which appeared and to optimise the quality of life. Integrally moving the therapeutic space into the online environment has also brought changes to the evolution's dynamic of the process. Besides the pandemic's novelty and its anxiety-evoking potential, the therapeutic endeavour's difficulty comes from the multiple and diverse issues that appeared. These are multiple losses (of daily comfort, of the possibility of going out, of the social space and of the personal definitions regarding the important life's plans) and the discomfort of doing numerous activities only online, of hanging out with the same people daily, etc. These led to diminishing the people's well-being and, temporarily, to various forms of existential dead ends. The study's objectives were centred around diminishing the problems and finding viable solutions in the long run for the new conditions.

Keywords: Therapy, quality of life, stress, anxiety, pandemic, online

New situations bring the stress of adapting in our lives, and those with a large element of novelty and that intervene suddenly in our lives make adaptation even harder. One of the definitions of stress starts from looking at it as an interactional body-environment configuration. Coping with it can then be the ensemble of mechanisms and conduits that the individual puts between themselves and the events perceived as stressor agents in order to diminish, tolerate them and take control of the effect these have over his physical or mental comfort. In a definition taken taken over for this coping notion, Jurcău specifies the fact that this is an ensemble of our cognitive and behavioural efforts that are destined to control stressors, in situations that surpass our resources (Jurcău, 2003). For each of us, this is realised in a personal style and has a dose of flexibility, which reflects personal attitudes tied to what we know about ourselves to be able to do in the given situation, the efficacity of our coping, but also the personal intention to have adequate behaviours related to this. The flexibility of our coping needs most likely to be tied to the mental adjustment in stressful situations rather than to the intention to give socially desirable answers (Cheng,

2001). In these moments that have intervened in our lives, once the pandemic hit, we all had to make proof of flexibility to adapt to certain conditions which were completely new, for all of us. The crises in our century are different than up to this point and can be registered under the name of "unthinkable" or "unbelievable" or "inconceivable" because some of them are unexpected and unencountered up until this moment. Thus, they are unspecific and almost not studied at all, as they have never happened before. Some of these crises have been the diseases brought in by contamination – BSE (bivine spongiform encephalopathy) (mad cow disease), SARS, avian flu (Rodriguez, Quarantelli, & Dynes, 2007). But even so, with a few known crises, however not known well enough, the one that the pandemic brought over has elements of novelty, by it developing across the globe, and through the fact that everyone has been affected one way or another, through the fact that temporarily everyone was in a lockdown. Its lack of specificity and its novelty make is hard to go through. In this case, it is not about simple coping mechanisms but about adapting to extreme conditions – the unknown of the novelty, insecurity for long periods of time, a new economic and financial dynamic, a new social dynamic, deprived of habitual social contacts, to new and foreign situations that we haven't encountered so far. Resilience, in a simple acceptance, is exactly adapting to conditions of shock, to adversities (after Muntean, Munteanu, 2011). Resilience makes reference to our capacity to succeed in an acceptable way when our life conditions are dramatically changed, and it always assumes the existence of suffering. In successfully finalizing this process, the person's potential when going through the situation, they wish to give this experience a significance and not to quit and they wish to find a balance in the new conditions, the capacity to believe in his or her own resources and the possibility to activate the feeling of control over one's own life. Out of reality is one that is built, and this is realised through communication and social dynamics, and it is built in the socially historical and cultural space we live in (Cristea, 2015). While in these moments, specifically out habitual social dynamic has been completely modified by the existence of the emergency state and this thing brought through destabilisation, stress and anxiety. If we are to look at the stress-control relationship, then Atkinson sustains that an event, as much as it is hard to control, or even uncontrollable, it is as much more likely to be perceived as stressful (Atkinson, 2002). Many of the research done in this domain of stress have been oriented towards the cognitive processes that take place when people are confronted with a risk, precisely the errors (the biases) that an individual makes or has when taking a decision which involves a certain degree of risk. When they are asked to think of their chances to confront a risk, people have the unrealistic tendency to imagine that their future reserves them very few unhappy events, and they await for these events to hit other people, and not them (Joffe, 2003). This phenomenon was called the illusion of invulnerability, which can appear both in individual conditions for decision-making as well as in group conditions, as a factor of the group's thinking. This concept results in the fact that people compare themselves with others exposed to the same stressful or intensely stressful situations in order to maintain a sense of their own personal risk, which is lower, and at the same time underestimate their own abilities that they would need in order to successfully go through this situation that involves risk or overloading. At the start of the pandemic, we have all gone through these sentiments and reactions due to the novelty element of the situation. Our ways to cope, the adaptative ones assume the immediate mobilisation, and the body can nuance its decisions in the right way, while the maladaptive ones assume manifestations that are not appropriate for the context (Crocq, 2014). The difficulty in adapting ourselves successively throughout this period was given by the constant change of the life contexts that we were going through (some things changed in our day-to-day life quicker, while others slower). Throughout these multiple and little known changes, stress and anxiety accentuated.

A resilience model that we have is the one built by Pourtois, Humbeeck and Desmet which presents the development of this double axis concept – resilience – vulnerability and resistance – acceptance. The four concepts encompass the strategies for "solutioning" found by the people that live through averse events. On the resilience–vulnerability axis, resilience would be given by the processes of freeing development, adaptative reactions, thus avoiding the identity collapse, and the person comes out of this situation transformed, in an actual progress. On the contrary side, the lack of resilience brings in maladaptive processes and alienated development which lead to the person's lack of organization, alienation, to following a social countersense, isolation, or renegating the existence and importance of others for their own self. On the resistance–acceptance axis, resistance would mean adaptative processes, through which the person that opposes with a real force the events he or she is going through, so that in the end they can take back their life, go back on their road as before the obstacles were met. If we look at the problematic of acceptance, then we have processes of giving up, of misunderstanding one's potential to develop, of living a personal fragility, partial or total disinterest towards one's own possibilities for finding solutions to the situations that have come about. In the case of resistance, the person opposes the averse factors, but the ways through which they do so are different (after Pourtois, Humbeeck, Desmet, 2013).

Objectives

Objective 1. Finding the modifications that appeared in the emergency state from the point of view of stressors, quality of life, anxiety and one's own definitions. One of the things that changed in our life when we stayed in the emergency state was our definition on multiple dimensions – that of our career, of our free time, of the significant or less significant relationships and of significant things for ourselves.

Objective 2. Emphasising the role of the therapeutic endeavour in tackling the emergency state period, dominating the role of stressors and diminishing anxiety while growing the quality of life.

Hypotheses

Hypothesis 1. The existence of the emergency state leads to major changes in our life, and this will bring with it an augmentation of the levels of stress and anxiety (expected changes) and the loss of one's own definition (unexpected changes).

Hypothesis 2. The therapeutic endeavour contributes to diminishing the symptoms that appeared due to the emergency state (stress, anxiety, modifications in the quality of life) and also contributes to building one's own definition in the new conditions.

Participants and Tools

The study had 17 participants, the ones who have solicited psychotherapy during this time, with their age range between 32 and 54 years old. In order to collect the data to describe the sample (age, occupation, number of children, etc.), we have applied a questionnaire and in order to identify the starting values of the levels of stress, anxiety and quality of life, we have applied a second questionnaire. The latter, which targets the autoperceived level of stress, anxiety and quality of life, was repeated every week. The evaluation of stress, anxiety and quality of life was done on a scale of 1 to 5, where 1 was the lowest level and 5 the highest. In addition to this, we have pointed out to the participants that the term of quality of life makes reference to multiple areas of their life, and at the same time, while when they note down their quality of life, they are actually noting down the perceptions of these areas as a whole. These specific areas were specified to them as being part of the auto-evaluation of their quality of life, and they are as follows: health, occupation, couple, relationships with their children (in case they have them), living space and free time.

Results and Discussions

Hypothesis 1. From the questionnaire to auto-evaluate stress, anxiety and quality of life, the results obtained are: for the level of stress, the subjects perceive it as follows: 35 % on a medium level, 29 % on a high level and 24 % on a very high level (they have all self-evaluated the stress as average or over); for the level of anxiety they perceive it as follows: 30 % on a medium level and 35 % on a very high level (the level of anxiety perceived by all subjects is average or above); for the quality of life: very low levels 25 %, low levels 41 % and average 47 % (all participants perceive their quality of life as under average). These measurements represent indicators for fixing certain objectives for therapy which will take us onto balancing the levels of stress and anxiety, but also of their own perception on their quality of life. The evaluation of these three dimensions is done every week in the pandemic and ascertains that the values of stress and anxiety have augmented in week four or five for all subjects and also has drastically diminished the value for the subjects' quality of life. The values obtained for stress are 24 % average level, 35 % high level and 41 % very high level; the values for anxiety are 18 % average level, 35 % high level and 47 % very high level; and the values for quality of life are 33 % very low level, 40 % low level and 27 % average level. The values from week five have changed in terms of the values obtained with a percentage or two in each category; they have self-evaluated staying quite high in terms of stress and anxiety and rather low in terms of quality of life. A possible explanation for this is the fact that the emergency state was initially announced after 30 days, and in week four, this was prolonged for another month, and also the fact that there was a particular case for each person involved (the context of life in which they were caught in). The emotional state of each person living in this country has been deeply tried, but on top of this, one can superimpose for each of us our own context of life with its specificity. As a therapist, one often confronts themselves with the difficult experiences of people who are going through a difficult situation and when they temporarily can't find solutions. All of these are inscribed on each person's emotional continuum which contains a large and varied space of emotions (Burgo, 2019). Once the emergency state appeared, our movement freedom has been drastically limited, and to this one can add a constant state of fear, given by the multiplication of new cases in our country, but also by the worrisome international situation from the point of view of the number of cases registered. On top of this, we have also noticed dimensions of each participant's personal case, like for example:

- Each family member's state of health (vulnerable or not) – the danger of this new virus is also given by the other health concerns each one has, and thus, the perception of one's own health as a robust one, or not, brings in certain degrees of perceiving stress and anxiety. Reported to this, there are people who, at the beginning of the emergency state were following treatments for post-operatory issues or for chronic diseases, and this added an extra stress tied to taking part in their own treatment (in case this was happening at a clinic), the access to medicine (getting the referral, going to get medicine or ordering these online, which was all made harder by the restrictions) or even the impossibility to follow treatments.
- If in the family there were elders (whether they lived together or not) – the main concern was that of protecting them, which often added a strong stressor (the thought that you might be a source of disease or death for a loved one), and another problem was that of the limited amount of hours in which the elderly could get out of the house (a limited amount of hours makes walking or procuring supplied difficult for those who could get out of the house); if they did not live in the same house, there was also an added issue of provisions (the possibilities to make the trip were reduced, making it difficult to supply provisions in several locations, depending on where each person's parents lived in; the elderly have less friends, relatives being in general people who socialise less often). If the parents and grandparents lived far, then to all these difficulties one can add the impossibility to temporarily visit, and if the elderly were in a care center, one can also add the impossibility to visit for the fear of making anyone sick (all the people in a care center are vulnerable, so the possibility of them contracting the disease is higher than in other areas, or for other population categories).
- If they had children and however old they were – small children understood less the absence of walks, going out to the playground, why they couldn't see friends, the space to play has moved inside the house and usually a parent or both are taken as play partners. In terms of kindergarten activities – moving these online has brought through a real issue with regards to the children's patience and the fact that they were accompanied to "class" by a parent, which meant that the parent was temporarily off their usual work. For the older children, the main stressor was the absence of friends, but also online schooling – the way in which the classes happened, the way they studied for each subject and the possibility to get grades in order to finish the year well, and for those in terminal years the way in which they will graduate or pass their final exams. For the children, and also for the parents, sharing the same space to "work" brought in constant difficulties – if there are enough

devices in the house for each to be able to appoint themselves one, if the space was sufficient for each person to have the silence they needed to follow their activity, if the time frame for work/free time was adequately split for the activities to be able to happen (parents' work would finish later than the one of the kids, and the latter can derange through games, happiness, running, etc.).

- The possibility to work in an online space (which in certain cases brought after itself furlough or loss of job) – not all jobs are properly done online, so for many there was also the issue of furlough or loss of job. The difficulty of such news brings in financial difficulties for the long term (implications in the family budget, its well-being, projection of a future – tied to health, children's schooling, holidays, in general all that ties to future plans).
- The existence of enough space in the house – living space split so that each person can work in their personal space without stepping over someone else's working space. If in the same home there were also some people in case, who were constantly in bed, the difficulty the family faced to operate the space and the work in the house grew considerably.
- The impossibility to constantly supply provisions and necessary items – due to the impossibility to go out shopping or by the breaks in purveyance (in grand terms this was also present due to the fact that Romanians do not supply provisions most of the time through online services that deliver at home, and also the courier services were vastly overbooked by the amount of people who needed to use them which grew suddenly, from one day to another).
- The impossibility to make future plans – these could only comprise the immediate reality, and that was an unusual thing for each of us. The future was no longer described as concrete for the next few months, but mostly for the next few days, maximum one week. This has added another dimension to how our lives were destabilized – the dimension in which we perceive the future and the illusion of invulnerability.
- Our balanced perception about our life's future is a positive one, which makes us take the decisions for our future – we image a beneficial, optimistic and positive future for ourselves, and that is how we think about ourselves (we do not believe that any catastrophe will happen to us). When asked to think about their chances of confronting with a risk, a problem, people have the unrealistic proclivity to imagine that the future will not be full of undesirable events and they believe that this type of situations would happen in somebody else's life. This phenomenon was named the illusion of invulnerability. When the pandemic struck, it was difficult for all of us to think that

our future will be a safe one, so unbalanced reactions occurred one after the other.

- Losing some personal definitions – it is widely known that we define ourselves through the dimensions of our life's main roles (sons, daughters, parents, the ones illustrated by our jobs, the roles highlighted by each group in which we are involved, etc.). Suddenly, some roles temporarily disappeared from our lives each day, and questions appeared – who am I without this job? Or without this role (whichever it may be)? If the dimension was not completely lost then it surely suffered an alteration due to the provisional limitation of movement – so questions appeared in this case too – how can I define myself if I work differently? Which are the changes for me at this point? Or how do I define myself as a student via online school? Or how is my role as a parent defined now? Which are my challenges? All these types of questions brought with them stress, unsettlement and anxiety.
- Making the trust fragile – throughout the lockdown, in every household, for the family members, various ways of perceiving stress and anxiety, as well as different ways of coping with them, were highlighted. This often led to conflict which made their mutual trust fragile. The families that coped well with the situation were the ones that found an authentic way of communicating with the others and managed to support and offer emotional comfort to each other. Having a beneficial affective resonance before this situation contributed to this aspect.
- The appearance of boredom – the feeling of losing touch with the usual routine (usual activities, going to school, the job, household activities or job-related activities, going to the park with the children, with friends, sports activities, going to get the groceries, visits, going out with friends, etc.) all of these led to the appearance of boredom. To this were added the feeling of uselessness, the frustration related to self-monitoring your own health, to cope with multiple stressors, the limited social and physical contact with the others, perceiving the resentment of the loved ones (who might think that they would need to self-isolate due to physical contact with us).
- The appearance of the lack of motivation – we are bonded to our goals and the meaning we give to the things in our life and the pandemic confronted us with the loss of some of the goals and meanings, hence leading to the loss of motivation. Another contributing factor was that our life's distress was resolved abruptly and was replaced with less work, extremely rare outgoings, and an unpredictable future. For some time we thought this was a well-deserved rest but then acknowledging the loss of multiple plans led to the constant lack of motivation.

- The loss of control – regarding the abrupt realisation of how little things we can control. The future of our job, our studies, our activities, etc. seemed like they were in our control and suddenly they were not anymore. We found out that numerous things, big or small, which we controlled were not accessible anymore (from what food I could order to who I could meet, or where I could go on vacation).
- Awareness and tiredness – when we find ourselves constantly being careful, our preventive behaviour, having a sense of obligation towards ourselves, towards the loved ones, and a constant wish for vigilance regarding what we are doing, tiredness can occur in the long term.
- The realisation and deepening perception of being alone – the isolation period deepened this inner perception of being alone, which made us vulnerable and anxious. The lack of social interaction made us perceive our loneliness and isolation more truthful than ever before. Most of our individual needs are satisfied through human interactions: love, inclusiveness, gratefulness, esteem, security, and status. These needs' dynamic is influencing us personally and socially, but throughout the pandemic, these needs have suddenly shifted.
- Constant cohabitation with the fear – this is something that we have never experienced before, or if we did, it did not have so many sources of fear. These sources were manifold – regarding health, the fear of being infected and without symptoms, of infecting others, the fear of objects and surfaces (the virus's novelty made it unknown on which surfaces and for how long was it contagious in the beginning), the fear of loneliness, the decrease in unobstructed movement, the lack of supplies, the incapacity of purveyance, the lack of information (the situation was new to the governments as well), the lack of our own definitions and the unpredictable future regarding various plans.
- To all of this it could have been added (but it was not the case for these subjects) quarantining, being brought to the hospital to be isolated when coming from another country, being send to another location if they were infected afterwards. Another stressor could have been the fact that some people have gone to another country and, for various reasons, missed their return slot. This brought with it stress, financial problems and, usually, survival issues.

For these subjects, the stress and anxiety problems, and the perception on the quality of life changed weekly, culminating with the numbers recorded on the fourth and fifth week, detrimental weeks for these people. The issue related to their adaptability was multifaceted depending on their life's context. The mix of stress, financial, social and motorically restrictive factors brought each family in contact with what was functional or not, as well as with each individual's role in the family's dynamic. Another important aspect leading to the recording of the initial data was the fact that no individual worked in the health system, a field of work that could have led to more stress throughout this period. The fourth and fifth weeks showcased data correlated to their means of adaptability, each family's flexibility, and ways of offering support and psychological comfort – the lack of the last two being the main detrimental factors for each family. Throughout this whole period, we had various teachings to learn from our life and about our life, teachings which were constantly changing. This led to difficult times in our existence because learning something is not an easy task as the process of learning brings us in contact with our inabilities initially (Badea, 2019).

Hypothesis 2. Starting from the three dimensions' evaluation – stress and anxiety levels, quality of life and the evaluation of the symptomatological, existential and familial plans, the psychotherapy revolved around the next objectives:

- Taping into personal resources;
- Enabling decisional flexibility and adequacy to multiple changes;
- Defining new routines;
- Activating creativity;
- Enabling a sanogenuous way of living;
- The evaluation and optimisation of the affective resonance;
- The re-evaluation of the future plans and the development of a new, more in tune with the present moment, future (plans related to the closer future with a shorter span in time);
- The repositioning process regarding the idea of success and failure;
- Clarifying the personal image and one's role within the family;
- The losses' management (people, roles, freedoms and definitions);
- The situations' management (for every person, depending on their life's context, which was different, various situations appeared);
- Clarifying the possibilities from this very moment and this very situation for the future;
- Redefining the roles within the family, towards friends, at work or school;
- The construction of new personal definitions.

The therapeutic endeavour comprises a plethora of problems, starting from the established objectives; so the people that benefit from them can find their own solutions, unlock their potential and use it plenarily (Mitrofan, 2008). After the psychotherapy sessions, the measurements taken in the eighth week from the beginning of therapy showcased the following: the stress level decreased with around 15–20 %, anxiety level decreased with about 9–17 % and the quality of life improved by 12–20 %. The therapeutic endeavour brought out different means of action in everyone's life, acknowledging the new duties regarding home, actively participating in family activities, constructing a new, smaller routine which would maintain the family's equilibrium throughout the pandemic, bonding with the family, increasing the engagement level towards the family and their common activities, the capacity of making decisions based on various situations, while being able to adjust them if the context changes, the capacity of seeking new methods of performing one's job, the adjustment to working in an online environment, facilitating online meetings with their friends (maintaining the usual means of meeting up with friends and stimulating creativity in order to find solutions that would enable them to be done in the online environment), strengthening the support grid of each individual and their relationships, marring the feeling of isolation through actively participating in leisure time manifestations in the online medium (concerts, classes and events), the propagation of hope, experiencing empathy and solidarity more frequently. One of the main dysfunctions was given by their personal definition, which shifted from career to nothing stable, temporarily. We are all defining ourselves by the things and activities that we undergo, through our significant relationships, so a personal definition in adulthood is the one regarding the career. We have all suffered during the pandemic and lockdown, especially relating to the career. Some of us have redefined their way of working while others have redefined everything as they have lost their job. So, one of the main personal definitions has been affected, and this led to a personal loss for everyone. This affected all the person's other action plans because of its importance in our life temporarily. Each human being experiences the implicative with his or her own explanation. By doing this they fully understand what is happening with them. Through new symbols we understand all that is interacting with the implicative, hence it receives new meanings for us, and it is uncovered to us. The explicit meaning of things, of the definitions, of what is happening with us, is born with the interaction felt by ourselves and through our own symbols, built throughout my life. Each individual's symbols, their way of expressing them, illustrate each person's implicit method of putting themselves into that situation (Vanaerschot, 2011).

The therapeutic endeavour is centred on finding a new meaning to their career's definition, as well as defining all the other personal planes (to redefine their role within the family, with the significant other or the ones relating to household activities and friends).

Conclusions: The gathered data points out the fact that throughout the pandemic, the main problems adhered to the stress and anxiety's spheres, problems which can be arise in therapy. This endeavour brings data relating to the possibilities regarding the problem's resolutions that occurred in our life, the real possibilities of a resolution, and of the multifaceted impact on our life.

The study's limitations. The study's main limitation is related to the small number of participants, while another one was related to the tight time span in which the therapy was done. The therapeutic endeavour continued after the eighth week of the study, implicating all the participants, but the data gathered then is not present within this study. The main challenge regarding the therapeutic work was the shift from a face-to-face environment to an online one, implying – limited possibilities regarding the devices used (the internet's speed, the connection quality, etc.) restrained possibilities of interaction and the big difference between the physical and virtual interaction.

Bibliografie

Atkinson, R.L., Atkinson, R.C., Smith, E.E., Bem, D.J. (2002). *Introducere în psihologie*, Editura Tehnică, Bucureşti

Badea, M. (2019). *Dor. O perspectivă psihologică asupra experienţelor de separare din viaţă*. Editura Sper, Bucureşti

Burgo, J. (2019). *De ce fac asta? Mecanismele psihice de apărare şi căile ascunse prin care ne schimbă viaţa*. Editura Trei Bucureşti

Cheng, C. (2001). Assesing Coping Flexibility in Real-Life and Laboratory Settings: A Multimethod Approach. Journal of Personality and Social Psychology, nr. 80

Cristea, D. (2015). *Tratat de psihologie socială*, Editura Trei, Bucureşti

Crocq, L. (2014). *16 conferinţe despre traumă*, Editura Trei, Bucureşti

Joffe, H. (2003). *Risk: from perception to social representation*, British Journal of Social Psychology, No.42, pp. 55–73.

Jurcău, N. (2003). *Psihologie inginerească,* UTPRE S, Cluj-Napoca

Mitrofan, I. (2008). *Psihoterapie. Repere teoretice, metodologice şi aplicative.* Editura Sper, Bucureşti

Muntean, A., Munteanu, A. (2011). *Violenţă, traumă, rezilienţă*, Editura Polirom, Bucureşti

Pourtois, J.P., Humbeeck, B., Desmet, H. (2013). *Rezistență și reziliență asistate: o contribuție la susținerea educativă și psihosocială*, în Tratat de reziliență asistată, coord Ionescu, Ş., Editura Trei, Bucureşti, pag 58–79

Rodriguez, H., Quarantelli, E.L., Dynes, R. (2007). *Handbook of Sociology and Social Research,* Springer Science+Busines Media, LLC

Vanaeschot, G. (2011). Rezonanța empatică – sursă a intervențiilor pentru intensificarea experienței, în vol coord. Bohart, A., Greensberg, L.S., *Empatia în psihologie*, Editura Trei, Bucureşti

Laura Elena NĂSTASĂ and Oana POPA

4 Designed to Connect! Building a Secure Base for a Resilient and Satisfactory Life

Abstract Recognizing attachment needs, communicating them consistently to significant people, and accepting responsibility for one's emotions are the path to self-realization of human potential, safety, and physical or mental health. This research aims to study the relationship between attachment, resilience, emotional regulation, and life satisfaction. Seventy-seven students aged between 18 and 24 were involved. They were asked to complete online: the Inventory of Parent and Peer Attachment (Armsdein & Greenberg, 1989), Adolescent Resilience Scale (Oshio et al., 2003), and Satisfaction with Life Scale (Diener et al., 2013). The results support the need to design and implement intervention programs that: (1) capitalize on the trusted relationships that students have built with peers and family members and (2) foster the development of resilience and increase their satisfaction with life, thus contributing to the successful adaptation and to the well-being of young adults.

Keywords: Attachment, emotional regulation, resilience, life satisfaction and well-being

Attachment – a Base for Emotion Regulation

The quality of our familial and social relationships represents an important factor for the physical, mental, and emotional health (Johnson, 2008). Bowlby (2011) argues that healthy, happy, and confident adolescents and young adults are the product of stable and functional families, in which both partners support each other and are willing to share their time and attention with their children to help them grow.

Physical or mental health and social relationships are influenced by the way in which young adults are able to deal with their own emotions. Emotion regulation requires an emotional response to a given situation and, also, the person's voluntary or automatic endeavor to decide on the right emotions and the right context in which these are allowed to be felt, but, mostly, to decide on the way these emotions are expressed (Mauss et al., 2007). While behavior regulation means to be able to modulate the behavior as a response to a given emotion, emotion regulation is the ability to initiate, maintain, and modulate the appearance and the intensity of the subjective feelings and physiological processes that accompany the emotion. As people internalize behavioral norms and standards, they learn to inhibit the emotional impulses and to postpone gratifications (Denham, 2007). In most cases, people learn to regulate their emotions and their behaviors by discovering different ways to deal with anxiety, to defend themselves, to tolerate frustration or loneliness, and to negotiate the quality of interpersonal relationships. Emotion regulation is integrated through the life experiences that require human interaction, through behavior modeling and through various day-to-day learning contexts. The most frequently used emotion regulation strategies are: avoidance, expressive suppression (one's effort to inhibit or reduce the behavioral manifestation of the emotions), attention distraction, rumination (repetitive negative thoughts) or worrying, acceptance, mindfulness, problem solving, and cognitive re-evaluation (modifying the emotional meaning by reinterpreting a lived experience). Naragon-Gainey et al. (2017) analyzed several studies, which targeted the correlation between different emotion regulation strategies used by people to deal with negative emotions. They suggested that people tend to rely on more than one strategy at the same time. These strategies were grouped into three categories as follows: (1) emotional disengagement – includes attention distraction, and avoidance. With the help of these two strategies, one may try to experience more pleasant emotions, by focusing thoughts and attention away from the present moment; (2) focus on negative emotions (the aversive cognitive preservation) includes rumination, thus the person gets stuck in the repetitive negative thoughts concerning self-blaming and failures; (3) adaptive engagement is centered on solving real-life problems or on accepting that a specific situation cannot be changed, and thus, the person becomes more flexible and tries to experience more pleasant, adaptive emotions. The authors suggest that the best strategies are those that focus on the adaptive engagement but also that the others, too, may be useful in certain contexts: for example, the intense reflection and analysis of personal problems could lead to exploring different alternatives and finding solutions to those problems. The purpose of the emotion regulation is to reduce the intensity and the duration of the dysfunctional emotions. Grouping the strategies in smaller categories may offer more efficient ways and instruments for regulating one's own emotions.

The way in which young people experience and regulate their emotions is based on the attachment style shaped from early childhood until adulthood, when it becomes relatively stable. Human attachment is the inherent tendency to be near the attachment figures in stressful situations, in the most difficult moments of life. In Siegel's vision (2014), it can be understood through four major components: the need to be seen and to feel safe, comforted, and secure. Thus, attachment is like a basic, permanent, innate human need that aims at survival; therefore, it is not a typical child dependency that can be overcome with growth. Ruppert (2012) claims that, through attachment, two people come to develop a common soul structure. In the author's opinion, human attachment is a psychic process that develops even before birth between a mother and her would-be child, the child reacting sensitively to the mother's movements, touches, dispositions, heart rate, and intonations.

Bowlby (1973, 1980, 1982) used the term *working model* to describe the individual's internal representation of the world, of the significant others in their lives and of themselves. These representations are rooted in early childhood and are assumed to be determined by the emotional availability of the significant others and by the extent to which they meet the children's needs (Bretherton, 1985; Sroufe & Waters, 1977). According to Main et al. (1985), the child's early working models consist of a scheme that, in fact, represents the child's attempts to gain comfort and security. These specific experiences become, over time, more and more abstract, turning into generalized beliefs and expectations about how people are supposed to react, in terms of warmth and responses in relationships, and also about one's personal value. Once formed, these beliefs can be used to predict and interpret the others' behavior and to act in new situations, without necessarily needing their rigorous evaluation. A person can have more than one attachment model, and these models are activated automatically, without intent or awareness, at specific moments that resemble a particular attachment relationship from the past (Siegel, 2014).

The attachment theory supports two main types of attachment models: secure and insecure. From these two, three styles of attachment or general patterns of social interaction and emotional adjustment that characterize a person emerge.

The first pattern is the secure attachment in which young adults are confident that the attachment figure is available, attentive to their needs and responds with affection, providing protection or comfort when faced with difficult situations. Secure individuals feel comfortable in intimacy, are warm, loving, and eager to bravely explore various new life contexts.

The second pattern is the attachment characterized by anxiety and resistance in which young people are not certain that the attachment figure will be available or responsive when needed. Anxious people are constantly prone to separation anxiety, very eager for intimacy, being particularly concerned about the relationships they have and always worried about their partner's ability to love them just as hard as they do.

The third pattern is the attachment characterized by anxiety and avoidance in which young adults do not have the faith that they will be answered and helped when seeking protection or relief; on the contrary, they expect to be categorically refused. Avoidant individuals place the mark of equality between intimacy and loss of personal independence, constantly trying to limit their closeness to their partner. There are also cases where they try to live their lives without the love and support of others, striving to become emotionally independent, as a result of repeated previous rejections (Bowlby, 2011).

Emotional Expression according to the Attachment Styles

The way in which people experience life and choose to express their own emotions is influenced by the secure attachment (source of resilience), anxious attachment (seeking, with insecurity, the other's attention in order to receive emotional support), or avoidant-insecure attachment (the distrust pattern). These attachment styles are associated with the following patterns.

People with a secure attachment style learned in childhood that expressing their emotions was acceptable for those around them, so, they let themselves be open about their own feelings because they are confident that the others are receptive and their needs will be met. Research shows that these people are more resilient when it comes to the hardships of life, as this attachment style provides them with a secure base essential for surviving the emotionally negative moments and helps them regulate their emotions and socially adapt and maintain their mental health (Mikulincer & Shaver, 2016a, 2016b, 2002). Also, they are more optimistic, rarely resort to catastrophic evaluations of the dangers around them and are more confident in their abilities to face daily struggles. As a rule, they freely express their feelings, without any distortion, and they make use of adaptive emotion regulation strategies such as problem solving, re-evaluation, or seeking the help of others.

People with an anxious attachment style know, from experience, that there is an inconsistent response to their emotional expressions. Therefore, they developed a strategy of exaggeratedly expressing their feelings, especially the negative ones, because, in this way, they would draw attention onto themselves. Also, they tend to focus on the exacerbation of negative feelings as they are in accordance with their seeking of closeness and hyper-activation of attachment needs and on the vulnerability and helplessness feelings as well as on the seriousness of the threats to make their entourage give more attention, support, and protection. While intensifying negative emotions and focusing on the internal indicators of the distress, these persons underestimate their own resources and over evaluate the danger, which lead to a hyperactivity of their own anxiety. In this way, a vicious circle is created, which maintains the threat perception even after its actual disappearance, preserving also the feeling of vulnerability in the face of real or potential dangers.

People with an avoidant attachment style have developed a strategy to help them hide their feelings in order not to be ignored or despised, as they have a history of repeated rejections of their emotional expressions, especially the negative ones, and their needs were poorly met or not met at all by their significant others. They associate fear, anxiety, sadness, anger, shame, guilt, rejection, treason, or separation with their own vulnerability. So they tend to block or inhibit these emotions as well as the emotional reactions to the attachment figure's availability, because such potential or real threats could reactivate unwanted attachment needs (Fraley & Shaver, 2000). At the same time, they make a great effort to defend themselves from the conscious feeling and expression of the unpleasant emotions and use of strategies such as suppression and distraction in order to avoid the emotional reactivity. These mechanisms lead to a decrease in the likelihood that the emotional experience be integrated in the existent cognitive-affective structures which, then, could determine the changing of the pattern already learnt and could allow the subsequent use of this information in a social context.

Young adults with an anxious attachment style are worried about others not being available for them when needed, so they constantly seek their support and love; while the ones with an avoidant attachment style do not trust the others' intentions, and they have a compulsive self-confidence. They know, from their childhood experiences, how to adjust their behavior to the requests of the significant other, whose availability was either erratic or constantly not available. These attachment patterns become, in time, maladaptive because they do not challenge them to obtain the support and interdependence that would bring reward and maintain well-being. When it comes to interpersonal relationships, these young adults do not feel safe as the vulnerabilities that come with this type of attachment style keep them in a repetitive state of activation and also trigger the suppression of negative emotions, maintain a distorted image of themselves and others. Thus, their mental and physical health are more vulnerable because they did not learn how to properly regulate distress and, at the same time, their internal resources did not develop in order to successfully help them deal with adversity. While young anxious adults show a high commitment for rumination, which intensifies the feeling of distress, they also tend to distance themselves, emotionally and cognitively. In terms of emotional memory, those with an anxious attachment can rapidly access sad memories and those linked to anxiety, while the avoidant type have a reduced access to those memories. The ability to suppress the thoughts correlated to separation is low in the anxious type and high in the avoidant one. The mechanism, used by the latter, to defend themselves against experiencing unpleasant emotions is quite fragile and, therefore, these individuals feel overwhelmed especially when a cognitive load is also present besides the material to suppress (Goldberg, 2000; Mikulincer & Shaver, 2019).

Both emotion regulation and mental health are associated with leaving the negative experiences behind. The individuals who forget the negative memories have a greater success in focusing on the positive aspects of life because they manage not to be burdened by past regrets and failures. Thus, forgetting represents a part of mnemonic emotion regulation, and it refers to those instances in which people regulate their emotions by changing, emphasizing, or forgetting some of the unpleasant events. Furthermore, some individuals forget the negative memories in a selective way (the unimportant memories, those that cannot be changed or those which prevent personal growth), wanting to avoid negative emotions and trying to facilitate the appearance of positive ones. Focusing on the positive aspect promotes an optimistic interpretation of the neutral events and increases the chance of experiencing positive emotions and, as a consequence, individuals are more open to engage in experiences that might offer them the opportunity to develop their intellectual, physical, and social abilities (Nørby, 2018).

Building Emotions and a Secure Attachment

Recent neuroscience studies suggest that emotions are assumptions built by the brain, (Barrett, 2017). The human brain predicts and creates the personal experience; it gives new meanings and determines actions based on the available sensory information and past history. The theory of constructed emotions is based on these studies, and it unveils the way the brain works, explaining the vast diversity of the emotional experiences and human perceptions. The way in which people experience their own and others' emotions is based on predictions. These are helpful for a better and faster understanding of the outside world because they make a connection between inner, bodily sensations and outer events. The author suggests that people have control over and are responsible for their own emotions in order to be able to embrace change because the actions and experiences created in the present moment become the brain's predictions for the future.

According to this theory, people are the architects of their own emotions, being able to build more nuanced emotional experiences. Young adults capable of discerning between different emotions and able to flexibly recognize that in a certain situation they may experience diverse emotions are experts in emotions. Emotion regulation involves acquiring new emotional concepts and improving the existing ones by learning new words (Barrett & Bliss-Moreau, 2009). Labeling emotions can have the same effects as other emotional adjustment strategies and consists of talking about emotions or describing what creates anger using emotional language. There is research that proves the following beneficial effects of emotion labeling: it decreases positive and negative emotions, decreases emotional reactivity, decreases the difficulty of talking about emotional experiences, increases task performance in people with test anxiety, and encourages exposure in the case of simple phobia. Labeling emotions help young adults reduce their uncertainty and clarify ambivalent and conflicting situations. At the same time, it requires reflection on one's own emotional states, leading to introspection, which, in turn, causes an increase in the activity of the ventrolateral prefrontal cortex (responsible for the regulation of the amygdala) and a decrease in the activity of the amygdala (responsible for emotional reactivity). Moreover, through language, the emotional stimulus or emotional experience is transformed into a symbolic representation, thus diminishing the emotional experience (Torre & Lieberman, 2018). The more nuanced the human vocabulary, the more precisely the brain succeeds, through its predictions, to calibrate the body budget, according to its real needs. Young adults able to make predictions and build facets of emotions suitable for each specific situation are more flexible in regulating their own emotions (Barrett et al., 2001), less prone to excessive alcohol consumption when they go through a stressful period (Kashdan et al., 2010), less aggressive toward those who harm them (Pond et al., 2012) and more able to choose the right action in social situations (Kimhy et al., 2014). Those less able to discern the negative emotions tend to experience more anxiety and more depressive states (Mennin et al., 2005; Erbas et al., 2014). The pleasant personal experiences adjust the conceptual system because they reinforce the concepts of those positive events and increase their potency in the created mental model. Writing details of these experiences in a personal journal leads to the development of concepts and fosters the prediction of new positive events, which leads to the adoption of a positive attitude (Emmons & McCullough, 2003; Frohn et al., 2008).

If the secure attachment models are characterized by flexibility, self-understanding, and an effortless creation of satisfying relationships, the insecure models occur in many forms (avoidant, ambivalent, and disorganized) and represent a challenge for one's ability to form authentic relationships with others.

A connection marked by love is the only certainty that nature offers to the human beings, and the attachment theory supports the idea that the significant attachment figure represents that secure base where one can always find comfort when needed. When the significant other (parent or romantic partner) is not available or emotionally responsive, it created a situation similar to being left helplessly alone in the coldness of the dark (Johnson, 2008). The consequences of a traumatic experience are extensive, the world becomes an unsafe place to be in, and losing the connection with the loved one threatens the feeling of security. This type of event may cause attachment disorders and could increase the likelihood of suffering a personal traumatic experience or of inflicting trauma to others (Ruppert, 2012).

The attachment models formed in early childhood have a continuous influence throughout the life span. These models have an impact on the private and social life, on the professional relationships, on the stress management, on the physical and psychological health, and on the cognitive development. Although the psychological benefits of the secure attachment seem to be stable in time, the lines of research remain open. Most studies suggest that secure attachment is a stable trait over time and has long-lasting effects on the mental functioning (Bartholomew & Shaver, 1998; Shapiro & Levendosky, 1999). However, results of some research studies indicate that this attachment type tends to vary, depending on the major life events and on the stressful experiences (Davila & Sargent, 2003). According to Baldwin and Fehr (1995), 30 % of the participants change their attachment style over a period of a few months. Even more, Mikulincer and Shaver (2007), noticed that, although the secure attachment is conceptualized as a stable trait, it has its origin in a complex network that includes many attachment representations related to context and relationships. In fact, studies show that the feeling of security could be altered in time (Mikulincer & Shaver, 2001). In the same way in which the attachment style is learnt, the opposite is possible. The attachment style can be modified and, in fact, it changes (Baldwin & Fehr, 1995), continuing to be shaped by life experience (Carnelley & Janoff-Bulman, 1992). A painful breakup could transform a secured, until that moment, individual into an insecure one; on the other hand, a happy, harmonious, functional relationship may empower a person with a sense of security, who, until that time, had an avoidant attachment style (Kirkpatrick & Hazen, 1994). More than a third of the individuals have the possibility to really change their attachment style, within a two year period (Fuller & Fincham, 1995). Davila et al. (1997) suggest that insecure attachment styles (mostly avoidant and ambivalent) are more prone to change than the secure ones. A study conducted by Waters et al. (2000) confirms that, during childhood, depending on the life situations experienced, representations of the attachment stay open to adjustment.

The Secure Attachment, the Resilience Builder for a Life Lived with Satisfaction

The link between the parent's responsiveness and the child's functioning makes an impact on various developmental areas. A secure attachment model correlates with positive socio-emotional achievements (Clark & Ladd, 2000). Specifically, the parent-child connection is associated with social acceptance (Cohn, 1990), satisfying friendships (Kerns et al., 1996), and high levels of altruism and moral development (MacDonald, 1992). Moreover, the way parents relate to their own child/adolescent is reflected on the child's ability to identify, express, understand, and manage their own emotions, as well as on the way in which they choose to act as part of a relationship (Năstasă & Sala, 2012). The individual's ability to receive the emotional information and to acknowledge the meaning of those emotions in order to use them for solving problems and accomplish abstract judgments is associated with professional achievement, life satisfaction, and a reduced emotional stress, mostly where their jobs imply frequent human contacts (Van Rooy & Viswesvaran, 2004; Daus & Ashkanasy; 2005; Năstasă & Farcaş, 2015; Cazan & Năstasă, 2015).

The efficient attachment, the emotional bond between the attachment figure and the child, offer, for the latter, a sense of security, assuring them that the caregiver will always be available when it comes to difficult times (Pianta & Walsh, 1996). Creating an emotional connection is closely linked with the quality and the quantity of the caregiver's feedback given to the child (Epstein et al., 1993). A full of warmth, gentleness, and sensitive response to the child's needs facilitates the development of resilience and healthy adaptability (Maccoby & Martin, 1983). The ability to recover from negative emotional experiences and to flexibly adapt to the stressful events is essential for the individual's well-being and satisfaction with life (Tugade & Fredrickson, 2004).

The above considerations have outlined the theme and, eventually, have given birth to the present research, which was aimed at studying the relation between attachment, resilience, emotion regulation, and satisfaction with life. The design was correlational and the following hypothesis were formulated:

1. A high level of resilience predicts a high level of attachment.
2. A high level of attachment predicts a high level of satisfaction with life.
3. Resilience predicts a high level of satisfaction with life.

4. Attachment positively correlates with emotion regulation.
5. Parent attachment is associated with positive future orientation.

Seventy-seven psychology students from Transylvania University in Brasov were recruited for this study, out of which 68 were female and 9 male, with ages between 18 and 24, with an average of 20.4 years old. In order to comply with the professional conduct rules, the participants gave their consent regarding their involvement in this research. The questionnaires were answered online, were anonymous, and did not imply any kind of compensation. The results are confidential and are used only for the purpose of this study. Participants were invited to answer the following three psychological tests:

(1) *Inventory of Parent and Peer Attachment* – IPPA assesses the positive and negative affective and cognitive dimensions of adolescents' relationships with their parents and close friends. The theoretical background of this instrument is the attachment theory, and the results represent indicators regarding the psychological safety level. The inventory consists of two scales: parent attachment relationship (PAR1) and peer attachment relationship (PAR2), each containing 25 items, measured on a five-point Likert scale. For each of the parent and peer scales of the IPPA, items are included to assess three dimensions of attachment including trust – 10 items, communication – 9 items, and alienation – 6 items. In their psychometric investigation of the IPPA, as concerning the alpha Cronbach coefficient, its authors found significant inter-correlations between all subscales, with values ranging between .72 and .91 (Armsdein & Greenberg, 1989). The present study reported excellent internal consistency for the IPPA with Cronbach's alpha coefficient of .91 for both the parent and peer attachment sub-scales. Past research found that attachment, as assessed with the IPPA, is associated with several personality variables. Among mid-to-late adolescents and young adults, the parent and peer attachment is correlated with positivity and stability of self-esteem, as well as with satisfaction with life and emotional state. The respondents who described their relationships with parents as being respectful (trust) and committed (communication) and who rated minimum values at the alienation dimension were nominated as having a high level of secure attachment. In contrast, the ones whose relationships with parents were marked by lack of trust and interest, but full of anger and detachment, were nominated as having a low secure attachment. The authors found that the participants who had a high level of secure attachment, reported a higher self-satisfaction, a higher probability

to seek help from others and less inadequate reactions toward the negative life events (Vivona, 2000).

(2) *The Adolescent Resilience Scale* – ARS measures the psychological features of resilient young individuals and consists of 21 items, covering three factors: Novelty Seeking (the ability to be interested in a wide variety of events), Emotion Regulation (the ability to remain calm and to properly manage emotions), and Positive Future Orientation (the effort of achieving one's goals). The construct validity of ARS was determined in a study conducted with a group of 207 Japanese undergraduates and the results suggest that mentally healthy individuals, who had fewer negative life events had high resilience scores (Oshio et al., 2003). The present study reported a good internal consistency, with Cronbach's alpha coefficient of .87 for the entire scale, a .82 alpha coefficient for the Positive Future Orientation factor, an acceptable .76 and .70 alpha coefficient for the Novelty Seeking factor and, respectively, for the Emotion Regulation factor.

(3) *The Satisfaction with Life Scale* – SWLS is focused on assessing global life satisfaction and does not target related constructs such as positive affects or loneliness. This scale was based on the idea that it is necessary to ask the individuals for their overall judgment of their life, rather than obtaining a measure of the life satisfaction as a concept. The presence of this subjectivity is important because individuals are different in terms of country of origin, religion, and values; additionally, there is a large variety of personal perspectives and ways to be in the world so that it would be impossible to split this concept into certain specific domains (Diener et al. 2013). SWLS consists of 5 items on a 7-point Likert scale. The SWLS is shown to be a valid and reliable measure of life satisfaction, suited for the use with a wide range of age groups and applications (Pavot et al., 1991). The scale has a good internal consistency, with Cronbach's alpha coefficient between .79 and .89. Test-retest correlations proved to have good results (.84, .80) within a month period (Diener et al., 1985). The present study reported a good internal consistency as well, with Cronbach's alpha coefficient of .85.

The analysis of the results suggests a positive correlation between resilience and the level of attachment ($r = .37$, $p = .001$). Young adults who score high in resilience are able to build parent and peer positive relationships, and they also have a high level of attachment. The regression analysis model is statistically significant ($F = 12.34$, $p = .001$) and resilience represents a significant predictor for the attachment level ($t = 3.51$, $p = .001$). According to the linear regression analysis,

14 % (R^2 = .14) of the variation in the secure attachment level is explained by resilience.

The data obtained emphasizes that there is a statistically significant association between the predictor (attachment level) and the criterion (satisfaction with life) (r = .46, p = .001). Young adults who develop positive relationships, both with parents and peers, and who have a high level of attachment, will also have a high level of satisfaction with life. The mean value of the coefficient indicates that the attachment level is not the only factor that can explain the level of satisfaction with life; the latter could also be partially determined by personality traits, genetic factors, social-cognitive mechanisms, purpose-related activities, self-efficacy, expectations regarding the achievements, and the environment's support and resources. The linear regression analysis confirms that 21 % (R^2 = .21) of the satisfaction with life variation is explained by the attachment level. Therefore, besides the external, environmental factors and the personality traits, the attachment level represents an important dimension for explaining satisfaction with life, among young adults. The regression model is statistically significant (F = 20.27, p = .001), and the attachment level is a significant predictor for the level of satisfaction with life (t= 4.50, p = .001).

A positive strong correlation between the resilience level and satisfaction with life is to be noted (r = .67, p = .001). The regression analysis model is statistically significant (F = 64.16, p = .001), resilience being a significant predictor for satisfaction with life (t = 8.01, p = .001). The collected data prove that 46 % (R^2 = .46) of the satisfaction with life variation is explained by resilience. This result is in line with recent studies that suggest that a change in resilience predicts a change in the level of life satisfaction (Cohn et al., 2009).

As regarding the relation between the attachment level and emotion regulation, the results show that an increased level of the parent attachment is associated with emotion regulation (r = .27, p = .01); there is also a positive correlation, statistically significant, between the peer attachment level and emotion regulation (r = .34, p < .01). Students with a high level of secure parent and peer attachment level have the ability to understand and manage their own emotions, which stands as one of the greatest challenges of life itself (Gross, 2002); this means that these individuals are aware of the emotions they experience, they pay attention to the emotions' evolution in time, and they are able to correctly name and categorize them; all these skills help people direct and modify their emotions toward the achievement of their goals and the creation of healthy, functional, human relationships.

The results of the study also indicate the existence of a positive association between the parent attachment level and the positive future orientation, as a dimension of resilience ($r = .40$, $p = .001$). The confirmation of this last hypothesis is supported by the Kauai longitudinal study and by the Parent-Child Minnesota project, which suggested that an early personal history marked by a positive adjustment and by a protective and consistent care represents a powerful and long-lasting influence on the child's ability to adapt, offering the opportunity to use formal and informal support resources throughout the entire life. The empirical evidence illustrates that a loving and supportive relationship with a parent or with another family member represents one of the most powerful resilience processes during childhood and adolescence (Fergus & Zimmerman, 2005; Werner, 2005; Drapeau et al., 2007).

The results of the study suggest that a secure attachment, the parents' emotional support and the development of reliable, trustworthy relationships contribute to the creation of resilience and satisfaction with life, among young adults. The research hypothesis complete the attachment, resilience, and satisfaction with life studies and the results are consistent with previous research. Therefore, the confirmation of the hypothesis is in accordance with Bowlby (1969), who considers that the family environment is essential for developing a person's attachment style, well-being, and life satisfaction. Furthermore, the secure attachment is positively correlated with positive emotions (Torquati & Raffaelli, 2004) and with well-being (La Guardia et al., 2000). Feeney (1999) suggests that individuals with a secure attachment style, unlike those with an insecure attachment, tend to be more satisfied with the relationships with others. According to Haddadi Koohsara and Bonab (2011), satisfaction with life can be predicted by the quality of the attachment style. They noticed that participants with an anxious attachment style obtained lower scores at the satisfaction with life scale than those with a secure attachment style. In a study conducted by Steger and Kashdan (2009), the relation between the need to belong and well-being is statistically significant, which means a higher life satisfaction. Also, satisfaction with life is influenced by some personality variables; by the degree of satisfaction one feels about certain life domains, by the involvement in everyday tasks that value life, by the goals which aim to progress and personal growth, and by resilience (Lent et al., 2009).

The results of the present study are consistent with the abovementioned research, so, we can assume, in line with the presented hypothesis, that: (1) fourteen percent of the variation in the attachment level is explained by resilience; therefore, resilience represents a significant predictor for a high level of secure parent and peer attachment style, among young adults; (2) twenty-one percent of the variation in satisfaction with life is predicted by the attachment style; as a result, the attachment style is a significant predictor for satisfaction with life, among young adults; (3) forty-six percent of the satisfaction with life variation is explained by resilience, which becomes a significant predictor for life satisfaction; (4) young adults who developed a parent and peer secure attachment style are able to identify, understand, properly label, and manage emotions, too, by resorting to healthy emotion regulation strategies; (5) young adults who have a secure parent attachment style adapt successfully to very stressful situations or negative events, adopting a positive perspective of the future and striving to achieve their goals.

Evidence from previous research confirms that healthy relationships represent a great support for those who are experiencing stressful events and potentially traumatic circumstances. Secure attachments – those relationships in which there is a responsive, calm, loving, and thoughtful adult – empower the children's nervous system with the greatest resilience. Children and young adults who have a secure attachment style learn to develop a well-balanced state of mind, integrating both the cognitive and the emotional memory into a coherent personal history; they also learn to be confident in their parents' availability when needed, and they know that this protective source will become a personal resource for possible future life-threatening situations. Of those people who grow up in extreme poverty, abuse, or neglect, the ones who best recover and who, in a certain way, overcome their condition are the people who have around them at least one person who takes care of them and who, on a regular basis, is emotionally available. Research focuses on the central role that parents and significant figures have during early childhood, when small children are more willing to ask for support. Furthermore, it is important to emphasize the parents' role in facilitating a secure peer attachment, which, in turn, is associated with positive achievements (Allen & Land, 1999).

Fonagy et al. (1991, 1994) studied the relation between secure attachment and resilience and came to the conclusion that this obvious relation between the two variables is also associated with meta-cognition and with self-reflection, two central aspects of psychological health. Letourneau (1997) comes to the conclusion that a highly qualitative parent-child interaction is very important for fostering resilience in children, suggesting that this kind of interaction should be the central topic of early intervention programs for families.

The limits of this research must be taken into account: there was a small number of respondents and the vast majority of them was female; the participants were psychology students, and this may have influenced the results; other uncontrollable factors, such as recent experiences (in their family or in the peer group), could have biased some of the answers, especially those included in the IPPA. Taking all these aspects into account for a future reference, it is preferable to conduct a longitudinal and potentially mixed research for studying the relation between attachment, resilience, and satisfaction with life. It would be interesting to follow the evolution of the attachment level during the college years, for a large number of participants, male and female, since all three variables are too complex to be interpreted using only a simple test application.

Taking into account the results of the studies that reveal the negative impact of the insecure attachment on children's development and analyzing the data of the longitudinal studies which confirm that the insecure attachment represents one of the most vulnerable factors for a growing person, the need to intervene and to promote the secure attachment comes naturally and has to become a priority. Moreover, it was noted that the researchers or clinicians who studied the attachment ended up pleading for children's rights, trying to leave a mark on the health system and the social politics (Azar, 1995). Whether we are talking about low self-esteem, a lack of trust, or severe emotion regulation difficulties, the insecure attachments represent psycho-social disabilities, not only creating the right environment for children and adolescents to internalize and externalize problems but also generating the possibility of developing, at an adult age, an incapacity to solve problems. Considering that the attachment schemes formed in early childhood could have behavioral consequences beyond adolescence – as shown in the present study and in the previous ones – we cannot underestimate the importance of the secure attachment for children's growth. Therefore, it becomes a goal in itself to establish a secure base for children by facilitating this process for parents to consciously recognize the importance of their relationships for the child's future.

A future implication of the study concerns the possibility of designing contingency plans able to help develop resilience and, therefore, life satisfaction, contributing to a successful adaptation. Young adults, with an increased resilience level, seem to have more control over their skills and over their internal and external resources in order to cope with difficulties, which, in turn, lead to higher levels of satisfaction with life. Thus, as a result of such research, the education system could integrate programs which aim, on the one hand, to develop stress management strategies among students, taking into account, on the other hand, their family dynamics and the nature of their parent and peer trust relationships. The educational programs' efficiency depends, to a large extent, on how the specialist in psychology will emotionally support participants to deconstruct the childhood attachment patterns and form new ones within the therapeutic relationship. As the initial attachment relationship allows the child to develop, the attachment relationship built within the psychological intervention causes young adults to change because it provides a safety base that enables them to take the risk of feeling what they would not want to feel and to discover what they have long avoided to know (Wallin, 2010).

Johnson (2020) argues that young adults, who can afford to depend on reliable individuals, created a personal secure base, a source of power and resilience, which gives them the freedom to explore the opportunities around them, to take risks and develop autonomously. Validating the attachment needs, confessing them to the significant figures in a coherent manner, and accepting the responsibility for experiencing their own emotions (followed by clear identification and appropriate labeling of the emotional inner world, their discrimination, and emotion processing) represent the way to human potential self-realization, personal and professional self-fulfillment, creativity, authenticity and spontaneity (Năstasă, 2010), abilities so necessary for gaining security and life satisfaction.

References

Allen, J. P., & Land, D. (1999). Attachment in adolescence. In J. Cassidy & P.R. Shaver (Eds.), *Handbook of attachment theory and research* (pp. 319–335). New York: Guilford.

Armsdein, G. C., & Greenberg, M. T. (1989). *Inventory of parent and peer attachment (IPPA)*. Seattle, WA: University of Washington.

Azar, H. (1995). Attitudes toward deafness and security of attachment relationships among young deaf children and their parents. *Early Education and Development*, 6(2), 181–191.

Baldwin, M. W., & Fehr, B. (1995). On the instability of attachment style ratings. *Personal Relationships*, 2, 247–261.

Barrett, L. F. (2017). *How emotions are made: The secret life of the brain*. Cluj-Napoca: ASCR.

Barrett, L. F., & Bliss-Moreau, E. (2009). Affect as a psychological primitive. *Advances in Experimental Social Psychology*, 41, 167–218.

Barrett, L. F., Gross, J., Christensen, T. C., & Benvenuto, M. (2001). Knowing what you're feeling and knowing what to do about it: Mapping the relation between emotion differentiation and emotion regulation. *Cognition and Emotion*, 15(6), 713–724.

Bartholomew, K., & Shaver, P. R. (1998). Methods of assessing adult attachment: Do they converge? In J. A. Simpson, & S. Rholes (Eds.), *Attachment theory and close relationships* (pp. 25–45). New York: Guilford Press.

Bowlby, J. (1969). *Attachment and loss: Vol. 1. Attachment*. New York: Basic Books.

Bowlby, J. (1973). *Attachment and loss: Vol. 2. Separation, anxiety and anger* (2nd ed.) New York: Basic Books.

Bowlby, J. (1980). *Attachment and loss: Vol. 3. Loss.* New York: Basic Books.

Bowlby, J. (1982). *Attachment and loss, Vol. 1 Attachment* (2nd ed.). London: Hogarth Press.

Bowlby, J. (2011). *A secure base. Clinical applications of attachment theory.* Bucharest: Trei.

Bretherton, I. (1985). Attachment theory: Retrospect and prospect. *Monographs of the Society for Research in Child Development,* 50, 3–35.

Carnelley, K., & Janoff-Bulman, R. (1992). Optimism about love relationships: General vs. specific lessons from one's personal experiences. *Journal of Social and Personality Relationships*, 9, 5–20.

Cazan, A. M., & Năstasă L. E. (2015). Emotional intelligence, satisfaction with life and burnout among university students. *Procedia of Social and Behavioral Sciences*, 180(5), 1574–1578.

Clark, K. E., & Ladd, G. W. (2000). Connectedness and autonomy support in parent-child relationships: Links to children's socioemotional orientation and peer relationships. *Developmental Psychology*, 36, 485–98.

Cohn, M., Frederickson, B., Brown, S., Mikels, J., & Conway, A. (2009). Happiness unpacked: Positive emotions increase life satisfaction by building resilience. *Emotion,* 9, 361–368.

Daus, C. S., & Ashkanasy, N. M. (2005). The case for an ability-based model of emotional intelligence in organizational behavior. *Journal of Organizational Behavior*, 26, 453–466.

Davila, J., Burge, D., & Hammen, C. (1997). Why does attachment style change? *Journal of Personality and Social Psychology*, 73, 826–838.

Davila, J., & Sargent, E. (2003). The meaning of life (events) predicts changes in attachment security. *Personality and Social Psychology Bulletin*, 29, 1383–1395.

Denham, S. A. (2007). Dealing with feelings: How children negotiate the worlds of emotions and social relationships. *Cognition, Brain and Behavior*, 11(1), 1–48.

Diener, E., Emmons, R. A., Larsen, R. J., & Griffin, S. (1985). The satisfaction with life scale. *Journal of Personality Assessment*, 49, 71–75.

Diener, E., Inglehart, R. F., & Tay, L. (2013). Theory and validity of life satisfaction scales. *Social Indicators Research*, 112, 497–527.

Drapeau, S., Saint-Jacques, M.-C., Lépine, R., Bégin, G., & Bernard, M. (2007). Processes that contribute to resilience among youth in foster care. *Journal of Adolescence*, 30(6), 977–999.

Emmons, R. A., & McCullough, M. E. (2003). Counting blessings versus burdens: An experimental investigation of gratitude and subjective well-being in daily life. *Journal of Personality and Social Psychology*, 84 (2), 377–389.

Epstein, N. B., Bishop, D., Ryan, C, Miller, I., & Keitner G. (1993). The McMaster Model: view of healthy family functioning. In F. Walsh (Ed.), *Normal family processes* (pp. 138–160). New York: Guilford.

Erbas, Y., Ceulemans, E., Lee Pe, M., Koval, P., & Kuppens, P. (2014). Negative emotion differentiation: Its personality and well-being correlates and a comparison of different assessment methods. *Cognition and Emotion*, 28(7), 1196–1213.

Feeney, J. A. (1999). Adult romantic attachment and couple relationships. In J. Cassidy & P. R. Shaver (Eds.), *Handbook of attachment: Theory, research, and clinical applications* (pp. 355–377). New York: Guilford.

Fergus, S., & Zimmerman, M. A. (2005). Adolescent resilience: A framework for understanding healthy development in the face of risk. *Annual Review of Public Health* 26, 399–419.

Fonagy, P., Steele, H., & Steele, M. (1991). Maternal representations of attachments during pregnancy predict the organisation of infant-mother attachment at one year of age. *Child development*, 62, 891–905.

Fonagy, P., Steele, H., Steele, M., Higgitt, A., & Target, M. (1994). The Emanuel Miller Memorial Lecture 1992: The theory and practice of resilience. *Child Psychology & Psychiatry & Allied Disciplines*, 35, 231–257.

Fraley, R. C., & Shaver, P. R. (2000). Adult romantic attachment: Teoretical developments, emerging controversies, and unanswered questions. *Review of General Psychology*, 4, 132–154.

Froh, J. J, Sefick, W. J., & Emmons, R. A. (2008). Counting blessings in early adolescents: An experimental study of gratitude and subjective well-being. *Journal of School Psychology*, 46, 213–233.

Fuller, T., & Fincham, F. (1995). Attachment style in married couples: Relation to current marital functioning, stability over time, and method of assessment. *Personal Relationships*, 2, 17--34.

Goldberg, S. (2000). *Attachment and development*. London: Arnold.

Gross, J. J. (2002). Emotion regulation: Affective, cognitive and social consequences. *Psychophysiology*, 39, 281–291.

Haddadi Koohsara, A. A., & Bonab, B. G. (2011). Relation between quality of attachment and life satisfaction in high school administrators. *Procedia – Social and Behavioral Sciences*, 30, 954 – 958.

Johnson, S. M. (2008). *Hold me tight: Seven conversations for a lifetime of love.* New York: Little & Brown.

Johnson, S. M. (2020). *Attachment theory in practice: Emotionally Focused Therapy (EFT) with individuals, couples, and families.* Bucharest: Trei.

Kashdan, T. B., Ferssizidis, P., Collins, R. L., & Muraven, M. (2010). Emotion differentiation as resilience against excessive alcohol use: An ecological momentary assessment in underage social drinkers. *Psychological Science*, 21(9), 1341–1347.

Kerns, K. A., Klepac, L., & Cole, A. (1996). Peer relationships and preadolescents' perception of security in the child-mother relationship. *Developmental Psychology*, 32, 457–466.

Kimhy, D., Vakhrusheva, J., Khan, S., Chang, R. W., Hansen, M. C., Ballon, J. S., Malaspina, D., & Gross, J. J. (2014). Emotional granularity and social functioning in individuals with Schizophrenia: An experience sampling study. *Journal of Psychiatric Research*, 53, 141–148.

Kirkpatrick, L., & Hazen, C. (1994). Attachment styles and close relationships: A four year prospective study. *Personal Relationships*, 1, 123–142.

La Guardia, J. G., Ryan, R. M., Couchman, C. E., & Deci, E. L. (2000). Within-person variation in security of attachment: A self-determination theory perspective on attachment, need fulfillment, and well-being. *Journal of Personality and Social Psychology*, 79, 367–384.

Lent, R. W., Taveira, M. B., Sheu, H. B., & Singley, D. (2009). Social cognitive predictors of academic adjustment and life satisfaction in portuguese college students: A longitudinal analysis, *Journal of Vocational Behavior*, 74, 190–198.

Letourneau, N. (1997). Fostering resiliency in infants and young children through parent infant interaction. *Infants and Young Children*, 9(3), 36–45.

Main, M., Kaplan, N., & Cassidy, J. (1985). Security in infancy, childhood, and adulthood: A move to the level of representation. *Monographs of the Society for Research in Child Development*, 50, 66–104.

Mauss, I. B., Bunge, S. A., & Gross, J. J. (2007). Automatic emotion regulation. *Social and Personality Psychology Compass*, 1, 1–22.

Maccoby, E. E., & Martin, J. A. (1983). Socialization in the context of the family: Parent-childinteraction. In E. M. Hetherington (Ed.), *Handbook of child psychology*: Vol. 4, Socialization, personality, and social development (pp. 469–546). New York: Wiley.

MacDonald, K. (1992). Warmth as a developmental construct: An evolutionary analysis. *Child Development*, 63, 753–773.

Mennin, D. S., Heimberg, R. G., Turk, C. L., & Fresco, D. M. (2005). Preliminary evidence for an emotion dysregulation model of generalized anxiety disorder. *Behaviour Research and Therapy*, 43(10), 1281–1310.

Mikulincer, M., & Shaver, P. R. (2001). Attachment theory and intergroup bias: Evidence that priming the secure base schema attenuates negative reactions to out-groups. *Journal of Personality and Social Psychology*, 81, 97–115.

Mikulincer, M., & Shaver, P. R. (2007). Boosting attachment security to promote mental health, prosocial values, and inter-group tolerance. *Psychological Inquiry*, 18, 139 156.

Mikulincer, M., & Shaver, P. R. (2016a). *Attachment in adulthood: Structure, dynamics, and change*. New York: Guilford Press.

Mikulincer, M., & Shaver, P. R. (2016b). Adult attachment and emotion regulation. In J. Cassidy, & P. R. Shaver (Eds.), *Handbook of attachment: Theory, research and clinical applications* (pp. 507–533). New York: Guilford Press.

Mikulincer, M., & Shaver, P. R. (2019). Attachment orientations and emotion regulation. *Current opinion in psychology*, 25, 6–10.

Naragon-Gainey, K., McMahon, T. P., & Chacko, T. P. (2017). The structure of common emotion regulation strategies: A meta-analytic examination. *Psychological Bulletin*, 143(4), 384–427.

Năstasă, L. E. (2010). Developing emotional intelligence of students in psychology through the experiential group. In I. Mitrofan (ed.). *Validation studies and applied research of psychology and psychotherapy unification – in education, personal development and clinical* (pp. 565–802). Bucharest: Bucharest University Press.

Năstasă L. E., & Farcaş A. D. (2015). The effect of emotional intelligence on burnout in health care professionals. *Procedia of Social and Behavioral Sciences*, 167, 78–82.

Năstasă, L. E., & Sala, K. (2012). Adolescents' emotional intelligence and parental styles. *Procedia of Social and Behavioral Sciences*, 33, 478–482.

Nørby, S. (2018). Forgetting and emotion regulation in mental health, anxiety and depression. *Memory*, 26(3), 342–363.

Oshio, A., Kaneko, H., Nagamine, S., & Nakaya, M. (2003). Construct validity of the adolescent resilience scale. *Psychological Reports*, 93, 1217–1222.

Pavot, W. G., Diener, E., Colvin, C. R., & Sandvik, E. (1991). Further validation of the satisfaction with life scale: Evidence for the cross-method convergence of well being measures. *Journal of Personality Assessment*, 57, 149–161.

Pianta, R. C., & Walsh, D. J. (1996). *High-risk children in schools: Constructing sustaining relationships*. New York: Routledge.

Pond, R. S., Kashdan, T. B., DeWall, C. N., Farmer, A. S., Lambert, N. M., & Fincham, F. D. (2012). Emotion differentiation moderates aggressive tendencies in angry people: A daily diary analysis. *Emotion*, 12(2), 326–337.

Ruppert, F. (2012). *Trauma, bonding & family constellations: Understanding and healing injuries of the soul*. Bucharest: Trei.

Shapiro, D. L., & Levendosky, A. A. (1999). Adolescent survivors of childhood sexual abuse: The mediating role of attachment style and coping in psychological and interpersonal functioning. *Child Abuse and Neglect*, 23(11), 1175–1191.

Shaver, P. R., & Mikulincer, M. (2002). Attachment-related psychodynamics. *Attachment & Human Development*, 4(2), 133–161.

Siegel, D. J. (2014). *The power and purpose of the teenage brain*. Bucharest: Herald.

Sroufe, L. A., & Waters, E. (1977). Attachment as an organizational construct. *Child Development*. 48, 1184–1199.

Steger, M. F., & Kashdan, T. B. (2009). Depression and everyday social activity, belonging and well-being. *Journal of Counseling Psychology*, 56(2), 289–300.

Torquati, J. C., & Raffaelli, M. (2004). Daily experiences of emotions and social contexts of securely and insecurely attached young adults. *Journal of Adolescent Research*, 19, 740–758.

Torre, J. B., & Lieberman, M. D. (2018). Putting feelings into words: Affect labeling as implicit emotion regulation. *Emotion Review*, 10(2), 116–124.

Van Rooy, D. L., & Viswesvaran, C. (2004). Emotional intelligence: A meta-analytic investigation of predictive validity and nomological net. *Journal of Vocational Behavior*, 65, 71–95.

Vivona, J. M. (2000). Parental attachment styles of late adolescents: Qualities of attachment relationships and consequences for adjustment. *Journal of Counseling Psychology*, 47(3), 316–329.

Wallin, D. J. (2010). *Attachment in psychotherapy*. Bucharest: Trei.

Waters, E., Merrick, S., Treboux, D., Crowell, J., & Albersheim, L. (2000). Attachment security in infancy and early adulthood: A twenty-year longitudinal study. *Child Development*, 71, 684–689.

Werner, E. (2005). 'What can we learn about resilience from large-scale longitudinal studies?'. In S. Goldstein & R. Brooks (Eds.), *Handbook of resilience in children* (pp. 91–106). New York: Kluwer Academic/Plenum.

Ramona HENTER and Cristina NICOLAU

5 Teachers' Superpowers: Being Mindful. Being Positive. Being in the Flow – a Basis for Their Well-Being

Abstract Teaching depends not only on teachers' scientific and psycho-pedagogic abilities, but also on their ability to finely analyze what is going on in their classroom and in their students' minds; hence, the necessity of metacognitive training, doubled by the development of personal abilities such as perseverance, receptivity, and acceptance that can be attained through mindful practices. Mindfulness, the ability to draw one's attention to the experiences occurring in the present moment without judging them (Kabat-Zinn, 1990), brings about optimism, seen by Seligman (1991) as having a general positive feeling about the future and fosters the state of flow, defined as an intense and focused concentration on the present moment (Nakamura & Csikszentmihályi, 2001). Teacher training mainly focuses on pedagogical abilities and psychological content aiming to guide students' development, but the above abilities offer support for both a focus on students' individual differences and teachers' personal well-being.

Keywords: Mindfulness, positive psychology, metacognition, flow, optimism

1. Being Aware while Teaching

Awareness highlights the processes that are going on in our mind while finding solutions for daily challenges. We can be aware of our cognitive or affective processes and a teacher should be aware of both, meaning that they should use metacognitive abilities while solving problems (as these require cognitive skills that can be directed by metacognition) and at the same time, they should be mindful by having a complete image of what is going on in their body and mind as regarding the feeling associated with the activity. Teachers' personal resources are needed to offer them the sources of optimism, positivity, and the possibility to fully engage in their teaching, to feel appreciated and to live the whole teaching experience as an activity full of joy, to feel its importance, and to take advantage of everything else while in front of the students.

Teaching has become a very strenuous profession, and successful teachers are defined not only by their scientific and psycho-pedagogic abilities, but also by their ability to be aware of everything that is going on in their classroom and in their students' minds; hence, the necessity of metacognitive training

(Henter, 2014) for the cognitive part, doubled by the development of personal abilities such as perseverance, receptivity, tolerance, and acceptance that can be attained through mindful practices.

1.1. Metacognition

The concept of metacognition introduced by John Flavell in 1976 defined metacognition as "knowledge of cognitive phenomena" (Flavell, 1979), awareness of the thinking process: what we think, how we think about a particular task or situation, and why we think in a certain way. Metacognition also includes the ability to monitor these processes (Goh, 2008). Further development and use of the term metacognition remained relatively faithful to this initial sense. Many researchers point out that metacognition is best defined by recognizing that it represents both knowledge and control over thought processes (Armour-Thomas & Allen, 1990; Mayer, 2003). Metacognition is "the ability to reflect on what you do or not do about what you know or do not know, leading to critical reflection and assessment of thinking, which can lead to changes in learning" (Anderson, 2005).

After Flavell (1979), metacognition takes the form of metacognitive experiences, metacognitive knowledge, goals, and activities or strategies. The research based on Flavell's model of metacognition revealed the existence of two dimensions of metacognition: knowledge of cognition and regulation of cognition (Mayer, 2003; Schraw & Moshman, 1995).

Knowledge about cognition can be divided into three factors: declarative knowledge ("knowing that"), procedural knowledge ("knowing how," where we can include the learning strategies), and conditional knowledge (knowing where, when, and why someone uses a certain strategy). Several researchers have used the concepts of declarative and procedural knowledge to distinguish types of cognitive knowledge (Mayer, 2003; Schraw & Moshman, 1995). Kuhn and Dean (2004) characterize declarative cognitive knowledge as being, broadly speaking, the epistemological understanding or the understanding of one's own way of thinking and knowing in general. Schraw et al. (2006) portray cognitive declarative knowledge as the learner' self-knowledge, as well as factors that could influence one's performance. On the other hand, procedural knowledge involves awareness and management of knowledge, including knowledge about strategies (Kuhn & Dean, 2004; Schraw et al., 2006). Schraw et al. (2006) distinguish another category, that of conditional cognitive knowledge, which is the knowledge of the reason and the moment of using a certain strategy. Researchers noted that although the ability to explicitly articulate cognitive knowledge tends to improve with age, many adults fail to explain what they know about their thinking, which may suggest that this cognitive knowledge does not need to be explicit for people to be able to access and use it.

Cognitive regulation includes planning (selecting appropriate strategies and allocating the resources needed to carry out the task), monitoring (comprehension about the level of understanding and solving the task during its implementation), testing (putting into practice), reviewing and evaluating strategies (including the evaluation of the methods used, but also of the objectives and the results) (Schraw & Moshman, 1995). Many researchers have argued that it includes planning, monitoring, and regulation activities, as well as evaluation (Mayer, 2003; Schraw & Moshman, 1995; Schraw et al., 2006). Planning involves identifying and selecting the right strategies and appropriately allocating resources and may include setting goals, activating general knowledge, and setting time resources. Monitoring involves active and conscious participation in understanding and accomplishing the task and may include self-testing. Flavell (1979) discusses cognitive monitoring in the context of "cognitive experiences" represented by perceptions or inward gazes during the processes of knowledge, expressed in phrases such as "I do not understand this." Flavell notes that these experiences can serve as "quality control," which helps students revise their goals. Finally, evaluation is defined as "assessment of regulatory products and processes of learning" and includes the review of one's goals (Schraw et al., 2006).

1.2. Mindfulness

Mindfulness can be defined as the ability to participate in a non-evaluative manner in one's own physical and mental processes during normal daily tasks. It can be seen both as a human trait that is present in all individuals, in varying proportions, and as a skill that can be learned through the practice of meditation (van Son et al., 2015; Sharf, 2014).

Mindfulness meditation requires focusing only on the present moment, on what is happening to us now or on our thoughts, and to observe all these events with some detachment – that is, to be aware of their existence, but not to judge them. Once we are aware of our experiences, they can no longer exert the same influence on us because, although we do not evaluate them as good or bad, pleasant or unpleasant, we analyze them and our reaction will be more appropriate, given that most of us act impulsively. Instead of reacting as usual, mindfulness helps us stop and look at the situation, as well as the emotions and thoughts that it provokes; it prevents us from falling into the mesh of the old story we tell ourselves with regarding similar events (that we have experienced or imagined) and helps us identify a new scenario, a more adaptive one (Loucks et al., 2019). Therefore, it helps teachers treat each situation with a fresh perspective, preventing them from keeping grudges and offer them the space for creatively solving any problem. Being present in the moment and noticing thoughts and emotions without judgment is aimed at reducing stress (Kabat-Zinn, 1990).

Mindfulness as an ability is conceptualized as the set of meditation techniques that can be learned by anyone (Mantzios & Wilson, 2013). It can be practiced formally – making time daily to practice using, perhaps, guided meditations, performed by a specialist to guide you throughout the exercise – or informally – to allow these practices to penetrate into all the areas of life, in an unplanned and natural way, meaning becoming aware of everything that is in you and around you in all areas of life (Kabat-Zinn, 2016).

Such skills were integrated into special programs based on mindfulness, both for alleviating suffering, mindfulness-based interventions having been shown to be effective in improving people's well-being, including lowering general stress, anxiety, and depression symptoms and for offering protection against the influence of stressful events on emotional well-being, acting as a buffer (van Son High, 2017). Mindfulness training for teachers is scarce, although the need for instruments to help teachers handle the stress and emotional rollercoaster or teaching has been long present. As "the thoughts and emotions of both students and teachers play a critical role in the teaching and learning process" (Marzano & Marzano, 2015, p. 3), teachers can improve the level of students' learning outcomes by regulating their own inner world. Also, "the relationship between what teachers are thinking and feeling at any point in time and their actions at the same point in time" (Marzano & Marzano, 2015, p. 2) influences both the teaching activity and teachers' well-being: positive teacher emotions lead to effective teaching strategies, while negative teacher emotions lead to low motivation in teachers, which, in turn, inhibited student learning (Garner, 2010). Not surprisingly, frustration mainly felt by teachers (Garner, 2010) and burnout is present in school personnel (Chang, 2009). If teachers do not have effective coping skills to manage the daily stresses of teaching, they act in overly punitive ways and are not able to offer a supportive and nurturing environment for students (Jennings, 2011).

As Viktor E. Frankl said, "between stimulus and response there is a space. In that space is our power to choose our response. In our response lies our growth and our happiness." That space represents our ability to use metacognitive and/or mindfulness skills to better adjust to the situation. "The psychological capacity to stay wilfully present with one's experiences, with a non-judgmental or accepting attitude, engendering a warm and friendly openness and curiosity" (Kabat-Zinn, 2003) represented by mindfulness should be trained early during the teacher training so as to offer personal constructs able to sustain the process of awareness during teaching, awareness toward all that is happening in the classroom, with the students and in the teachers' mind. The opposite, mindlessness means being on autopilot with little conscious awareness and allowing old, habitual responses to take over, instead of offering each situation the peculiar response it needs. Neurosciences (Woodyard, 2011; Russo, Santarelli, & O'Rourke, 2017) showed that breathing triggers the parasympathetic nervous system – the opposite of fight or flight response – which slows heart rate and makes blood pressure go down. So, the breathing techniques of mindfulness can contribute to a better adaptation to the situation. What is essential in facilitating positive change through mindfulness is intention, which sets the stage for what is possible, reminding us from moment to moment of why one is practicing mindfulness in the first place (Kabat-Zinn, 1990).

Jennings (2011) and other researchers have specifically proposed mindfulness as a tool to prevent burnout and promote well-being in teachers. Chang (2009) suggested that teachers be trained to deal with emotional domains with effective emotional regulation and coping strategies as an antidote to burnout. Meiklejohn et al. (2012) found that mindfulness was a cost-effective way for school systems to build resilience and reduce burnout in teachers. Moreover, Roeser et al. (2013) proposed that using mindfulness as a mechanism to build habits of mind, teachers showed improved well-being, occupational health, engagement, and student relationships. Marzano and Marzano (2015) stated mindfulness was "quite obviously related to managing inner world" (p. 51) and intimated that "managing the inner world is attainable by all teachers with the proper understanding of the human mind and the requisite practice" (p. 55). Additionally, Greenberg et al. (2016) reported that "mindfulness practices can lead to reductions in psychological stress" (p. 9).

Taking time to turn focus onto yourself so that you can better respond to various challenges in the classroom may seem as impossible to do for some teachers who see time a scarce resource so that every new task becomes an urgency. Time urgency leads to time pressure, which spawns a chronic state of impatience, accompanied by hurry and maybe negative thoughts when projecting into the future the failure of accomplishing the task in the minimum of time allotted. These behaviors have a negative impact on one's own work and relationships as they trick the body to enter a flight or fight response state as a stress-related response. The autonomic nervous system (ANS) and the hypothalamic-pituitary-adrenal (HPA) axis are two major systems that respond to stressors by regulating the function of internal organs. During stress situations, the activity of the sympathetic branch increases, while the activity of the parasympathetic branch decreases, leading to alterations in the activity of innervated organs (e.g., increased cardiac activity). At the same time, the HPA axis regulates the release of cortisol, which influences many bodily functions such as metabolic, psychological, and immunological functions. These bodily responses shift one's attention to the internal organ functioning from the activity that was being done (from teaching and from paying attention to the children's real words and actions) and lead in time to specific disease such as depression or cardiovascular disease (Wettstein, Kühne, Tschacher, & La Marca, 2020). Thus, time management should be considered a myth – we cannot manage something over which we have no control, we can only manage our reaction to time passing. Mindfulness helps us stay in the present moment and fully make use of it.

Mindfulness is also envisioned as realizing freedom from delusion, hatred, and greed (Kabat-Zinn, 2003) and as increasing the participant's capacity of observing, describing, acting with awareness, non-judging, and non-reactivity (Baer et al., 2008). Kabat-Zinn (2003) conveyed that mindfulness was an "inherent human capacity" (p. 146), and Rechtschaffen (2014) stated, "the beauty of mindfulness for our modern use is that all we need is our breath, our bodies, our minds, and our hearts" (p. 36). Significantly, mindfulness has a non-harming orientation, akin to the medical Hippocratic Oath, such that mindfulness has been described as bidirectional with ethics (Kabat-Zinn, 2003).

Metacognitive and mindfulness skills can be taught (Efklides & Metallidou, 2020; Jones, Milton, Mostazir, & Adlam, 2019; Norton, Griffith, 2020; Laukkonen, Leggett, Gallagher, Biddell, Mrazek, Slagter, & Mrazek, 2020), but they are useful on a solid cognitive skills base – the abilities trained in any teaching program.

2. Being Positive while Teaching

The thoughts and emotions of both students and teachers play a critical role in the teaching and learning process (Marzano & Marzano, 2015). The goal of positive psychology is to guide people toward positive functioning and flourishing (Seligman, 2011). Teachers should have this goal for all their students, but first of all, they must be able to apply positive psychology skills on themselves. A flourishing-based approach means having a clear goal and intention to increase positive variables, by identifying and mobilizing human assets to help moderate dysfunctional emotions, cognitions, and behaviors; to prepare individuals with the skills and confidence to address life's challenges; and to foster and maintain an optimal state of well-being. Seligman's (2011) concept of PERMA summarizes this concept in the acronym: **P**ositive emotion, **E**ngagement, **R**elationships, **M**eaning, and **A**ccomplishment, all characteristics needed in teaching for fostering the development of children's strengths. Martin Seligman's (1991) theory of optimism focuses having a general positive feeling about the future, while the roots of that feeling are embedded in the way we explain to ourselves why things happen. Optimists believe that the causes of bad events and the causes of good events are permanent; that the causes of bad events are constrained to a particular area of life, and they tend to take credit for good events and attribute bad events to external causes. These characteristics, permanence, pervasiveness, and personalization offers optimists a view on life that enables them to pursue bolder goals, feeling valuable and deserving.

Being Mindful and Positive while Teaching

Being mindful and positive means combining the awareness about what is going on in the classroom, with the children and in the teachers' own mind and at the same time with the compassion and optimism for what is going on there. Teachers should focus on the PERMA concepts as they help both students to develop and teachers to enter the flow state.

3. Being in the Flow while Teaching

The flow is a mental state of operation where a person is fully immersed in an activity and experiences a feeling of extreme energized focus, complete involvement, and success in the activity or simply explained, completely focused motivation (Csikszentmihalyi, 1990). When in the flow, teachers don't feel as if they are working; they are energetic and able to focus on each detail of the class and the lesson taught.

Many teachers will recognize the experience of "flow" in their classrooms, when a teachable moment occurs serendipitously or when careful planning results in an authentic memorable learning experience for both teacher and students. However, when understanding the multiple, complex relationships in a classroom, we can better prepare for a flow experience. Fairness and happiness become emotional motivating factors in achieving a state of flow (Masterson, 2011).

4. Starting Being Mindful, Positive, and in the Flow Early on in the Teaching Career

Learning the skills that promote well-being early in life can prevent both turnovers in career and job associated disease. Preservice teachers' well-being skills are trained in their mock-classes, without previous academic support (as far as the Romanian education system is concerned). Preservice teachers do not have experience and are under continuous observation; therefore, they face many anxiogenic situations that can shape their professional persona. Anxiety is one of the main stress factor for any public-related profession, putting more strain on novices. One proven way to reduce anxiety is being mindful.

Preservice teachers are all the students preparing to become teachers and attending special teacher training courses, which include teaching practicum. Therefore, they may feel more anxiety and stress related to teaching the mock-classes (as part of their assignments) and being in front of a class of pupils (a state) or it be part of the student's personality (trait). Trait-anxiety is innate and manifests itself both through the predisposition to feel fear under the action of stimuli that for other people are less anxiogenic, or at least anxiogenic, and by the development of conditioned fears under the action of stimuli that are not anxiogenic (Larousse, 2006). Some occasional anxious reactions caused by factors such as the presence of a real danger, an examination or the health problems are normal and may even play a protective role and inhibit the possible inappropriate actions of the subject. In general, anxiety manifests in the absence of a concrete and valid reason and is a major problem that clinicians are trying to evaluate, having to rely on self-report questionnaires.

We designed a study aimed to identify the relationship between mindfulness and anxiety and to measure whether high levels of mindfulness skills are associated with less anxiety. Also, we thought that metacognitive awareness, which can be considered a special type of mindfulness (the ability to be present in your mind and identify the thoughts/strategies you use during a task), may also be linked to anxiety levels. Our hypothesis was that preservice teachers with high levels of mindfulness skills are less anxious during their teaching activities, and they feel greater levels of well-being than those not practicing mindfulness. Students preparing to become teachers were given mindfulness and anxiety inventories. The findings are discussed below.

The participants were first year students from Transilvania University of Brasov, including 124 female and 35 male students, preparing to become teachers. Their mean age was of 22.2 years old. Only 30 students were attending distance education, the rest being full-time students, and 108 were from humanistic faculties and 51 from engineering ones.

We used three self-report questionnaires to assess constructs of anxiety, mindfulness, and metacognition. The generalized anxiety disorder questionnaire (GAD-7) is a brief clinical measure for assessing the generalized anxiety disorder, developed by Robert L. Spitzer, Kurt Kroenke, Janet B. W. Williams, and Bernd Lowe (2006). It consists of 7 items, with a reported internal consistency of Cronbach alpha =.92, while for the present sample it was similar, Cronbach alpha =.903. The authors also report good criterion, construct, factorial, and procedural validity. The scale asks the respondents to say how often they had the presented symptoms during the last two weeks: not at all, on several days, more than half the days or nearly every day.

In order to assess the level of mindfulness, we used the Mindful Attention Awareness Scale (MAAS), a 15-item scale designed to assess mindfulness through its core concept a receptive state of mind in which attention, informed by a sensitive awareness of what is occurring in the present, simply observes what is taking place (Brown & Ryan, 2003). MAAS respondents indicate how frequently they have the experience described in each statement using a 6-point Likert scale from 1 (almost always) to 6 (almost never), where high scores reflect more mindfulness. The Cronbach alpha for the entire scale is of .856.

A metacognitive report was added to gain more knowledge about the factors influencing anxiety. The Metacognitive Awareness Inventory (MAI), developed by Schraw and Dennison (1994), was used. It has two main factors, the knowledge of cognition and regulation of cognition. The first factor has three components: declarative knowledge, procedural knowledge, and conditional knowledge, while the latter has five components: planning, information management, monitoring, debugging, and evaluation. The Cronbach alpha for the entire scale is of .949.

The data analysis started with calculating the Pearson correlation coefficients for the main variables involved in this research. The level of anxiety correlates negatively with all the other variables; thus, we can say that high levels of anxiety are associated with low levels of metacognitive awareness ($r=-.223$, $p=0.01$ for the relation with metacognitive knowledge, $r=-.157$, $p=0.05$ for the relation with metacognitive regulation, and $r=-.188$, $p=0.05$ for the relation with total metacognition) and mindfulness ($r=-.332$, $p=0.01$). We also found that age is strongly related to metacognition ($r=.187$, $p=0.05$) and its dimensions ($r=.220$, $p=0.01$ for metacognitive knowledge and $r=.158$, $p=0.05$ for metacognitive regulation), anxiety ($r=-330$, $p=0.01$), and mindfulness ($r=.268$, $p=0.01$).

As expected, grade point average correlates with the metacognitive skills: r=.184, p=0.01 for the general metacognition, r=.181, p=0.01 for metacognitive knowledge and r=.175, p=0.01 for metacognitive regulation, as metacognition clearly supports academic achievement.

We also aimed at finding whether self-analysis and self-knowledge were specific only to students coming from faculties where introspection and self-awareness is valued (such as Psychology or Education majors). There were not identified any statistically significant differences between the results obtained by students from humanistic and engineering faculties: t(157)=1.106, p=.270 for mindfulness and t(157)=.749, p=.455 for anxiety. Thus, we can assume that mindfulness and anxiety are not dependent on the field of education, but they are trait dependent.

Also, there were not identified any statistically significant differences between the results obtained by male and female students: t(157)=.654, p=.514 for mindfulness and t(157)= −1.797, p=.074 for anxiety. Thus, we can assume that the levels of mindfulness and anxiety experienced by the male and female students in our study are not statistically different significantly, although female students tend to show more anxiety.

The relationship between anxiety and mindfulness was addressed in previous research with findings suggesting that facets of trait mindfulness moderated the relationship between social anxiety schemas and responses to a social anxiety stressor task (Parsons, Luebbe, & Clerkin, 2017) or that mindfulness could reduce psychological distress caused by social stressors, such as job- or school-related ones (Ohu, Laguda, & Ogunyemi, 2018; Van Gordon, Shonin, Zangeneh, & Griffiths, 2014), or by disease (Kabat-Zinn, 1982; Loucks et al., 2019). Also, mindfulness, at least partially, can have beneficial effects in reducing depression and anxiety through reducing stress (Valikhani, Goodarzi, & Hashemi, 2019).

Students preparing to become teachers may feel more anxious when they are not sure of what is expected of them to do or whether are enough prepared to teach pupils. Mindfulness claims to help us stay in the present moment, without any judgment of what is happening – so we can give our full attention to pupil while teaching and not ruminate of what may happen if the unexpected drops in during teaching (which seems to be one of the greatest fears preservice teachers have). Hence, in preparing students to become good teachers, there could be introduced self-management classes, starting from the principles of mindfulness and metacognition. Learning prevails when the future teacher is able to plan and monitor his cognitive enterprises, in order to find the best answer to give a pupil or find the alternative teaching strategy, meaning that they have a high level of metacognitive awareness, which, in turn, is associated with low levels of anxiety. This can be helpful for educational policies – teaching metacognitive skills may result in improving teaching and learning. We can also argue that the older the future teacher, the more mindful and less anxious he is. Although they were unexperienced in the educational field, it seems that skills based on self-knowledge develop in time. If we consider metacognition and mindfulness related, being mindful, receptive at every signal from the class may be just another description of the ideal teacher. In conclusion, the development of programs that enhance mindfulness skills could be part of a larger curricula for future teachers.

References

Anderson, N. J. (2005). L2 strategy research. In E. Hinkel (Ed.), *Handbook of research in second language teaching and learning* (pp. 757–772). Mahwah, NJ: Lawrence Erlbaum Associates.

Armour-Thomas, E., & Allen, B. A. (1990). Componential analysis of analogical-reasoning performance of high and low achievers. *Psychology in the Schools, 27*(3), 269–275.

Baer, R. A., Smith, G. T., Lykins, E., Button, D., Krietemeyer, J., Sauer, S., & Williams, J. M. G. (2008). Construct validity of the five facet mindfulness questionnaire in meditating and non-meditating samples. *Assessment, 15*(3), 329–342.

Brown, K. W., & Ryan, R. M. (2003). The benefits of being present: Mindfulness and its role in psychological well-being. *Journal of Personality and Social Psychology, 84,* 822–848.

Chang, M. (2009). An appraisal perspective of teacher burnout: Examining the emotional work of teachers. *Educational Psychology Review, 21*, 193–218 doi:10.1007/s10648-009-9106-y.

Csikszentmihalyi, M. (1990). *Flow: The psychology of optimal experience.* New York: Harper and Row.

Efklides, A., & Metallidou, P. (2020). *Applying metacognition and self-regulated learning in the classroom.* Oxford, England: Oxford Research Encyclopedia of Education.

Flavell, J. H. (1979). Metacognition and cognitive monitoring: A new area of cognitive-developmental inquiry. *American Psychologist, 34*, 906–911.

Garner, P. W. (2010). Emotional competence and its influences on teaching and learning. *Educational Psychology Review, 22*, 297–321. doi:10.1007/s10648-010-9129-4.

Goh, C. (2008). Metacognitive instruction for second language listening development: Theory, practice and research implications. *Regiona English Language Centre Journal, 39*(2), 188. doi:10.1177/0033688208092184.

Greenberg, M. T., Brown, J. L., & Abenavoli, R. M. (2016). *Teacher stress and health effects on teachers, students, and schools.* University Park: Edna Bennett Pierce Prevention Research Center, Pennsylvania State University.

Henter, R. (2014) *Metacogniţia. O abordare psiho-pedagogică.* Cluj-Napoca: Presa Universitară Clujeană. e-book: http://www.editura.ubbcluj.ro/php/download.php?f=1951&ex=pdf

Henter, R., & Indreica, E. S. (2014). Metacognitive training for students preparing to be kindergarten and primary school teachers. *Perspectives of a Higher Quality Level of the Training of Specialists for Early Education and Primary Schooling "(PERFORMER)", Brasov, Romania, 2014.*

Jennings, P. A. (2011). Promoting teachers' social and emotional competencies to support performance and reduce burnout. In A. Cohan & A. Honigsfeld (Eds.), *Breaking the mold of preservice and inservice teacher education: Innovative and successful practices for the twenty-first century* (pp. 133–144). Lanham, MD, USA: Rowman & Littlefield Education.

Jones, J., Milton, F., Mostazir, M., & Adlam, A. (2019). The academic outcomes of working memory and metacognitive strategy training in children: A double-blind randomized controlled trial. *Developmental Science,* 23: e12870. doi:10.1111/desc.12870.

Kabat-Zinn, J. (1982). An outpatient program in behavioral medicine for chronic pain patients based on the practice of mindfulness meditation: Theoretical considerations and preliminary results. *General Hospital Psychiatry, 4*(1), 33–47.

Kabat-Zinn, J. (1990). *Full catastrophe living: Using the wisdom of your body and mind to face stress, pain and illness.* New York: Delacorte

Kabat-Zinn, J. (2003). Mindfulness: The heart of rehabilitation. In E. Leskowitz (Ed.), *Complementary and alternative medicine in rehabilitation* (pp. xi–xv). Saint Louis: Churchill Livingstone.

Kabat-Zinn, J. (2016). *Mindfulness pentru începători.* Bucureşti: Editura Trei.

Kuhn, D., & Dean, D. (2004). Metacognition: A bridge between cognitive psychology and educational practice. *Theory Into Practice* 43(4), 268–273. Ohio State University College of Education. Retrieved July 18, 2014, from Project MUSE database.

Laukkonen, R. E., Leggett, J. M., Gallagher, R. M., Biddell, H. L., Mrazek, A. J., Slagter, H. A., & Mrazek, M. D. (2020). *The science of mindfulness-based interventions and learning: A review for educators. Future of education and skills 2030: Curriculum analysis.* OECD Future of Education and Skills 2030: https://www.oecd.org/education/2030-project/

Loucks, E. B., Britton, W. B., Howe, C. J., Gutman, R., Gilman, S. E., Brewer, J., et al. (2019). Associations of dispositional mindfulness with obesity and central adiposity: The New England family study. *International Journal of Behavioral Medicine, 23*, 224–233.

Managing Workplace Stress in S. Dhiman et al. (Eds.), *The Palgrave handbook of workplace spirituality and fulfillment.* Springer International Publishing AG. doi:10.1007/978-3-319-61929-3_7-1.

Mantzios, M., & Wilson, J. C. (2015). Mindfulness, eating behaviours, and obesity: A review and reflection on current findings. *Current Obesity Reports, 4*(1), 141–6.

Marzano, R. J., & Marzano, S. J. (2015). *Managing the inner world of teaching: Emotions, interpretations, and actions.* Bloomington, IL: Marzano Research. ISBN: 9780990345831.

Masterson, S. S. (2001). A trickle-down model of organizational justice: Relating employees' and customers' perceptions of and reactions to fairness. *Journal of Applied Psychology, 86* (4), 594–604.

Mayer, R. E. (2003). Memory and information processes. In I. B. Weiner (ed.), *Handbook of psychology.* New York, NY: John Wiley & Sons.

Meiklejohn, J., Phillips, C., Freedman, L., Griffin, M. L., Biegel, G. M., Roach A., et al. (2012). Integrating mindfulness training into K-12 education: Fostering the resilience of teachers and students. *Mindfulness 3*, 291–307. doi:10.1007/s12671-012-0094-5.

Nakamura, J., & Csikszentmihályi, M. (2001). Flow theory and research. In C. R. Snyder Erik Wright, and Shane J. Lopez (ed.), *Handbook of positive psychology* (pp. 195–206). Oxford University Press. ISBN 978-0-19-803094-2.

Norton, K. R., & Griffith, G. M. (2020). The impact of delivering mindfulness-based programmes in schools: A qualitative study. *Journal of Child and Family Studies, 29*, 2623–2636. doi:10.1007/s10826-020-01717-1.

Ohu, E., Laguda, E., Ogunyemi, K. (2018). Mindfulness and stress reduction: Managing workplace stress. In S. Dhiman, G. Roberts, and J. Crossman (eds.), *The Palgrave handbook of workplace spirituality and fulfillment.* Cham: Palgrave Macmillan. doi:10.1007/978-3-319-61929-3_7-1Parsons, E. M., Luebbe, A. M., & Clerkin, E. M. (2017). Testing the relationship between social anxiety schemas, mindfulness facets, and state and trait social anxiety symptoms. *Mindfulness, 8*(6), 1634–1643.

Rechtschaffen, D. (2014). *The way of mindful education: Cultivating well-being in teachers and students.* New York, NY: W. W. Norton.

Roeser, R. W., Schonert-Reichl, K. A., Jha, A., Cullen, M., Wallace, L., Wilensky, R., et al. (2013). Mindfulness training and reductions in teacher stress and burnout: Results from two randomized, waitlist-control field trials. *Journal of Educational Psychology, 105*, 787–804. doi:10.137/a0032093.

Russo, M. A., Santarelli, D. M., & O'Rourke, D. (2017). The physiological effects of slow breathing in the healthy human. *Breathe (Sheff), 13*(4), 298–309. doi:10.1183/20734735.009817.

Schraw, G., Crippen, K. J., & Hartley, K. (2006). Promoting self-regulation in science education: Metacognition as part of a broader perspective on learning. *Research in Science Education, 36*(1–2), 111–139.

Schraw, G., & Dennison, R. S. (1994). Assessing metacognitive awareness. *Contemporary Educational Psychology, 19*, 460–475.

Schraw, G., & Moshman, D. (1995). Metacognitive theories. *Education Psychology Review, 7* (14), 351–371.

Seligman, M. E. P. (1991). *Learned optimism*. New York: Knopf.

Seligman, M. E. P. (2011). *Flourish: A visionary new understanding of happiness and well-being*. New York, NY, US: Free Press.

Sharf, R. H. (2014). Is mindfulness Buddhist? *Transcultural Psychiatry, 52*(4), 470–484.

Spitzer, R. L., Kroenke, K., Williams, J. B. W., & Lowe, B. (2006). A brief measure for assessing generalized anxiety disorder. The GAD-7. *Archives of Internal Medicine, 166*, 1092–1097.

Valikhani, A., Goodarzi, M. A., & Hashemi, R. (2019). Psychometric properties of dispositional selfregulation scale in Iranian population and predicting inhibitory/initiatory self-control on the basis of it. *Current Psychology, 38*(1), 154–164.

Van Gordon, W., Shonin, E., Zangeneh, M., & Griffiths, M. D. (2014). Work-related mental health and job performance: Can mindfulness help?. *International Journal of Mental Health and Addiction, 12*(2), 129–137.

van Son, J., Nyklicek, I., Nefs, G., Speight, J., Pop, V. J., & Pouwer, F. (2015). The association between mindfulness and emotional distress in adults with diabetes: Could mindfulness serve as a buffer? Results from Diabetes MILES: The Netherlands. *Journal of Behavioral Medicine, 38*, 251–260.

Wettstein, A., Kühne, F., Tschacher, W., & La Marca, R. (2020). Ambulatory assessment of psychological and physiological stress on workdays and free days among teachers. A preliminary study. *Frontiers in neuroscience, 14*, 112. doi: 10.3389/fnins.2020.00112.

Woodyard C. (2011). Exploring the therapeutic effects of yoga and its ability to increase quality of life. *International journal of yoga, 4*(2), 49–54. doi: 10.4103/0973-6131.85485.

Rajit NAIR and Preeti Sharma NAIR

6 Psychological Path to Access the Effectiveness of Digital Well-Being

Abstract Technology is used in almost every area of daily life. Besides being a medium for practical everyday tasks, technology can serve as a medium for psychological needs such as popularity, bonding, and self-improving. We attempt to investigate digital media users to explore how they handle their increasing knowledge overload for social relationships. They need to learn how to turn digital data into information that can be used for individuals' gain. We firmly agree that these harmful side effects pose a significant threat to people's well-being. This chapter will discuss the basic psychological needs theory that can be extended to medical systems to improve digital well-being. The approach integrates the Motivation, Engagement, and Thriving in User Experience and focuses on six fundamental needs of users' culture and experiences. The chapter will also represent a model that can measure the effectiveness of digital well-being features.

Keywords: Overconsumption, Self-Determination Theory (SDT), digital wellness skills, multitasking, technostress

1. Introduction

The definition of "digital skills" has continually expanded following the emergence of newer digital technology and implementations. We also observed a theoretical expansion of "media literacy." In the 1980s and 1990s, digital skills are seen as only being computer-related skills (van Dijk, 2005). This methodology was applied during the development of the European Computer Driving Licence (ECDL). With the dissemination of the Internet, the ability to browse, pick, and filter information quickly appeared as a new competence to the previously obsolete world of print. In this particular step, the dimension of "informational skills" or "information literacy" has become more critical after the Internet's evolution. This is also because of the progression from web 1.0 to web 2.0, as skills linked to communication and sharing online increased in value (Hargittai, 2008).

Furthermore, artistic content such as music and video creation has become an integral part of specialized applications like art galleries and amusement parks. Finally, several research has considered using digital media for personal and professional purposes (Martin and Grudziecki, 2006). In this same topic, a quick scan of the twelve most popular digital skills theories identifies six major categories of digital skills: organizational, technological, formal, information, cognition, and digital communication. The government's new way of thinking will affect future developments. This trait is linked to dealing with the negative impact of "constant communication overabundance," "too much information," and "information overload" (Levitin, 2014). We experience difficulties keeping ourselves successful at present while multi-tasking, fragmenting, and overconsuming knowledge. This is seen in the papers published regarding digital media's detrimental impact (Bevilacqua, 2014; Fernández Pedemonte, 2012; Rheingold, 2012). However, it has been far ignored in digital literacy systems and – even more broadly – media literacy studies. It is understood that many of the causes of mental illness in modern societies contribute to the heavy use of computers and the Internet. These economic and environmental challenges are becoming a danger to our quality of life. We show that internet communication overabundance skills are a new level in digital skills – a collection of skills designed to contribute to a productive and happy life. We address why the skill of self-control is both a true and general competence. Therefore, digital literacy needs to be at the center of a universal media education program. When talking about individual well-being, you must recognize the digital effect presence can have on everyone's economic life. Often, over-consumption can be triggered more by the frame of mind than particular skills. For a proper social study, it must include both psychological and physiological aspects. We should value the multicultural dimension of digital well-being in terms of a deep-rooted culture of digital well-being. "Digital well-being" is a digital version of the value of "general well-being" ideals of particular groups of people.

Well-being is culturally differentiated because it relies on the beliefs and conventions of a specific social context. To build a theory on "digital well-being," we propose considering both the individual skills of users and culture-specific values and norms within which those skills are described. We explore how to operationalize digital wellness skills and digital well-being norms. Finally, you will hear about some of the effects of creating these systems for socio-cultural study, media studies, education, and public policies.

The critical point of the chapter is to explore how social features ought to be taken into account. Digital well-being can be sought by the user when they apply digital media in many ways. We have only understood the sense of the word "digital well-being" in two respects. When Nansen et al. (2012) introduced the concept within an ethnographic analysis of children's online use, they bridge the gap between health and inclusion-driven structures. A philosophy of wellness and the internet's role is keyed to children's interpersonal relationships, education, play, and social development. The author also supports the benefits of digital engagement because of "the potential risks of digital engagement as well as the potential benefits." Sumersale mentions a variety of adverse effects caused by the digital culture. She also states that online behavior needs to be monitored, and the pressure of work can be very heavy after hours of work. In this context, we aim to structure for a better understanding of the term. We describe "digital well-being" as the state where subjective well-being is held in an atmosphere with too much digital communication. With a stable online environment, people can use the internet to eliminate their health issues. This condition is beneficial due to the unique knowledge and wisdom a person possesses.

"Digital well-being" is not only linked to a subject's economic life but also social activities like family, job, and so on (Ryan and Deci, 2001). A person's health is not merely about enjoyment. It also concerns the willingness to use modern technology to one's advantage (eudaimonic dimension). In the short-term, digital well-being can be looked at to manage "technostress" and negative physical factors associated with the use of modern media. Current social media is directly essential to individual well-being (Ryff and Singer, 2008). It is well-known that conventional digital skills and internet access greatly lead to subjective well-being. It refers to using digital technology to compensate for stress, anxiety, depression, loneliness, a sense of isolation, and finally, concentration. It seems that citizens have become involved in health because of the atmosphere of over-affluence, where extreme wealth has already been attained. Eating disorders and overconsumption have very similar characteristics from an economic viewpoint since supply has gradually increased (Gui and Argentin, 2011). We claim that digital health is evolving when there is a surplus of contact triggers, as never before. It's crucial to integrate digital well-being into social science and policy because of the rising amount of time spent in front of a computer. All these we can attain only if we accept digital resources.

According to Interface, smartphone use is more prevalent during school times and at home with a family dinner in a less advantaged group of children. This issue may involve a new sort of digital and social inequality. In light of recent studies, deprived consumers are engaged in digital contact instead of decreasing this form of operation. We need to investigate whether the increased use of digital technologies by less advantaged society segments is generating more disparities. We will see the same patterns of contact in eating disorders that we see in eating disorders.

"Digital skills" is an important subject, which has become one of the dimensions of "digital inequality" (van Deursen and van Dijk, 2014; Hargittai,

2002)and should be linked to social inclusion. How can the definition be implemented into metrics and variables? We think that "Digital Well-being" can be tested from both the subjective and objective yardsticks. Test clients' experience of tension when they regularly watch on the internet or an application. It is also the route pursued by surveys like Ofcom 2016 and academic studies (Lutz et al., 2014). This can be used to aid us with assessments of digital health. In this category of metrics, we should think about how our activities a day and space. Factors such as the number of switches from one program to another every day and the number of emails reviewed every hour may be some factors that can be regarded as potential variables (Reid and Thomas, 2017). We may interpret such actions as manifestations of attention to the use of computer technology. The final thing to note is the motivation for people to pay special attention to their digital health. In this scenario, bottom-up innovation may influence cultural habits. It can diminish and slacken the drive for success and multitasking.

Specific programs (e.g., RescueTime or ManicTime) may be used to record this data. One of the main source of data on digital well-being skills may come from observing safe or good practices in the medical and psychological literature. Actions such as "strategically selecting contacts and information channels to follow" and "knowing how to change the Instant Messaging app settings to eliminate sound notifications for group chats" are most important. Nevertheless, we need to broaden our study of these metrics to the social context as well. Digital community well-being expectations are crucial steps toward world unity. As an example, we might suggest controlling and regulating actions further with the use of "netiquette" codes and individual human moderators in social media sites. The final thing to note is the motivation for people to pay special attention to their digital health. This bottom-up approach could enable people to prioritize the quality of life and diminish the rush to contribute to productivity and multi-tasking. Schools can play a vital role in socializing children to critical and balanced use of the media in everyday life. The relationship between digital skills and quality of life can be very clearly established by this research and offer a new way to understand the different issues. Future research would need to provide a more precise definition of risks to well-being related to connected devices' overabundance. This area of research would also study how media consumption is legitimized. Furthermore, social science needs to guide policy to disseminate information about "the clinical flip-sides of the use of ICTs" and "nudge" toward cultural reflexivity about what is good for the digital world.

2. Background Study

Digital overconsumption:

In the first sentence, we will include a literature review of the most critical details regarding such problems. These topics are very relevant for those that specifically relate to new media. It is possible to define two significant dimensions to this issue. Studies reveal the subject of "overconsumption" and "TV overconsumption" with social network addiction and another problem stated in the lecture is multitasking. Both of these issues arise concurrently in digital media consumption. Despite their seemingly similar characteristics, this is possible to differentiate them by feature or intention. We concentrate on each literature individually.

2.1 Social Network Addiction

There have been concerns from internet users that they do not get as much time for Internet use. "Internet addiction" or "problematic internet use" have been investigated as an ill condition affecting a small sub-group of digital media consumers (Christakis et al., 2011). Beyond a few severe cases, many people suffer from the "too much information" issue both at work and in their personal life. Fifty percent of English internet users spend longer than intended on the internet (OFCOM, 2016). Forty-eight percent of Internet users seemed to think that digital overconsumption caused them to neglect housework, lost sleep, or becoming exhausted the next day (47 %). Those individuals aged between sixteen and twenty-four were most likely to have illicit drug use (OFCOM, 2016). The main concern for teachers in Italian secondary schools is whether their students are overusing the internet and videogames.

Sherry Turkle (2016) cautioned that there was a loss of relationships with people in messages and mediated contact. Her research has found that too much smartphone use can seriously harm the quality of people's lives. According to a study, to stick to a smartphone is negatively connected with well-being. There are also differences in information and communication technology in the job market. Researchers have also found difficulty in managing digital communication among employees. It depicts how workers are suffering from persistent and unnecessary use of emerging technologies. With so much information available, it is understandable that users want to turn to various outlets, lest they miss something important. For businesses with more than 50 workers, a new law in France ("Loi Travail") obliges them to agree with the internal trade unions the hours and amount of computer time employees will use per day. The analysis of "Mettling, 2015" found that less than 25 % of managers who were surveyed stopped email and job contact when they had free time. These habits demonstrate how digital technology has induced sensory exhaustion.

2.2 Multitasking

It has been revealed that digital media use has a negative impact on the attention span of people. The main issue of this discussion regards the effective management of publicity. New media implement such strategies that alter attentional behaviors. A noteworthy characteristic of digital media is the ability to open many different programs at the same time. As a consequence, you get to do multiple things at the same time. We also run various programs and documents at the same time. Multitasking generates distractions such that we cannot pay careful attention to multiple items (Ophir et al., 2009).

Multitasking can be risky in an educational setting because it means an increased risk of injuries. A sufficient period will help individuals concentrate on learning a task (Rosen et al., 2013). Here's another explanation of why multitasking isn't good for us. This happens to many people. Even this adverse effect impacts our cognitive outputs (Stothart et al., 2015). People find themselves frustrated because of repeated interruptions or multitasking. "Technostress" arises as a result of these behaviors (Lee et al., 2014) speak about some empirical studies, which support the association between cellular phone use and anxiety (Beranuy et al., 2009; Bianchi and Phillips, 2005; Lu et al., 2011). We have to learn how to maintain our focus to control its impact on our everyday life. This chapter essentially shows that we could be entering an age in which human frailties stop advancement from emerging technology.

Nowadays, "Digital Well-being" is emerging gradually as another way to address these problems. Besides, this topic has not been viewed directly by digital skills literature and social science. In this case, this paragraph aims to provide elements for constructing theoretical concepts of "digital well-being skills" and "digital well-being." We will split this down into two parts: individual skills and the culture stage. As of yet, references to the potential of neutralizing harmful effects of digital communication are entirely implicit. In the initial version of the European system DIGCOMP (Pérez-Escoda and Fernández-Villavicencio, 2016), there is a problem called "protecting health" that focuses on the "health risks linked with the use of technology in terms of the threats to physical and psychological well-being." In the second version of the system, Well-being 2.0 (Vuorikari et al., 2016), this definition is mentioned in a different field, "Protecting health and well-being." Also, Ferrari et al. (2014) and Vuorikari et al. (2016) research area is related to problem-solving capacity. Both van Dijk

(2005) and Van Deursen et al. (2014) claimed that commitment to personal objectives was challenging when using the internet. "Strategic Internet skills" provide the skill to use digital technology to pursue unique benefits. A similar concept seems to hold well for the times. This is a more critical skill nowadays, mainly when using the internet.

One may object that self-control has always been an important problem in any human activities, and it's more relevant to human characteristics than capability. With the increased complexity of modern culture, it is almost difficult to manage our self-control issues. Before digitalization, pre-eminence in academic practices has been already an outcome of self-control (Mischel et al., 2011). However, we are constantly constricted by our small inputs and large variety of other necessary inputs. We claim that, irrespective of users' characteristics, digital media world drives people to quick paced information and communication use. The said climate is not conducive for forming satisfactory relationships. Technology has the ability to nudge people in a particular direction.

Living in the digital society produces dynamic patterns of stimuli and individual reactions that humans are still difficult to deal with. This goal can be accomplished only when a new collection of information, views, and organizational skills is employed. That's why digital communication really brings technology-specific psychological issues such as self-control and preference. Why is Digital Well-being Needed? We consider the following features of digital environments: (i) the abundance of possibilities, (ii) the ease to concentrate on any singular task, (iii) the monetary exploitation of attention of human beings, (iv) the convergence of different concerns in the same device, and (v) the consistency of the above situation until the end of the day. This is a highly specific and special setting that cannot be found anywhere else. "The very things that make IT useful – reliability, portability, userfriendliness and fast processing – may also be undermining employee productivity, innovation and well-being." I will argue that "mass use of portable media involve a major change in digital studies." Many who possess informational, social, and production digital skills will still struggle as there can be many repercussion of knowledge overconsumption.

We describe digital well-being skills as the strategies required to cope with the negative effects of excessive digital communication. Digital well-being skills can be understood as the skills of strategic attention concentrating in everyday life and reducing the stress generated by the excessive flow of information and minimizing the wastes of time and attention on all things that do not deserve them. To implement this, digital stimuli must be designed so as to be systematically mediated to an individual's well-being. The skills required for digital well-being are both cognitive and metacognitive. Additional skills are needed to avoid attention being diverted. These skills are often important for a successful negotiator. The internet stimulates us; but, some people learn how to delay them by using "pre-commitment strategies" (Elster, 2002). These meta-cognitive strategies envisage "constraints which an agent imposes upon himself in pursuit of some imagined advantage to himself." We can regulate our internet use by implementing software (e.g., Freedom) that restricts our internet access for a given duration. Putting phone in silent mode to fend off interruptions is a simpler technique compared to other preconceived strategies. We avoid disturbances by sustained focus and participate in capacity of interrupting by meta-cognitive abilities.

There are some skills needed to include meta-cognitive techniques on setting by yourself. It would be very helpful to know how to silence instant messaging chat groups or knowing how to toggle on the Facebook timeline check. It is crucial for organizations to have some knowledge of how web 2.0 and social networks operate, particularly when it comes to understanding when and how to use the technological and strategic skills described above. While digital well-being is critical for individuals, a "good" use of digital media has expanded concerns outside of mental well-being. First we should recognize the role of digital professionals in designing the online world. Sometimes in media messages are specially and scientifically designed to attract people's attention. "As much as a person might need to have willpower, responsibility and self-control, but we also need to acknowledge that the other side of the street also has to consider themselves morally accountable."

According to David Harris, major tech companies have one hundred of the brightest mathematical analysts and computer scientists, who have gone to top universities, whose mission is to crack your willpower (Schulson, 2017). Putting well-being in mind implies to account for the consequences of a specific digital architecture. A minimalistic homepage, a selection of links and links with banners and social network to share private information, has various impacts on the users. This is an ethical concern emerging from the need to embed the fundamental human values of social responsibility and protection. In addition, this encourages the perception of human digital well-being beyond the individual. If instantaneity, success, and multitasking are taught in our digital lifestyle, we will have contradictions between personal needs and societal needs. In terms of web design, there has been lack of importance of user privacy and privacy has been replaced by "visibility," "transparency," and "exposure" (Cohen, 2008).

New media is creating tension between digital society perceptions and the well-being of young people (Saidel, 2017). Moreover, young boys and girls who prefer to avoid video games are disadvantaged due to such adolescent social sanctions (Mai et al., 2015). From this viewpoint, community ideals have a significant impact on digital well-being. Therefore, digital media can either work for or against them. Here is a historical example that deals with online community management and topic of moderation: Netiquette and Moderation. The third understanding concerns a sense of health within the digital world. Therefore, we have to create the relationship between physiological and social studies to discover the meaning of "well-being." Indeed, the cultural context plays a significant role in the formulation of particular customs and values (Keeffe and Andrews, 2015). When we discuss "digital well-being," we have to take into account people's socio-cognitive trend, and position of well-being values in it. With that we can see how well-being's influence can reflect into the digital world and how this influence may have an impact to the conception of general/human well-being. Thus, the perception of duties regarding self-care can vary between cultures because of different environments.

These considerations help to incorporate some communal reflections in dealing with public speaking abilities. Digital well-being can become a condition pursued by the person, both morally and ethically, by their digital media uses. But digital well-being often affects larger groups whose norms and values may contribute to their members' comfort, protection, happiness, and fulfillment when they use digital media. As far as we are aware, "digital well-being" has been used in two studies. Nansen et al. (2012) use this concept within an ethnographic analysis of children's online use within an eHealth service. To explain the importance of the Internet and social relationships, scholars used the idea of wellness to analyze online threats. The author highlights the benefits of digital interaction between educators and students and the possible dangers of the technology. There are several issues listed in the below chapters, which, if not treated, can lead to deterioration of digital well-being. For instance, she refers to students' inability to understand whether the online activity was illegal. She also talks about universities' responsiveness when it comes to regarding both employees and students and the tension associated with being locked up in the office all day. We will offer a more structured account, later on. We describe digital well-being as the state where subjective well-being is obtained in an atmosphere in which digital communication overcrowds dominate. A condition where individuals can channel their media use toward ease, protection, happiness, and fulfillment can benefit their well-being. Socio-cultural environments may have a strong impact on substantially individuals' awareness and skills. We assume that the rise in digital well-being can lead to general well-being in both hedonic and eudaimonic ways (Ryan and Deci, 2001). Digitally well-being pertains to attaining emotions and minimizing consequences on others (hedonic dimension) and is concerned with using new technology to give meaning to one's actions and understand one's potential in existence (eudaimonic dimension).

3. Model for the Evaluation of Digital Well-Being

This model may be beneficial since it comes from Self Determination Theory (SDT) and is also well suited to technology design. AIAAEC (Acquisition, Interface, Activities, Actions, Existence, Community) will teach us about technologies' impacts in terms of well-being. The definition of well-being focuses on the well-researched basic definition as "optimal psychological functioning and experience," as stated in American psychological researcher Ryan and Deci's (2001) characterize a well-being model by three important factors:

- Dexterity (feeling able and effective)
- Inter-subgroup collaboration (feeling connected to others, a sense of belonging)
- Autonomy (feeling entity, behaving in line with one's priorities and values),

In this chapter, there are six parameters which are considered for accessing the effectiveness of digital well-being. The parameters are:

1. Acquisition
2. Interface
3. Activities
4. Actions
5. Existence
6. Community

In the above six points, first five parameters are contained in the last parameter i.e., Community.

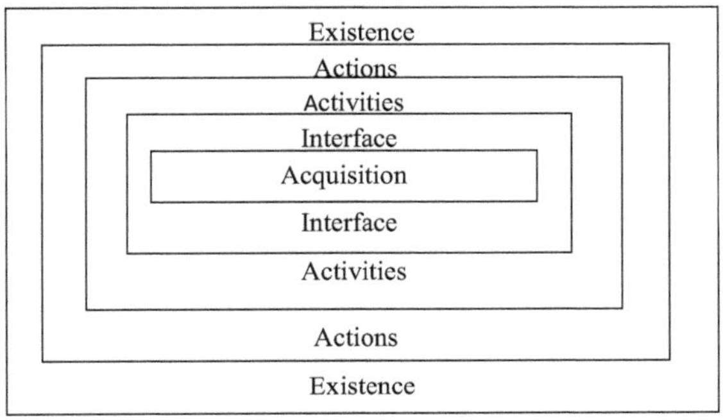

Hierarchy of parameters contained in the community

1. Acquisition – This parameter discusses the adoption of technology; various technologies are available today. So it depends on the user that what type of technology they adopt.
2. Interface – Interface is the important factor which is used to engage the user with a technology. The interface connects consumers with technology to the degree that their psychological needs for interaction are fulfilled. Needs satisfaction has to do with how functional something is and how open it is to the user. Bad usability will lead to dissatisfaction that, as we know, will affect both user engagement and user welfare. In the fitness app, there would be more capable of setting expectations and customized plans. Additionally, TENSINTERFACE questionnaire may provide insights on the need dissatisfaction at the interface stage.
3. Activities – Technology is used to help carry out different activities. An app could allow you to monitor the number of steps you have taken and gauge calorie consumption. Each of these activities might satisfy some psychological need or other: reading User Stories may cause you to feel more or less competent. Likewise, you can find step counting task boring or engaging. There are several different ways to track progress and how to show progress on the computer. The TENS-TASK questionnaire (Hargittai, 2008) can be used to expose intelligence-trained people's capabilities for human-made technologies.
4. Actions – Technology enforces any separable overarching intervention. Health apps can affect habits like taking exercise, healthy eating, and meditation. The distinction between these spheres is significant because technology may fulfill a user's needs concerning its use. Still, it may not affect the

user's behavior for what it's trying to solve. Unlike apps aimed at exercising, apps that promote social networking cannot result in the user exercising. We may use the Psychological Need Satisfaction in Exercise Scale (Bevilacqua, 2014) in calculating the degree of pleasure from exercising.

5. Existence – Existence may lead to a small shift in users' thinking regarding their feelings of competence and autonomy. It is normal to believe that a more powerful mindfulness app can change the existence to certain level. Thus, if technology goes beyond need fulfillment at the activities and interface factors to significantly impact people's overall well-being, it also depends on what the humans intended. Well-being touches the existence factor to determine addiction. A casual game can so please the gamer's senses, that in the life sphere, the most important activities such as work, relationships, and quality of life get crowded out so that the gamer feels so overshadowed and overwhelmed. Based on the focus on health, any technology claiming to support the energy must be assessed life. Users will be measured on the TENS-Life scale with questions about the kinds of technology they think have impacted their lives when they use the technology to a greater degree than required. A separate or supplementary assessment of life satisfaction and health may be used to track this technology's results.

Conclusion

In the coming ten years, it will become a customer standard that technologies value psychologists and therapists. The fear of damaging or unusual effects of the transition will continue to rise. An inevitable backlash against technology has begun. Design can't solve problems unless you alter how people communicate with technology. They would allow technology developers to bear the responsibility for their actions. Responding to a new market requires new approaches. I hope to create a future in which our technology is built to create wellness for all our people.

References

M. Beranuy, U. Oberst, X. Carbonell, and A. Chamarro, "Problematic Internet and mobile phone use and clinical symptoms in college students: The role of emotional intelligence," *Comput. Human Behav.*, 2009.

G. Bevilacqua, "La comunicazione scientifica: il delicato rapporto tra scienza, media e pubblico," *Testo, contesto ed Even. geomitologia una nuova Front. delle Sci. della Terra*, 2014.

A. Bianchi and J. G. Phillips, “Psychological predictors of problem mobile phone use,” *Cyberpsychology Behav.*, 2005.

D. A. Christakis, M. M. Moreno, L. Jelenchick, M. T. Myaing, and C. Zhou, “Problematic Internet usage in US college students: A pilot study,” *BMC Med.*, 2011.

J. E. Cohen, “Privacy, visibility, transparency, and exposure,” in *University of Chicago Law Review*, 2008.

A. J. A. M. van Deursen and J. A. G. M. van Dijk, “The digital divide shifts to differences in usage,” *New Media Soc.*, 2014.

J. A. G. M. van Dijk, *The deepening divide: Inequality in the information society*. 2005.

J. Elster, “Studies in rationality, precommitment, and constraints,” *Ethics*, 2002.

D. Fernández Pedemonte, “Turkle, Sherry. Alone together: Why we expect more from technology and less from each other?,” *Austral Comun.*, 2012.

A. Ferrari, B. Neza Brecko, and Y. Punie, “DIGCOMP: A framework for developing and,” *Elearning Pap.*, 2014.

M. Gui and G. Argentin, “Digital skills of internet natives: Different forms of digital literacy in a random sample of northern Italian high school students,” *New Media Soc.*, 2011.

E. Hargittai, “Second-level digital divide: Differences in people’s online skills,” *First Monday*, 2002.

E. Hargittai, “A framework for studying differences in people’s digital media uses,” in *Grenzenlose Cyberwelt?*, 2008.

M. Keeffe and D. Andrews, “Towards an adolescent friendly methodology: Accessing the authentic through collective reflection,” *Int. J. Res. Method Educ.*, 2015.

D. J. Levitin, “The organized mind: Thinking straight in the age of information overload,” *Sci. Am.*, 2014.

Y. K. Lee, C. T. Chang, Y. Lin, and Z. H. Cheng, “The dark side of smartphone usage: Psychological traits, compulsive behavior and technostress,” *Comput. Human Behav.*, 2014.

X. Lu, J. Watanabe, Q. Liu, M. Uji, M. Shono, and T. Kitamura, “Internet and mobile phone text-messaging dependency: Factor structure and correlation with dysphoric mood among Japanese adults,” in *Computers in Human Behavior*, 2011.

C. Lutz, G. Ranzini, and M. Meckel, “Stress 2.0: Social media overload among Swiss teenagers,” 2014.

L. M. Mai, R. Freudenthaler, F. M. Schneider, and P. Vorderer, "'i know you've seen it!' Individual and social factors for users' chatting behavior on Facebook," *Comput. Human Behav.*, 2015.

A. Martin and J. Grudziecki, "DigEuLit: Concepts and tools for digital literacy development," *Innov. Teach. Learn. Inf. Comput. Sci.*, 2006.

W. Mischel et al., "'Willpower' over the life span: Decomposing self-regulation," *Soc. Cogn. Affect. Neurosci.*, 2011.

B. Nansen, K. Chakraborty, L. Gibbs, C. MacDougall, and F. Vetere, "Children and digital wellbeing in Australia: Online regulation, conduct and competence," *J. Child. Media*, 2012.

OFCOM, "The communications market report – August 2016," *Ofcom*, 2016.

E. Ophir, C. Nass, and A. D. Wagner, "Cognitive control in media multitaskers," *Proc. Natl. Acad. Sci. U. S. A.*, 2009.

A. Pérez-Escoda and N. G. Fernández-Villavicencio, "Digital competence in use," 2016.

A. J. Reid and C. N. Thomas, "A case study in smartphone usage and gratification in the age of narcissism," *Int. J. Technol. Hum. Interact.*, 2017.

H. Rheingold, "Introduction: Why you need digital know-how – why we all need it," in *Net smart: How to thrive online*, 2012.

L. D. Rosen, L. Mark Carrier, and N. A. Cheever, "Facebook and texting made me do it: Media-induced task-switching while studying," *Comput. Human Behav.*, 2013.

R. M. Ryan and E. L. Deci, "On happiness and human potentials: A review of research on hedonic and eudaimonic well-being," *Annual Review of Psychology*. 2001.

C. D. Ryff and B. H. Singer, "Know thyself and become what you are: A eudaimonic approach to psychological well-being," *J. Happiness Stud.*, 2008.

E. Saidel, "Reclaiming conversation: The power of talk in a digital age," *New Media Soc.*, 2017.

M. Schulson, "User behaviour stochastic.Pdf," *Energy and Buildings*, 2017.

C. Stothart, A. Mitchum, and C. Yehnert, "The attentional cost of receiving a cell phone notification," *J. Exp. Psychol. Hum. Percept. Perform.*, 2015.

S. Turkle, "Reclaiming conversation.," *Camping Mag.*, 2016.

A. J. A. M. Van Deursen, E. J. Helsper, and R. Eynon, "Measuring digital skills. from digital skills to tangible outcomes project report.," *From Digit. Ski. to Tangible Outcomes Proj. report.*, 2014.

R. Vuorikari, Y. Punie, S. Carretero, and L. Van Den Brande, *DigComp 2.0: The Digital Competence Framework for Citizens*. 2016.

Roxana MAIER and Alina ROMAN

7 The Contact of the Institutionalized Elderly with Family, during the Pandemic and the Emergency State

Abstract This study's starting point is related to managing a difficult situation for the elders who are institutionalized in a care center once the lockdown is implemented. The difficulties that appeared were evoked by the family's impossibility of visiting the elderly and this comprised an anxiety-evoking and dysfunctional potential for both the seniors and their families. The study proposes an intervention to the level of the relationship's dynamic, in a care center. The intervention brought new possibilities of interaction among the participants, hence contributing to the normalisation of the negative aspects and the participants' well-being.

Keywords: Elderly, family, pandemic, care center, communication space

Aging is a natural general biological phenomenon, which manifests itself in all the functions of the body, on all levels, starting on a cellular, tissue, organ level, so on an organic level, up to the exterior manifestations such as behavioral manifestations, operation execution, daily tasks, and adaptive-behavioral capacities.

Aging is the final temporal segment of human existence, which brings after itself a manifold of changes, generally physical ones, but not only, which is where many difficulties stem from. From the point of view of each person's subjective perception, senescence is a number and there are people who, even though old in age, don't feel old, but also people who feel and act as if they were older than they are. Old age includes the third and fourth age, with relatively distinct delimitations between them, meaning that fourth age is considered as being formed of octogenarians, nonagenarians, and centenaries.

As a distinct age stage, old age represents a "period of profound degradations and involution of the main functions of the human body" (Cosmovici, 2003). From the WHO, adult health age is post 65 years old, and this age is variable depending on certain geographical areas and the social perception. In terms of geographical areas, the start of the third age is for Greeks 68 years old, but for Turkish 55 years old, and in some African countries, the start of this age is around 53–55 years of age. In terms of the start of this age depending on the social perception, this depends on the moment in the life of the respondents (how old they are when asked), their social status, and their health. If the person is asked around adolescence, they will situate old age around 50 years old, if the person is 75 years old, they will say that old age is around 72 years old. The people who have a higher social status and those who are more robust from a health perspective situate the beginning of old age later on (Man, 2017).

The process of getting old assumes a series of biological, mental, and social modifications and changes, which assume effort and adaptation from the person, and sometimes even acceptance. In the literature in this field of study, on the side of psychology and on the side of the medical profession, one can notice a series of disputes toward the concept of old age and the specific periods it entails, which lead on its own to several classifications. These differences appear depending on the criteria established and are generated by the fact that principally they target a person's involution in certain areas. It is thus known that aging is different from person to person, depending on the bioclimatic environment in which this person lives, on his or her health state prior to aging, on the sanogenetic factors and on the ways in which this person took care of oneself until that point. In addition, one cannot neglect the material factors, the standard of living, psychological factors, pollution of any kind, and maintaining certain professional and social preoccupations, which all influence aging (Verza, 1993).

Senescence does not represent only a phase in one's life, but also a period in our existence which manifests itself differently from person to person. The perception and the attitude toward older people have oscillated throughout time and in different geographical spaces between respect, veneration, esteem, and wisdom, and ignorance, marginalization, taunting, compassion, and pity (Crețu, 2001). This was also seen as an age of wisdom, an antechamber to death and stock-taking, a period of tolerance and reconciliation with others, of freedom, of vanity, and a counsel for a life of frugality for the younger generation (Malim, 2003). The fragmented and atomized family had, as a consequence, strengthening of the death taboo (older generations remind us of our own future disappearance) and the exclusion of old age. Erstwhile, grandchildren were used to seeing their grandparents under the same roof, but now, this is more and more seldom found. The elders were the guarantors of traditions, and at the same time those who shared from their wisdom, full of tenderness, what brought them their side of socialization, utility, respect, which, in turn, allowed a better acceptance of old age and of death (Barbier, 2003).

The stages of old age are characterized through the possible appearance of certain health issues, the appearance of decline, and the mental feeling of the terminal stage. Of course, all these depend on the native dowry of the person, on their way of living, on their education, culture and training, on what he or she has realized with and for their own being, on his or her concept of the world and life. In support of understanding the problems of the third and fourth age comes a good communication of the elder with his or her own family, but also a deep understanding of the changes that appear, from the side of the family. Thus, the family-elder and family-doctor communication should be constant, for a better understanding of the changes that appear. Older people can't identify the changes of their health state as they used to in younger years, or are not as agile in respecting the medical prescriptions, or they can't accept they are in the respective state, and this makes their health state deteriorate or makes the problems that appeared not subside. Family can offer them, through the concrete understanding of the changes that appeared, the good type of care or support so that it helps the elder do it him or herself.

The older people are more fragile through the deterioration of physical and mental functions, have a decreased adaptability and that is why a change that is not major can be perceived otherwise and can affect their balance. The elderly can become selfish, ego-centric, fiercely tied to objects they possess, are rigid, anchored in the past, which they constantly evoke. Their feelings are mostly from the past, they can be part of a conflict, become touch, staying very little in the action zone due to their physical limitations, and also due to their emotional limitations due to the little amount of emotionally significant people that are close to them.

In seniority, the relationships with people close to us (life partners, children, grandchildren, brothers, sisters, and friends) present certain particularities, and they increase in importance, as the number of persons dwindle, the relational and emotional contacts dwindle as well. To this we can add the changes that appear in terms of health, but also on an economical level and in the social roles, which, in turn, also make the elderly person more vulnerable.

For the elderly, communication can represent a sign of affection, a clear proof that the person is not forgotten and marginalized, a gesture of care. Psychological aging is in a direct connection with the elderly's capacity to communicate; thus, the change in the way he or she communicates with the family can represent a facilitating factor for the appearance of problems, or it cannot. Sporadic communication will increase the elderly's loneliness and he or she will believe they are forgotten, neglected, unimportant, condescending communication will make him or her think that they are more incapable than they really are, and he or she will not feel respected and appreciated. The majority of the elderly are feeling treated inappropriately when one uses when speaking to them a type of condescending communication in its two options – overaccommodative speaking, which is speaking to them in short, clear sentences, said slowly and loudly or baby talk, as if they were speaking to babies. On top of all this, one can add the communications dysfunctionalities that can appear in the elderly's memory problems, in dementia, vascular accidents, and other severe health issues, which involve temporal and spatial disorientation, or language dysfunctions.

The changes determined by old age do not appear in all individuals at the same chronological age or in the same proportions, but once they age, the vulnerability to disease grows, deterioration installs itself gradually and in different functions, the level of adaptability also deteriorates and some functions or capacities can never be recovered. Senescence characterizes itself through the decrease in functional capabilities.

General Characteristics of the Decline in Functions for Those in the Third Age

- Changes at a sensory state, the majority enter a decline (the auditive sense – at around 45 years old, the visual and tactile sense at around 55 years old, the sense of taste at around 65 years old, and the sense of smell at around 75 years old)
- Motor and movement difficulties (difficulties given by the rheumatic changes, by muscular or postural atrophy, but also by changes in the proprioceptive perceptions that bring in movement changes, the appreciation of space and dimension and balance)
- The decrease in the capacity of efficiency and mobility of intellectual functions
- The decrease in the capacity to master information
- An increasing difficulty in adapting toward new situations
- The reduction in control and in the affective reactions
- Resistance to change, psychorigidity, conservatism, excessive attachment to property

In the third age, the subjective well-being decreases due to the large possibility of the appearance of different deteriorations in different areas of the person's existence. On the psychopathological side, disorders pertaining to affection are dominant, and place their imprint on the whole behavior of the older person. In this context, depressive conditions are frequent, and they lead to inadaptation through the imbalance that appears on the internal plan and also by disturbing the relationships the elderly has with people around him or her.

A hypothesis has been accredited stating that, for most people of older age, depression is accompanied by an anxious state towards the idea of death and the regret for the happy periods that the person has loved through. These kinds of feelings accentuate after losing one's life partner or certain close people, especially when the number of losses outweighs the number of people living. There are situations when the older person feels useless, or when not enough attention is given to them by people around, which adds a tragic character to their loneliness and sadness, and increases the feelings of frustration. In these cases, elders become unhappy, pessimistic, inhibited, or even agitated, but on both situations, their negativity accentuates and their behavior is marked by inadaptability.

Old age and depression are frequently associated through a few similar characteristics that they share, which are:

- A somber vision of life
- A pain due to the loss of the person they love, of their life partner
- Physical and mental deterioration
- Loneliness
- Lack of perspective

The main physical afflictions that appear in third age are:

- Arthrosis – the deterioration of articular cartilages
- Different cardio-vascular afflictions
- Diabetes mellitus
- Osteoporosis
- Urinary issues
- Dementia
- Cancer

Old Age and Institutionalizing the Elderly

Besides all the changes that appear, once people get older, one can add other factors to making the elderly more vulnerable, such as poverty, the absence of certain measures of public health, economical situation, age-ism, discrimination, abuse, access to services, social isolation, and loneliness. From the groups of elderly, the most affected are those over 85 years old, those in residential centers, those with no children, those who suffer from severe afflictions or handicaps, elderly couples in which one of the members is severely ill and are alone.

Poverty is the main factor, which affects older people, as they do not dispose of enough resources to actively participate in public, social, and cultural life, in order for them to make decisions on their own life, and this obstructs or at least restricts the access to health and social services, but also the necessary care for their individual needs.

Social issues (retirement and isolation), economical issues (decrease in income, poverty, and lack of financial aid from children), moral issues (disrespecting legitimate rights, neglect, and abuse), all these aggravate health issues for the elderly, which adds extra tasks to the family, in case this exists, but also to health and social assistance.

In the third age, friends and social contacts decrease, as the individual is retired. He or she will often feel an acute sentiment of loneliness and sadness, which can be favoring factors for the start of depression. Some older people have the impression that their time has passed and are only waiting to die. The elderly stay at home most of the time, socialize very little because their social circle has dwindled, people no longer look for them, they no longer find a meaning and this saddens them and makes them even lonelier than before. Once the parents are getting older, their children become adults, create their own families, no longer depend on the parents, build new personal meanings and distance themselves from their parents' generation.

Elderly people suffer a series of modifications in terms of their roles, slowly dis-employing themselves from active social roles and adopting other passive roles (of dependence) or compensating roles such as widower, grandparent, retiree, and volunteer. Their motivation decreases, their future projects will be done on a short term. If grandchildren appear, they can compensate the affective frustration of the grandparents, offering them a long-term motivation that will sustain them.

Age progression assumes the loss of certain roles, rather than the acquisition of new ones (the role of a husband, of an active person), the role of the parent loses its content.

Retirement represents a major status and role change in the life of the elderly, and the arrival of this moment can constitute a major stress factor that determines adaptive disturbances. The significance of retirement and adapting to a new situation depend on the attitude toward work, the state of health, financial situation, and the relationships with those close. The disturbances determined by retirement affects men more, as they are more engaged in their professional life throughout life than women are, the latter being engaged in parallel in domestic activities in which they can fully transfer themselves after retirement.

In the urban environment, people tend to bear the moment of retirement harder than those in a rural space, as in their adult life they dedicated themselves exclusively to their professional life, while in the rural areas, retirement never happens all of a sudden or completely.

Some social issues are the result of the organization of the current society (the reduction of the potential for caring for older people via their families, or via the reduced number of family members or the distance between them, or because of the fact that women have been more and more involved in the labor market, many elderly end up living alone and to depend on paid care services, paid for by their children, and are not cared for by them) (Busoiu, 2003).

Through dimensions and values, variety, and the numerous challenges that arise, the elderly challenge end up not only belonging to the family, but also to the care services. For certain issues of the third and fourth age, the family can no longer offer a proper care at home and thus, the elderly end up in an institution. The problem of institutionalization is mainly for those who live on their own, but can also be added to those with a family, in the cases where at-home care is not possible (repetitive falls, bed-ridden cases, dementia, incontinence, etc.). Only certain families assume the task of at-home care for elderly in these situations, especially due to the difficulty their specific health issues pose. Such a decision – of institutionalizing the elderly – is a difficult decision for him or herself, and also for the entire family. A large number of older people register in retirement homes, or in the cases where they suffer from chronic disease, in hospital homes. Here, the prevalence of depression is far more increased by comparison to the general elderly population, it being 25–40 %. Institutionalized people often have the feeling that family brought them there to forget about them, and this brings sadness, loneliness, and sometimes even depression in the long run (Filimon, 2004). The decision to institutionalize is an act of great responsibility and the factors that contribute to this decision are:

- Family, for those who have it, if the health state is majorly deteriorated and care is no longer possible at home (with the elderly's agreement, or if this is not possible due to the elderly's cognitive deterioration, then without his or her consent). Any elderly needs, at some point, to be cared for and if family cannot offer this, then the choice of such a service or the institutionalization by the family makes sense.
- The elderly himself or herself, if conscious, left without a family or in distant relations with the family.

- The doctor, the public social assistance services, and community authorities.

An option which can prepare the elderly for institutionalization is to house them in a recovery center for a limited amount of time. Admitting them to the institution implies three major types of changes:

- Freedom of movement will be restricted; he or she will only be able to walk around the institution.
- Relational deprivation – he or she will see people who will offer care, but not be close daily, and will only have access to family and friends when they come to visit.
- Informational deprivation – the access to information will be limited – on the TV, only on the channels on the institution's cable, in the press, only certain publications, books, only a reduced amount, etc.

The elderly goes from a life organized after certain necessities, to a life lived with strangers, constrained to a schedule and a different diet, forced to respect certain rules necessary for an institution, deprived of his or her own intimacy, and freed of any familial obligations and responsibilities. To the stress of the admission in the institution, one can add the feeling of forsaking and loneliness, isolation and the loss of identity, amplified by the contact with multiple people who care for them in these centers, but are strangers. In these situations, the capacity to adapt of the elderly is put to a test, surpassing and sometimes irreversibly alternating their socio-psychosomatic balance.

The pandemic period was, for everyone, difficult, as nobody has gone through anything similar; however, for elderly people who are institutionalized, it was even more difficult as they could not benefit from any visit from their family, their friends, or any people who are close to them.

Starting from this difficulty, the study points out the social interaction between the institutionalized elderly and their children during the lockdown. During this period, both parties were hindered as follows:

- For institutionalized people – the difficulty to communicate between them and their family, depending on the conditions they have; managing the dysfunctional emotions knowing they were in a risk category, and knowing they cannot receive visits from their families, children, or relatives as usual; and the difficulty of wearing the mask.
- For the sons and daughters of those in the institutions – the difficulty to communicate with the elderly depending on the condition that they have; managing negative emotions arising from not being able to visit their parent; the inconvenience of talking over the phone for a limited time only (and for

some elders, such as the ones with dementia, where a phone call would be impossible).

This pandemic created obstacles for both the elderly and their families, and as a resolution was not found immediately, it increased the stress levels of both parties. All of these new ways to communicate and relate led to an increase in anxiety, stress, and vulnerability levels, which were reflected in health dysfunctions, especially for those in the institutions.

The investigative endeavor was realized in two dimensions:

- Building a secure environment to communicate between the institutionalized and their families (establishing a schedule which meets their expectations and the possibility to be visited, even if from a distance).
- Identifying the possibilities offered by the new reality brought by the pandemic, in order to create a space stimulative enough for the institutionalized people (in order for them not to lose their abilities, and memories with their loved ones by not being stimulated, or through not seeing them temporarily).

The results of the investigative endeavor are tied to identifying the real possibilities in the new reality in terms of communicating with the family, but especially in terms of adequate care throughout this period of the elderly (socialization, diminishing the feeling of abandonment, etc.)

Objectives

- Showcasing the starting figures in the endeavor to build a secure communication space – different among cases for the different stages of illness in the institutionalized elderly.
- Emphasizing the relational aspects that can be ameliorated, or at least maintained in the absence of significant members (children or close grandchildren) and also the indicators to follow in terms of stimulating certain aspects (memory, motor capacities, etc.) and stimulating others that are necessary to diminish (decreasing anxiety, better relationship with those in the care center, medical personnel, and institutionalized people).

The Study Hypotheses

- The relational dynamics between the institutionalized people and their children are enhanced once the constant communication schedule is put in place in the new pandemic conditions.

- The decrease in anxiety and stress and the improvement in relating to people in the care center are enhanced once a constant functioning schedule in terms of phone calls with their family and "visiting" hours is established.

The Description of the Sampled

In this study, the sample was composed of a total number of 39 elderly who are institutionalized in a care center, their age range being between 64 and 79 years old, and a part of their children (each had at least one child in the sample, totaling 45 people).

Instruments Used

The instruments used in this study are the questionnaire that evaluates the changes brought by the pandemic regarding the anxiety level's perception, a questionnaire to evaluate the demands of the family in the new conditions from the point of view of the relational and communication dynamic, anamnestic and treatment data for the institutionalized people in order to establish the best way to communicate and relate for this.

Results and Discussions

A first stem realized for this had two phases: phase one was the questionnaire to the institutionalized people and the second, the evaluation of the communication and relational demands of their children in these new pandemic conditions. The questionnaire for the elderly targeted a few aspects tied to their realistic possibilities of communication and interaction. The questionnaire for their families targeted the visitation possibilities and those of phone communication. The initial evaluation of the elderly included:

- The evaluation at an auto perceived level of anxiety tied to the pandemic period (on a scale of 1–5, where 1 means not anxious at all, and 5 means very anxious);
- The evaluation at an auto perceived level of stress in the new conditions of the pandemic in the care center (on a scale of 1–5, where 1 means not stressed at all, and 5 means very stressed);
- The evaluation of the communication with the family – how many times per week they would hear each other over the phone;
- The evaluation of the communication with the family – how many times they would see each other in face-to-face visits.

The initial evaluation of the elderly's family (especially their children) included:

- The time frame they could participate in video calls;
- The time frame they could participate in the visitation times (with the mention that the visitation timings have been established as follows: the family was met in the courtyard of the institution and could come to the window of the room in which the mother or the father were in, and thus they could see each other and could talk, but it was not a visit per se).

The questionnaire that was given to the elderly brought in the following results: 20 of them stated that their self-evaluated anxiety level was very high, 11 that their self-evaluated anxiety level was high, 7 stating that it was average and only one that it was low. In terms of the self-evaluated stress level, 16 stated that it was very high, 18 that it was high while 5 said that it was average. This evaluation was done during the first week after the lockdown was imposed. By analyzing the data, it is observed that the majority of people perceive the anxiety and stress levels as high (4 or 5, where 5 is the highest mark they can attribute).

We can see from the following data obtained that the majority of people perceive anxiety and stress on a high rate (4 or 5, where 5 is the maximum grade it can be attributed).

The questionnaire applied to the families of the institutionalized elderly sought to establish for each elderly and their family a real possibility to see each other, so that each individual's well-being can be maintained or at least to prevent it from deterring. In terms of the older people, not all knew how to use the telephone on the video call option, or not all had devices that allowed them to use them this way, and in the emergency state conditions, this was one of the few possibilities to see their family. Thus, the personnel in the center where these elderlies were institutionalized thought of how they could make this solution possible for all who were able to talk to their families. The questionnaire applied to the elderly shone a light on how many knew how to use such devices, but also how often they spoke to their family. For those who did not know how to use the devices, the center organized a timetable for them to be called and they were given the institution's telephone in their salon to have access to the communication with their family (they were also helped in the procedure to answer a video call).

The questionnaire applied to the family emphasized everyone's time availability to make these conversations possible. From this latter questionnaire resulted the possibility to establish a "visitation" timetable as well. The data collected contributed to making a strategy and a timetable possible, in such way that the elderly can have access to their family once every few days – either through a video call, or through a "visit." The biggest difficulty came for the persons who were cognitively deteriorated for whom it was more difficult to understand why their conditions to see their loved ones changed. For those who were bed ridden, a difficulty in terms of the visits appeared when they couldn't reach the window to see their family physically, and the visit was limited to a video call. Despite the fact that the emergency state imposed functioning conditions that were very different in the institution, for the fact that they found ways to communicate in the new conditions, one can observe certain improvements in the state of people who were institutionalized, and thus, four weeks later the questionnaires were applied once more to evaluate if the auto perceived levels of anxiety and stress have changed. The results thus obtained are as follows: out of all the respondents, the number of those who perceived the anxiety level as very high decreased by 41 %, those who perceive it as high decreased by 2 %, and those who perceived it as average increased by 33 %. Regarding the stress values, the data is as follows: the number of those who perceive it as very high decreased by 33 %, of those who perceive it as high by 23 %, and of those who perceived it as average or low increased by 56 %.

It can be observed from the following data obtained that for the majority of the elderly, the level of anxiety and stress has decreased; thus, their general state has improved. It is known that in the case of distress the main hormones that are released are catecholamine (especially noradrenaline and adrenaline) which can favor cardiovascular diseases and cortisol, which decrease the body's resistance to disease (Iamandescu, 2002). This emphasizes once more the wish for those in the care center, and also for the families, that their stress levels do not rise, and if possible for those to actually decrease.

Through the communication with others, the elderly managed to distance themselves from the concrete dysfunctional reality of their life's perception, to reformulate it, and to understand it differently as much as for those who found out more information about the pandemic, were, more often than not their children. Once the usual visits shifted toward online communication, for the elders the loneliness received other proportions. Besides other stressors, the one given by utilizing a device added, alongside the failure of using it or sometimes even the incapacity of using it. The personnel helped them overcome these obstacles. As the communication between them brought in more and more encouraging data (that the number of cases is not too big, that it does not rise from one day to another, that the situation is under control in terms of the measures taken, etc.), the elderly's experience gradually improves with constructive meanings, full of hope and the levels of anxiety and stress decrease. The new means of communication and the more restrained possibilities of achieving them have shone a light for families the true possibilities of supporting one another, the possibility to find resources of all kinds to face the situation that arose, the exploration of the role that each member of the family has in its dynamic in case of difficulties, the possibility to unite for a common goal, which is to ensure an optimistic vision for the elderly that is in the care home. This emphasized once again our capacity to think positively, to identify solutions, to find positive aspects of the situations we're confronted with (Holdevici, 2000). Besides the benefit of communications with the family, the institutionalized people also were aware of the endeavors made by those in the care center so that the elderly and their families could remain in contact. This manifestation of understanding and compassion from the personnel made the relationship between them and the elderly to change for the better.

The more notable results though, are the ones firstly obtained on a family dynamic level – where it didn't seem to have any solutions, efficient ones were discovered, and the families quickly found possibilities to organize themselves so that they are constantly present in the lives of the elderly in their family. Another notable result is the fact that the mere existence of the communication with the family made the restless state of the elderly decrease, increased their capacity to cope with the new conditions, made the future not be perceived in a somber manner, and the state of loneliness to be tolerated with more ease. The elderly couldn't participate in the group activities in the center, so that their cognitive and emotional stimulation could be done without an interruption, so their families were enlisted in various types of exercises during their visit (solving crossword puzzles together, doing certain logical or memory games, etc.). One of the activities that they were unable to put into practice was the walk in the courtyard and the garden of the center, which some of the institutionalized people used to do with those visiting. This was a problem they could not find a solution for, due to the restrictions given by the emergency state. In this relational space affected by the pandemic, they have done still many of the things that did not seem possible at the beginning of the emergency state and thus the dynamic of the whole family improved.

Limitations of the Study

The study started from the premise that the pandemic and the emergency state brings in data that were unknown so far, so that the solutions of this problematic are inaccessible and even unknown. But even so, in difficult situations, the family – personnel team in the care center has a better efficiency rate than just the care personnel. One of the limitations of the study is constituted by the small number of subjects who participated in the study, and the second is the reduced opportunity to gather data in a pandemic and in an emergency state in multiple centers.

Conclusions

Even with all the limitations, the results obtained were positive and appeared fairly quickly, showcasing this the participants' availability to find solutions in the new conditions imposed by the emergency state. Finding strategies to maintain a good communication between the elderly who are institutionalized and their families lead to a significant improvement of coping in isolation situations for the elderly. Family represents a system whose functioning is given by the way its members function as well, even if they are not sharing the same space or are not in the same place (Vasile, 2011). Thus the social support networks play an important role in going through catastrophic situations or perceived int his way, and in our case the support network formed by the family we could add, in time other people, such as friends (Mitrofan, Buzducea, 2002). Starting from a reality in which visits were face-to-face and in a time everyone chose for themselves depending on their availability, to "visits" via video call or the contact beyond a window, the state of presence of each person, but especially the social contact(hugs, touches, staying close, etc.) were tainted, and for this new situation, solutions needed to be found. In the care center it was thus created, even from the first week of the emergency state, a space of meeting in which the focus was on maintaining the elderly's contact with their family to contribute to their well-being and to their mental balance.

References

Barbier D. (2005). *Ieşirea din depresie medicamente sau psihoterapie*, Bucureşti, Editura Trei

Busoiu,O. (2003). *Psihologia pentru toţi,* Arad, Editura Gutemberg Univers

Cosmovici, A. (2003). *Psihologie generală,* Iaşi, Editura Polirom

Creţu, T. (2001). *Psihologia vârstelor,* Bucureşti Editura Credis

Filimon, L. (2004). *Psihoeducaţia în terapia depresiei*, Oradea, Editura Universităţii din Oradea

Holdevici, I. (2000) – *Gândirea pozitivă*, Bucureşti, Editura Dual Tech,

Iamandescu, I.B. (2002). *Stresul psihic – din perspectivă psihologică şi psihosomatică*, Editura Infomedica, Bucureşti

Malim, T. (2003). *Psihologie socială*, Bucureşti, Editura Tehnica

Man, G. M. (2017). *Psihologia vârstei a treia şi a patra*, Editura Trei, Bucureşti

Mitrofan, I., Buzducea, D. (2002). *Psihologia pierderii şi terapia durerii*, Editura Sper, Bucureşti

Vasile, D. L. (2011). *Trauma familială şi resursele compensatorii*, Editura Sper

Delia BÎRLE and Raluca ZARO

8 The Theory of Reasoned Action and Planned Behavior. Implications for the Intention to Use Condom in the Case of Students' Sexual Behavior

Abstract The goal of the present study was to predict the condom use in students' sexual behavior, based on the classic Theory of Reasoned Action and Planned Behavior. Variables like *attitudes, perceived norms, perceived behavioral control, experience, anticipated affects* (positive and negative), *gender*, the status of their love *relationship*, or the situation of their *co-tenants* were arranged in three blocks and tested in a hierarchical multilinear regression analysis, on 136 Romanian students from different universities. Significant contributions were found for the situation of co-tenants, the relationship status, the attitudes, the perceived norms, the anticipated positive affects and the experience.

Keywords: Theory of Reasoned Action, Theory of Planned Behavior, condom use predictors, perceived norms, anticipated affects

Introduction

The Theory of Planned Behavior (TPB; Ajzen, 1991) is a widely known social-cognitive model used for intention and behavior prediction (Ajzen & Cote, 2008). According to *the Theory of Reasoned Action* (TRA), which was proposed by Fishbein & Ajzen in 1975, the proximal predecessor of volitional behavior is the intention to perform the behavior (apud Conner & Sparks, 2005, pp. 170–171). *Intention* is the motivation to execute the behavior in question (Ajzen, 1991). As Fishbein & Ajzen (1975) affirm, the intention is influenced by two conceptually distinct antecedents: behavioral beliefs and normative beliefs (apud Madden, Ellen & Ajzen, 1992). In compliance with Ajzen & Cote (2008), *behavioral beliefs* represent the individual's view about the possible consequences the behavior involves and they establish the positive or negative value of the individual's *attitude toward the behavior* in question. Despite the large number of attitude definitions provided by the literature, Fishbein & Ajzen (2010a) assert that the literature reached to an agreement with respect to its conceptualization: "a latent disposition or tendency to respond with some degree of favorableness or unfavorableness to a psychological object." Ajzen & Cote (2008) state that *normative beliefs* are the subject's expectations concerning the significant people's approval or disapproval of the behavior to be performed. Those contribute in forming the *perceived norms* to the extent that the person is motivated enough to comply to the referent individuals or groups rules or principles. The perceived norms refer to one's perceived social pressure to engage or not in a given behavior (Ajzen, 1991; Conner & Sparks, 2005; Fishbein & Ajzen, 2010b).

Thereby, the behavioral intention is shaped by the individual's attitude and by the perceived norms concerning the behavior in question (Ajzen & Cote, 2008). In order to express intention in behavior, the behavior itself has to be under one's complete control, the individual must decide whether or not they are planning to exert effort in order to perform it (Ajzen, 1991). According to Conner & Sparks (2005), the TRA narrows itself to the prediction of volitional behaviors.

Ajzen (1985) extends the TRA by including the concept of *perceived behavioral control* among the immediate antecedents of intention and behavior (apud Madden et al., 1992), asserting that the TPB differs from the TRA due to the insertion of the PBC in the model (Ajzen, 1991). Thereby, the TPB enlarges the limits concerning the pure volitional control stipulated the TRA by embodying *control beliefs* (Madden et al., 1992). Those beliefs represent individual's perceived possibility that there are some factors (requisite resources as personal skills, money, opportunities, other's assistance, availability, or lack of time) that could facilitate or inhibit the behavioral performance (Ajzen & Cote, 2008). Control beliefs are the foundation of the PBC, which refers to "people's perception of the ease or difficulty of performing the behavior of interest" (Ajzen, 1991).

Pursuant to Ajzen & Fishbein (2005), the three immediate predecessors of intention vary due to a large group of *background factors* including age, gender, social and economic status, nationality, religion, skills, personal values, and educational status. Those factors exert an indirect influence on intention and behavior through their effect on the salient beliefs that compose attitudes, perceived norms, and PBC. Conjunctively, attitudes, perceived norms, and PBC influence behavioral intention, which leads up to behavioral performance (Ajzen, 2002; Ajzen & Cote, 2008). In 1991, Ajzen defines a set of general rules with respect to the model's mechanism: the more positive and favorable the attitudes and perceived norms about a specific behavior and the greater the perceived behavioral control, the stronger should be one's intention to engage in the behavior in question. Likewise, the stronger the intention, the more likely should be the performance of the behavior under consideration. Yet

Ajzen (1991) states that the influence of attitudes, perceived norms, and PBC vary across behavior type and situations under analysis. Therefore, the TPB is designed to explain and predict both volitional and non-volitional behavior (Conner & Armitage, 1998).

TPB Efficiency. Ajzen (2011) assert the fact that the TPB has become one of the most influential models in predicting behavior, being widely used in health-related behavior research (Godin & Kok, 1996; Armitage & Conner, 2001; McEachan, Conner, Taylor & Lawton, 2011; Tyson, Covey & Rosenthal, 2014). One issue assessed by the literature concerns the efficiency of this model in prediction of sexual risk behaviors including abstinence and condom use with casual partners and relationship partners (Reinecke, Schmidt & Ajzen, 1996; Cha, 2005; Sikkema et al., 2005; Carmack & Lewis-Moss, 2009; Montanaro & Bryan, 2014; Asare, 2015; Bednarchik, 2016). The predictive power of the TPB vary across the literature: in predicting intention to use condom the variance explained by the TPB fluctuate between 30 % and 64 %, and in predicting behavior (condom use) the values vary between 35 % and 63.9 %.

Additional variables. Turchik & Gidycz (2012) emphasize the importance of increasing the model's predictive power of sexual risk behavior by insertion of additional variables, resulting in a number of extended models of TPB for condom use. There is research that underline the role of additional variables in prediction of intention and behavior, especially the influence exerted by *anticipated affect* (Richard, van der Pligt & de Vries, 1995, 1996a, 1996b; Hynie, MacDonald & Marques, 2006; Sandberg & Conner, 2008; Rivis, Sheeran & Armitage, 2009; Durán, Ferraces, Rodríguez, Río & Sabucedo, 2017), *past behavior* (Albarracín, Fishbein & Middlestadt, 1998; Turchik & Gidycz, 2012; Durán et al., 2017), and even demographic variables as *gender* and *relationship status* (Richard & van der Pligt, 1991; Sheeran & Orbell, 1998; Wise, Goggin, Gerkovich, Metcalf & Kennedy, 2006; Turchik & Gidycz, 2012; Rich, Mullan, Sainsbury & Kuczmierczyk, 2014). These extended models including past behavior and anticipated affect account for values from 62 % to 76 % in explaining condom use intentions. Sutton (1994) argues that many of the one's present behaviors are determined by one's experience involving that behaviors rather than cognitions (apud Conner & Armitage, 1998). The past behavior account for 4 % (Albarracín et al., 1998), 5 % (McEachan et al., 2011), and 8.7 % (Durán et al., 2017) of the variance explained in intention. *Anticipated affect* refers to the possibility that one could experience positive or negative feelings after performing or not performing a behavior (Rivis et al., 2009). In 1998, Conner & Armitage suggest that one lack of the TPB is the exclusion of the affective processes, especially when the behavior's consequences are negative. Thus, if the individual contemplates the possibility of feeling regret or worry after a sexual encounter where the condom has not been used, it is more likely that the individual is going to use a condom during intercourse. In accordance with Abraham & Sheeran (2003), the *anticipated regret* refers to individual's beliefs that feelings of regret or upset would come immediately after not engaging in the behavior. van der Pligt & Richard (1994) state that "anticipated regret is used as a generic term to refer to the main psychological effects of the various regrets and worries that beset the individual before any negative consequences actually materialise." Fishbein & Ajzen (2010c) assert that anticipated affect is usually measured in the opposite way (frequently inaction, not engaging in behavior, e.g., not using a condom) than all the other components of the TPB, which are measured with respect to perform a certain behavior (e.g., using a condom). A number of studies focused on the role of anticipated negative feelings, especially anticipated regret, in prediction of condom use behavior among youth, using the TPB as a theoretical framework (Richard et al., 1996b; Sheeran & Orbel, 1999; Hynie et al., 2006; Sandberg & Conner; 2008; Rivis et al., 2009). It is shown that the anticipated affective reactions account for 4 % (Hynie et al., 2006), 4.1 % (Durán et al., 2017), 5 % (Rivis et al., 2009), and 7 % (Sandberg & Conner, 2008) of the variance explained for intention.

Method

Research Objectives

This research aims to emphasize the components of the planned sexual behavior related to the condom use. Identifying and measuring these components and their influence on the intention to use the condom in sexual relationship may be the starting point in designing efficient programs for preventing adolescent pregnancy and sexual transmission diseases.

Several research questions were addressed: do the *attitudes*, *perceived norms*, and the *perceived behavioral control* have an influence on the participants' intention to use the condom? Could the *experience* and the *anticipated affects* (positive and negative) influence the intention to use of condom? Would students' *gender*, the status of their love *relationship*, or the situation of their *co-tenants* may have a significant influence on the condom use?

The aim of this research, derived from the above questions, was to identify the variables that have an important contribution in explaining the students' intention to use the condom, as a component of the planned sexual behavior.

Research Hypothesis and Design

The focus of this research is on identifying the elements of the planned behavior theory and the influence of these elements on the intention to use the condom in the next two months. The interest is on controlling the three blocks of variables in order to establish the independent effect of these variables on the intention and, also, to establish their common influence on the same dependent variable – the intention to use the condom in the next two months during the sexual acts.

Measures of the Research Variables

The variable *attitudes* toward the protected sex was measured by the items elaborated by Fishbein & Ajzen (2010a), Duran et al. (2017), and Ajzen & Driver (1991) and adapted for the present study, having two subscales: one for the attitudes toward the protected sex with a stable partner and the second subscale measures the attitudes toward the protected sex with an occasional partner. The perceived *norms* toward the protected sex was measured using items elaborated by Fishbein & Ajzen (2010b) and adapted for the present research. The *perceived behavioral control* over the protected sex was measured using items proposed by Armitage & Conner (1999a, 1999b), adapted for this study, having one subscale for the stable partner and one for the occasional partner. The *anticipated affect* regarding the protected sex was measured by a scale adapted after Fishbein & Ajzen (2010c), Turchik & Gidycz (2012), Durán et al. (2017) şi Richard et al. (1995), having subscales for positive and negative affect, both for a stable and for an occasional partner. The *experience* refers to the use of condom in the past six months and was measured with a scale adapted after Turchik & Gidycz (2012), having two subscales, one for a stable partner, and one for an occasional partner. The *intention* was measured with a scale adapted after Turchik & Gidycz (2012), with the subscales: intention to use the condom with a stable partner for the next two months and the intention to use the condom with an occasional partner in the next two months.

The research hypothesis: the elements of the planned behavioral theory (attitudes, perceived norms, and perceived behavioral control) are significant predictors for the intention to use the condom; the anticipated affects (positive and negative) and the experience are significant predictors for the intention to use the condom; gender, the relationship status (stable or occasional), and the situation of the co-tenants are significant predictors of the condom use in the next two months

Participants

The participants (N=136) were aged between 19 and 25, m=21.67, s.d. =1.54, 75 (55.1 %) were females, in their great majority declared as being orthodox (89), but a significant number declared themselves atheists, students in Universities of Oradea, Târgu Mureş, Cluj-Napoca, all from Romania.

Procedure

The questionnaire was introduced in the Google Form platform, and it was filled online by the students. They received the online questionnaire on students groups. In the instructions, they were assured about the confidentiality of their responses.

Results

Hierarchical multilinear regression analysis was used to identify the isolated influence of three variables blocks (block one consists in demographic characteristics: gender, co-tenants, the relationship status; block two comprised the components of the planned behavior theory: the attitudes, the perceived behavioral control, and the perceived norms; the third block comprises additional variables like anticipated negative affect, anticipated positive affect, and the experience) on the intention to use condom in the next two months. Tab. 1 presents the descriptive statistics, Alpha Cronbach coefficients for internal consistency and r Pearson values for correlation between the research variables.

In the first step, we introduced the demographic variables (gender, co-tenants, and the relationship status) having as a first purpose to identify the extent to which those variables have a significant influence on the intention change; the second purpose is to control their effect. It was necessary to transform the variables into dummy variables, *male* was considered the reference class for gender, *alone* was the reference class for co-tenants, and *stable* was the reference class for the relationship status variable.

The planned behavior theory components – attitudes, the perceived behavioral control, and the perceived norms – were introduced in the second phase of the regression analysis and the additional variables (the anticipated positive and negative affects and the experience) in the third phase.

Tab. 1. Descriptive statistics and the correlations between the research variables

Var.	M	s.d.	α	1	2	3	4	5	6	7
1	53.50	12.72	.90	–						
2	22.64	4.68	.66	.33**	–					
3	17.16	3.41	.72	.49**	.37**	–				
4	28.19	8.46	.83	.57**	.22**	.44**	–			
5	22.29	8.35	.80	−.37**	−.04	−.22**	−.49**	–		
6	8.28	4.75	.78	.43**	.28**	.28**	.29**	−.12	–	
7	11.31	3.12		.69**	.24**	.49**	.52**	−.41**	.47**	–

** p<.01 (1 – attitudes; 2 – perceived behavioral control; 3 – perceived norms; 4 – anticipated negative affect; 5 – anticipated positive affect; 6 – experience; 7 – intention)

The explanatory model for the intention to use condom

H1. The elements of the planned behavior (attitudes, perceived norms, perceived behavioral control) are significant predictors of the intention to use the condom

H2. The negative and positive anticipated affects and the experience are significant predictors of the intention to use condom

H3. Gender, relationship status, and the situation of co-tenants are significant predictors of the intention to use condom.

Tab. 2 presents the results of the multiple hierarchical analysis, demonstrating the explanatory weights of the change of the intention to use condom in sexual acts in the next two months. In the first phase, the model proves its statistical significance, better than based on the observed means estimates ($F_{(3;132)}$ =5.32, p<.01), meaning that characteristics like gender, relationship status, and the situation of co-tenants explain 10.8 % of the variability in the intention to use condom (R=.328, R^2=.108). Introducing in the second phase, the components of the planned behavior theory brings a significant plus for the explanatory power, of 47.9 % (ΔR^2=.479). The cumulated effects of the first two blocks of variables offers an explanatory power of 58.7 % (R=.766, R^2=.587) in the variability of the intention to use condom, and there is a significant change from the initial model ($F_{(6;129)}$=30.50, p<.01). After including the variables *positive and negative anticipated affects* and *experience* in the third phase of the regression analysis, there was a significant increase of the explanatory power of the model at 64.0 % (R=.800, R^2=.640) when explaining the intention to use condom. The difference between the two coefficients of determination (ΔR^2=.054) shows that there is a plus of 5.4 % in the contribution of these variables for explaining the intention to use condom. This new extended model offers a significant change compared to the previous equation ($F_{(9;126)}$=24.91, p<.01).

Observing the values of the standardized regression coefficients, one may decide that gender, the perceived behavioral control, and the negative anticipated affect don't have a significant contribution in the intention to use condom, and, in consequence, they were eliminated from the final model. It is important to mention that the situation of co-tenants doesn't have a significant contribution in the first phase of the model, (β=–.161, p=.056), but it became significant in the second (β=–.119, p=.04) and in the third phase (β=–.12, p=.02).

Tab. 2. The results of the hierarchical regression analysis in estimating the intention to use condom in the next two months

Variables	R	R^2	ΔR^2	β	F	p
STEP 1	.328**	.108**	.108**		5.32	.002
Gender (=feminine)				.116		
Co-tenants (=single)				–.161		
Relation status (=stable)				–.315**		
STEP 2	.766**	.587**	.479**		30.50	.000
Gender (=feminine)				–.056		
Co-tenants (=single)				–.119*		
Relation status (=stable)				–.244**		
Attitudes				.616**		
Perceived behavioral control				–.045		
Perceived norms				.190**		
STEP 3	.800**	.640**	.054**		24.91	.000
Gender (=feminine)				–.042		
Co-tenants (=single)				–.122*		
Relation status (=stable)				–.228**		
Attitudes				.455**		
Peeceived behavioral control				–.051		
Perceived norms				.155*		
Anticipated negative affect				.069		
Anticipated positive affect				–.150*		
Experience				.187**		

* p<.05; ** p<.01

In the final model, the variable having the largest explanatory power was *the attitudes* (β=.45), followed by *the relationship status* (β=−.22), *the experience* (β=.18), *norms* (β=.15), *positive anticipated affect* (β=−.15), and, finally, *the co-tenants* (β=−.12).

Thus, the students having co-tenants, without a stable love relationship, having positive attitudes toward the condom use, having internalized favorable norms for the condom use, who less anticipate positive affects for the sexual contact without condom use, and who used condom for the last six months are more likely to use condom in the next two months.

Conclusions

As a conclusion, the current study confirms the explanatory power of the TPB-based models both original and extended for intention to use condom with both relationship and casual partners. These results are related with the ones obtained in the sexual risk behavior literature (Richard et al., 1995; Albarracín et al., 1998; Armitage & Conner, 2001; Hynie et al., 2006; Sandberg & Conner, 2008; Turchik & Gidycz, 2012; Rich et al., 2014; Asare, 2015; Durán et al., 2017). Attitudes and perceived norms are significant determinants in explaining condom use intention, unlike PBC, which was excluded from the resulted models (Albarracín et al., 1998; Hynie et al., 2006; Protogerou et al., 2013; Rich et al., 2014).

The contribution of additional variables in explaining intention is significant (Turchik & Gidycz, 2012; Durán et al., 2017). Although the negative anticipated affect is excluded from the model due to exceeding the significance limit – p-value (.05), the positive anticipated affect's β-value is significant and negative (β=−.155, p<.05), yet indicating the intuited course of the results. The past behavior remains too a significant antecedent of intention to use condom (McEachan et al., 2011; Turchik & Gidycz, 2012; Durán et al., 2017).

Also, the current research sought to examine the role that two demographic variables (relationship status and co-tenants situation) play in explaining the variance of condom use intention. The results show that intention to use condom is stronger for the single individuals, that are not involved in a stable romantic relationship. Future studies should focus on the impact that this variable could have on condom use behavior. The co-tenants situation represents a new concept proposed by the current research, which has not been a subject of anaylses in the literature before.

As a general conclusion, this chapter points out that the individuals who do not live by themselves, who are not involved in a stable romantic relationship, who have positive attitudes regarding condom use, who internalized more favorable norms about this contraception method, who anticipate less positive emotions after a sexual intercourse without a condom, and who used this method in the past, have stronger intentions to use the condom in the next two months.

References

Abraham, C., & Sheeran, P. (2003). Acting on intentions: The role of anticipated regret. *British Journal of Health Psychology*, 42, 495–511.

Abraham, C., Sheeran, P., Spears, R., & Abrams, D. (1992). Health beliefs and promotion of HIV-Preventive intentions among teenagers: A Scottish perspective. *Health Psychology*, 11*(6)*, 363–370.

Ajzen, I. (1991). The theory of planned behaviour. *Organizational Behavior and Human Decision Processes,* 50, 179–211.

Ajzen, I. (2002). Perceived behavioral control, self-efficacy, locus of control, and the theory of planned behavior. *Journal of Applied Social Psychology,* 32*(4)*, 665–683.

Ajzen, I. (2011). The theory of planned behaviour: Reactions and reflections. *Psychology & Health*, 26*(9)*, 1113–1127. doi:10.1080/08870446.2011.613995.

Ajzen, I., & Cote, N. G. (2008). Attitudes and the Prediction of Behavior. In: W. D. Crano & R. Prislin (Eds.), *Attitudes and Attitude Change* (pp. 289–311). New York: Psychology Press.

Ajzen, I., & Driver, B. L. (1991). Prediction of leisure participation from behavioral, normative, and control beliefs: An application of the theory of planned behavior. *Leisure Sciences*, 13, 185–204.

Ajzen, I., & Fishbein, M. (2005). The Influence of Attitudes on Behavior. In: D. Albarracín, B. T. Johnson, & M. P. Zanna (Eds.), *The Handbook of Attitudes* (pp. 173–221). Mahwah, NJ: Erlbaum.

Albarracín, D., Fishbein, M., & Middlestadt, S. (1998). Generalizing behavioral findings across times, samples, and measures: A study of condom use. *Journal of Applied Social Psychology*, 28*(8)*, 657–674.

Armitage, C. J., & Conner, M. (1999a). The theory of planned behaviour: Assessment of predictive validity and 'perceived control'. *British Journal of Social Psychology*, 38, 35–54.

Armitage, C. J., & Conner, M. (1999b). Predictive validity of the theory of planned behaviour: The role of questionnaire format and social desirability. *Journal of Community & Applied Social Psychology*, 9, 261–272.

Armitage, C. J., & Conner, M. (2001). Efficacy of the theory of planned behavior: A meta-analytic review. *British Journal of Social Psychology*, 40, 471–499.

Asare, M. (2015). Using the theory of planned behavior to determine the condom use behavior among college students. *American Journal of Health Studies*, 30*(1)*, 43–50.

Bednarchik, L. A. (2016). *Using the Theory of Planned Behavior to Predict College Students' Communication of Affirmative Sexual Consent.* Doctoral dissertation, Arizona State University.

Carmack, C. C., & Lewis-Moss, R. K. (2009). Examining the theory of planned behavior applied to condom use: The effect-indicator vs. causal-indicator models. *Journal of Primary Prevention*, 30*(6)*, 659–676.

Cha, E. S. (2005). *Predictors of Sexual Behavior among Korean College Students: Testing the Theory of Planned Behavior.* Unpublished doctoral dissertation, University of Pittsburgh.

Conner, M., & Armitage, C. J. (1998). Extending the theory of planned behavior: A review and avenues for further research. *Journal of Applied Social Psychology*, 28*(15)*, 1429–1464.

Conner, M., & Spraks, P. (2005). Theory of Planned Behaviour and Health Behaviour. In: M. Conner & P. Norman (Eds.), *Predicting health behaviour: Research and practice with social cognition models* (a doua ediţie) (pp. 170–222). Buckingham: Open University Press.

de Visser, R., & Smith, A. (2001). Relationship between sexual partners influences rates and correlates of condom use. *ADIS Education and Prevention*, 13*(5)*, 413–427.

Durán, M., Ferraces, M. J., Rodríguez, M., Río, A., & Sabucedo, J. M. (2017). Intention to have sexual intercourse without a condom. *Trames*, 21*(71/66)*, 1, 15–32.

Fishbein, M., & Ajzen, I. (2010a). Attitudes and Their Determinants. In: Fishbein, M., & Ajzen, I. (Eds.), *Predicting and Changing Behavior: The Reasoned Action Approach* (pp. 75–128). New York: Psychology Press.

Fishbein, M., & Ajzen, I. (2010b). Perceived Norms and Their Determinants. In: M. Fishbein & I. Ajzen (Eds.), *Predicting and Changing Behavior: The Reasoned Action Approach* (pp. 129–152). New York: Psychology Press.

Fishbein, M., & Ajzen, I. (2010c). Challenges to the Reasoned Action Approach. In: M. Fishbein & I. Ajzen (Eds.), *Predicting and Changing Behavior: The Reasoned Action Approach* (pp. 281–320). New York: Psychology Press.

Godin, G., & Kok, G. (1996). The theory of planned behavior: A review of its applications to health-related behaviors. *American Journal of Health Promotion*, 11*(2)*, 87–98.

Graves, K. L., & Leigh, B. C. (1995). The relationship of substance use to sexual activity among young adults in the United States. *Family Planning Perspectives*, 27*(1)*, 18–22.

Hynie, M., MacDonald, T. K., & Marques, S. (2006). Self-conscious emotions and self-regulation in the promotion of condom use. *Personality and Social Psychology Bulletin*, 32*(8)*, 1072–1084.

Madden, T. J., Ellen, P. M., & Ajzen, I. (1992). A comparison of the theory of planned behavior and the theory of reasoned action. *Personality and Social Psychology Bulletin*, 18*(1)*, 3–9.

McEachan, R. R. C., Conner, M., Taylor, N. J., & Lawton, R. J. (2011). Prospective prediction of health-related behaviours with the theory of planned behaviour: A meta-analysis. *Health Psychology Review*, 5, 97–144.

Montanaro, E. A., & Bryan, A. D. (2014). Comparing theory-based condom interventions: Health belief model versus theory of planned behavior. *Health Psychology*, 33*(10)*, 1251–1260.

Protogerou, C., Flisher, A. J., Wild, L. G., & Aarø, L. E. (2013). Predictors of condom use in South African university students: A prospective application of the theory of planned behaviour. *Journal of Applied Social Psychology*, 43, 23–36.

Reinecke, J., Schmidt, P., & Ajzen, I. (1996). Application of the theory of planned behavior to adolescents' condom use: A panel study. *Journal of Applied Social Psychology*, 26*(9)*, 749–772.

Rich, A., Mullan, B. A., Sainsbury, K., & Kuczmierczyk, A. R. (2014). The role of gender and sexual experience in predicting adolescent condom use intentions using the theory of planned behaviour. *The European Journal of Contraception and Reproductive Health Care*, 19, 295–306.

Richard, R., & van der Pligt, J. (1991). Factors affecting condom use among adolescents. *Journal of Community & Applied Social Psychology*, 1, 105–116.

Richard, R., van der Pligt, J., & de Vries, N. K. (1995). Anticipated affective reactions and prevention of AIDS. *British Journal of Social Psychology*, 34, 9–21.

Richard, R., van der Pligt, J., & de Vries, N. K. (1996a). Anticipated affect and behavioral choice. *Basic and Applied Social Psychology*, 18*(2)*, 111–129.

Richard, R., van der Pligt, J., & de Vries, N. K. (1996b). Anticipated regret and time perspective: Changing sexual risk-taking behavior. *Journal of Behavioral Decision Making*, 9, 185–199.

Rivis, A., Sheeran, P., & Armitage, C. J. (2009). Expanding the affective and normative components of the theory of planned behaviour: A meta-analysis of anticipated affect and moral norms. *Journal of Applied Social Psychology, 39(12)*, 2985–3019.

Sandberg, T., & Conner, M. (2008). Anticipated regret as an additional predictor in the theory of planned behavior: A meta-analysis. *British Journal of Social Psychology*, 47, 589–606.

Sheeran, P., & Orbell, S. (1998). Do intentions predict condom use? Meta-analysis and examination of six moderator variables. *British Journal of Social Psychology*, 37, 231–250.

Sheeran, P., & Orbell, S. (1999). Augmenting the theory of planned behaviour: Roles of anticipated regret and descriptive norms. *Journal of Applied Social Psychology, 29(10)*, 2107–2142.

Sikkema, K. J. et al. (2005). Outcomes of a randomized, controlled comunity-level HIV prevention intervention for adolescents in low-income housing developments. *AIDS*, 19, 1509–1516.

Turchik, J. A., & Gidycz, C. A. (2012). Prediction if sexual risk behaviors in college students using the theory of planned behaviour: A prospective analysis. *Journal of Social and Clinical Psychology*, 31*(1)*, 1–27.

Tyson, M., Covey, J., & Rosenthal, H. E. S. (2014). Theory of planned behavior interventions for reducing heterosexual risk behaviors: A meta-analysis. *Health Psychology*, 33*(12)*, 1454–1467.

van der Pligt, J., & Richard, R. (1994). Changing adolescents' sexual behavior: Perceived risk, self-efficacy and anticipated regret. *Patient Education and Counseling*, 23, 187–196.

Wilson, C. (2015). *Adolescent Sexual Risk Reduction and the Theory of Planned Behavior: Moderation Effects and the Role of Previous Experience*. Thesis, Georgia State University.

Wise, D., Goggin, K., Gerkovich, M., Metcalf, K., & Kennedy, S. (2006). Predicting intentions to use condoms using gender, sexual experience, and the theory of planned behavior. *American Journal of Health Education*, 37*(4)*, 210–218.

Ionel Nicu SAVA

9 The State of Well-Being and the Information Technology (IT) – Digital Well-Being

Abstract Changes are unavoidable in a life of a human being, and they can be performed by resorting to different energetic levels, according to the availability of each person to invest this energy in order to increase the state of well-being disturbed by the multiple life situations. The capacity of each person to value what the context is offering in order to solve the life situations is different, the difference is given by the availability to be open to new things, or to be conservative and more rigid and fearful in accepting new things. In both situations, one desires to keep and/or increase the state of well-being, if, in the case of the flexibility and the openness to new things, the state of well-being occurs through discovery, learning and the usage of new adaptative techniques, in the case of conservative people, one tries to preserve the previous state of well-being with the risk of remaining in the same state. From this perspective, the chapter is two-folded, it outlines the especially important role of the unprecedented development of the IT and the second perspective, regarding the influence this phenomenon has of the personal state of well-being.

Keywords: State of well-being, IT, flexibility, rigidity

Introduction into the Thematic Framework

The flexibility to change people can show is visible in the behavior adopted by these ones during their lifetime. It can be easily identified when factors which impose adaptation occur, such as the passing from a life cycle to another, the setting up of a family, the loss or the birth of a new member in the family system, the change of the residential or of the professional environment, a disease of a family member or of a significant person, the desire for personal development, which imposes the restructuring of one's own personality, and other factors that require certain repositioning and adaptation strategies. Other factors that required and are requiring adaptation are the ones related to the changes incurred by the progress of society in general, such as the industrialization, urbanization, globalization, and, more recently, the pandemics! Therefore, the state of well-being (as perceived by the subject at the moment of the occurrence of the disrupting factor) is threatened, and it claims a re-balancing and even a growth through diverse strategies, methods, and techniques, adequate for and available to the affected person. The sketching of the introductory framework into the theme of the chapter has as argument the arising of the curiosity in relation to the capacities of our peers to be flexible to the new (automated technology, epidemiologic context with risk of mass contamination, etc.) and the state of well-being.

The General Purpose of the Chapter

The theoretical approach of this material has as main objective the defining and the understanding of the concept of digital well-being, starting from the broader concept of state of well-being. For a better clarification of the content of the research, I specify that I do not propose myself to approach the implications created by the pandemic phenomenon on the state of well-being, but I shall try to identify how the information technology is involved into the decrease of the frustration created by the isolation measures and how it can compensate for the damages created. In such a situation, the need to adapt is claimed from two directions: on one side, it is imposed by the adjustment to the epidemic phenomenon and, on the other side, the accommodation with the IT-related skills (necessity expected also prior to the appearance of the new coronavirus), which, in any event, exceeded the rhythm of our peer to adapt to it. The pandemic effect has facilitated and even forced the rhythms of the familiarization with the information technology, which presupposes a dosed effort according to the capacity and to the availability of each of us, availability hampered by our unconscious resistance, which can diminish or even sabotage our natural capacity of adaptation and our potential openness to new through the level of flexibility we might show.

Under this subject, the resorting to the information technology, which is imposed with necessity, facilitates the transfer of information in accordance with the new needs arising from the restrictions imposed. Starting from the premise of the undeniable utility of the technological progress, one can state that the adaptation with its support helps the decrease of anxiety induced by new situations with disrupting potential. Therefore, I state that the digital technology contributes to the reinstatement of the psychological state of well-being as it is named in our time, the digital well-being.

But, in order to reach this composite concept, I shall synthesize several opinions related to the concept of well-being, stating that there is no consensus of the specialists in relation to its definition.

The Theoretical Framework for the Concept of *Well-Being*

Well-being – conceptualized uni- or multi-dimensionally, subjective or a combination between subjective and objective, with implications at the cognitive and emotional level. The state of well-being to positive emotions, such as pleasure or happiness, which can arise and develop in relation to what we do and with our relationships. Nevertheless, we must be careful that well-being does not refer to that state of happiness, which we can have in our passing moments from our lifetime, but to our general satisfaction toward life (King, 2016).

According to certain authors, the state of well-being refers to the subjective perceptions of the individual on his/her psychological health and on the quality of life on the cognitive and emotional level (Lubin şi Whitlock, 2004 *apud.* Landen şi Wang, 2009).

At its turn, well-being was assimilated to wellness, which refers to our capacity to live our lives as close as possible to the way we want and to the feeling that it is happening as such. It comprises the ability to have positive relationships, to promote a healthy life, and to feel the satisfaction of life.

The psychological well-being is closely related to the psychical well-being and means not only the absence of psychical diseases. The psychological health implies a state of psychical well-being, which goes closely together with the state of a healthy self (Keyes, Shapiro, 2004; Ryff, Singer, 1998, *apud* Papalia et al., 2010). This subjective state of good or happiness represent the self-assessment a person is doing in relation to his/her own life (Diener E., 2000, *apud* Papalia et al., 2010).

The psychological well-being can be illustrated by happiness, self-content, the felling of one's own identity, the decrease of the excessive stress, self-esteem, the spiritual wealth, and the feeling of safety. Wellness is given by the totality of the actions a person does so that to trigger a positive change in his/her life. Most often, wellness is associated with a form of material possession, but it signifies, actually, a philosophy of life, based on the acceptance of the idea that wellness resumes to being rich.

The specialists in the field of psychology not only have become more interested in the in-depth study and research of the psychological aspects related to the emotional wellness or to the state of *well-being*. The psychological wellness and the perception on it are the result of the "screening" of the events lived through the schemes of value judgments, which refer to the significance of *happiness* and of *life satisfaction*.

Despite the fact that the scientific study of happiness has seen a remarkable progress during the last three decades – which entitles certain researchers to qualify the topic as a true "wellness epidemiology" (George, 2010, *apud* Iluţ, 2015), it seems that the implicit semantics, which operates in the definition of happiness is still fairly limited (Biswas-Diener, Kashdan şi King, 2009, *apud* Iluţ, 2015). Despite these restrains, happiness is operationalized in the specialized literature on the basis of indicators, which bring rigor and precision.

One of the concepts most frequently assumed in psychology to designate happiness is the state of subjective (Diener, 2012, *apud* Iluţ, 2015). Thirty years ago, Diener (1984) pleaded for the scientific usage of the term of "subjective well-being," to the detriment of the term of happiness, which is, in his opinion, ambiguous, used in common language with different meanings for different people. The construct evoked refers to the subjective assessment of one's own life and it has two major components: life satisfaction and the emotional balance (Diener, 1984; Diener şi Larsen, 1993, *apud* Iluţ, 2015).

Life satisfaction refers to the cognitive overall assessment of one's own life, and it represents the cognitive component of the subjective well-being, while the emotional balance refers to the relative share of the positive emotions (pleasant emotional experiences) in relation to the negative emotions, and it represents the emotional component of the subjective well-being (Diener, 1984, *apud* Iluţ, 2015).

In the approaching of the subjective psychological well-being, there are two traditions: a hedonistic one, which refers to the notion of happiness as being the presence of positive feelings and emotions and the absence of the negative ones, as well as an eudaimonic one, focused on the life fully lived, in a satisfactory way (Ryan şi Deci, 2000, *apud* Iluţ, 2015).

The psychological wellness has been studied as a basic theme in the psychology during the last quarter of the century, as a notion focusing on the optimal psychological experience and functionality. A great influence in this sense was attributed to Diener (1984), according to whom, *the state of wellness of a person is considered subjective, because he/she evaluates himself/herself, in a general way, the extent to which he/she is living the wellness and confers a significance to it in agreement with his/her own experience* (Deiner, 1984, pp. 542–575).

An alternative conceptualization of happiness is the psychological wellness, which refers to the feeling of fulfillment gained following the overcoming of the life obstacles and the valorization of one's own potential (Keyes, Shmotkin şi Ryff, 2002, *apud* Iluţ, 2015). This concept was frequently used to designate the *eudaimonic* wellness, as it surprises aspects of a human positive functioning which exceed the simple cognitive and emotional assessment of a person, tying to incorporate a sequencing meaning of life.

Ryff (1989, *apud* Salami, 2011) operationalizes the state of psychological wellness and offers a multidimensional model of it. This model is based on the theories about human development and on the ones regarding the functionality, efficiency, and life satisfaction when growing old. Therefore, the author constructs a psychometric inventory based on six factors:

1. Autonomy – independence and self-determination. The great scores obtained at this factor indicate the fact that the respondent is independent and regulates his/her behavior independently from the social pressures. Example of this item is "I trust my beliefs, even if they are contrary to the general consensus."
2. Control over the environment – the ability with which the person is leading his/her life. Great scores indicate the fact that the respondent uses efficiently the opportunities offered by the environment and has a feeling of ownership in dealing with the management of the environment factors and activities, including the management of daily tasks and the creation of situations that should benefit from personal resources. Example of item for this factor is "Generally, I feel I am responsible for the situation I am living in."
3. Personal development – the openness to new experiences. The great scores indicate the fact that the respondent continues to develop, that he/she is open to new experiences and admits the improvement of the behavior and of his/her own self in time. An example of item for this factor: "I think that it is important to have new experiences which should contradict the way one thinks about oneself and about the world."
4. Positive relationships with the others – the possibility to have satisfying and good quality relationships with other persons. Great scores to this factor reflect the involvement of the respondent in significant relationships with the others, which include reciprocal empathy, intimacy, and affection. Example of item for this factor: "People would describe me as a giving person, available to spend his/her time with the others."
5. The purpose in life – the belief that life has a purpose. Great scores reflect a stronger orientation of the respondent and his/her belief that life has a meaning. Example of item for this factor: "Some people wander in life without a purpose, but I am not one of them."
6. Self-acceptance – positive attitude toward the past and the peers. Great scores at this factor reflect the positive attitude of the respondent toward him/herself. An example of item for this factor "I like most of the aspects of my personality."

Synthesizing the attempts to define operationally the concept of well-being by my predecessors, I understand that it is a subjective emotional state arisen from the feeling of living one's own life in consonance with one's own expectations and possibilities.

The Theoretical Framework for the Composite Concept of *Digital Well-Being*

While digital technologies entered our lives, their impact on our well-being was considered to be important. Therefore, concerns appeared with regards to the effect of digital communication, online networks, and mobile technologies on the sentiment of self and on our relationships with the others. Such concerns led to the appearance of a relatively new field of research, the one regarding the digital well-being.

The concept is an absolutely new one and has no equivalence in the Romanian language, being an expression borrowed from English. The concept refers to life quality in general and to the state of well-being a person can experiment in relation to the usage of information technology. The scientific world is still debating the field, the specialist not agreeing with a definition unanimously accepted. It is certain that the notion is on the working table of more sciences and their fields of research. The research developed until the present moment unveil a dynamic process, which refers to the obtaining, by the people, of a state of well-being, vitality, and autonomy, with the experimenting of actions impregnated with a lot of meaning, the accessing of good abilities to adapt to change, functional coping mechanisms, but also good skills, interrelational abilities, and communication with others. It is obvious that if a person succeeds in fulfilling the requirements from above, he/she can hope for a general state of well-being, which should satisfy him/her and to make possible the increase of the quality of his/her life. Therefore, the levels of self-confidence gain new dimensions, and the respective person can consider him/herself a fulfilled person, and his/her life is going to an adequate direction for him/herself and for his/her needs. Certainly, the central purpose of any person is to access and maintain a balance, challenge to which we all subject, more or less, sooner or later.

The term "digital well-being" is used at the present moment by the health specialists, and also by the researchers and technicians interested in the production of technical devices using information technology, and it designates the features of the interaction between all this technology and the people using it, either we speak about a smartphone, a laptop or a personal computer, or a digital wrist watch. The concept takes into consideration the fact that the experience of the usage of digital technologies is forced to focus on the maintaining, possibly on the improvement of the physical and psychical health indicators.

The central purpose followed by the concept of digital well-being is to design and build technologies so that they can promote and maintain the health state, through an economical usage, which should help the person maintain an optimal state of health. Therefore, the large companies that manufacture these technologies, on the background of the legal regulations in force, have focused on the development of certain functions for these devices in order to respect the personal time, to stop or to limit the notifications, especially the ones with a purely commercial character, but also the others, of the type of invitations, the choosing of usage options or purely the updating of the settings for the devices. All these steps occurred following the proliferation of the incidence of certain psychical disorders, such as the dependency on the information technology, recently introduced in the Diagnostic and Statistical Manual of Mental Disorders, but also in others, such as the attention disorder with hyperactivity, depression, increased levels of anxiety, the bad management of time, and impulsivity. From a somatic point of view, the most affected organs are the eyes, the bone system, and the muscular one, but also the digestive and the nervous ones. Especially in the case of children and adolescents, the passing of a longer period of time in front of a computer screen or laptop, more recently of a smartphone can produce serious disorders of the spine, of posture in general, but also of the development of the muscles. Obviously, the ophthalmologic disorders are also in the top of the problems one can confront with unless the time spent in front of a screen is not judiciously managed.

Therefore, the specialists and the designers from the IT business took measures to restraint the excess usage of the devices, through notifications regarding the period of time spent on them, the limitation of notifications for certain periods of time, etc. Therefore, the first concern regarding the well-being in relation to information technology came from the IT specialists, marking a new field of concern, digital well-being.

The composite concept of digital well-being could be understood through similarity as a digital state of wellness, which is often defined in terms of capacities and abilities a person claims in order to successfully use the digital technologies.

In September 2019, JISC published a report following a research performed by Mark Langer-Crame, Tabetha Newman, Helen Beetham, Clare Killen and Sarah Knight, on a lot of approximately 30,000 students from the United Kingdom regarding the digital experience. In this report, the authors offer a detailed image of the way in which the students are experimenting technology as part of learning. In the report, there are mentioned six areas of intervention as being essential to the digital well-being:

1. care for the personal health, safety, relationships, and the balance of the professional life in digital settings;
2. the usage of the digital tools for the following-up of the personal objectives (e.g., health and fitness) and in order to take part in social and community activities;
3. safety and responsibilities in the digital environments;
4. conflict resolution and negotiation;
5. the management of the volume of digital work regarding the overload and the distraction;
6. prudence in relation to inter-human relationships when digital instruments are used.

All these require an understanding of the benefits and risks of digital participation in relation to the results from health and wellness (JISC, 2019). Therefore, JISC recently revised their definition for digital well-being in order to catch one of the complexities of the subject, enlarging the concept coverage area from the individual aspects to the ones of the society (digitală society). As we advance in the knowledge and usage of digital technologies, the exploration and the research of digital society are required, in order to develop the understanding about the well-being and digital identity.

In the paper *"The Ethics of digital wellbeing: a multidisciplinary approach,"* the author links the usage of digital technologies with the online manipulation, relating one of the factors of the psychological well-being, the autonomy. The author states that the online manipulative actions have effect, most frequently, to the detriment of the well-being, submining the autonomy. The autonomy is part, as reminded, of the list of objective factors of psychological well-being (Ryff and Singer, 1998). For a person to maintain his/her autonomy, he/she should be treated with respect for his/her rationality (Levy, 2017), which should allow him/her to exert the capacities of rational being and, implicitly, responsible. To be responsible means to be receptive to the reasons of action and to its consequences (Fischer and Ravizza, 1998) and to resort to morality. To manipulate someone means to undermine his/her autonomy, to act immorally on him/her, trying to hide the true purpose of the interaction, directing that person toward a result foreseen by the manipulator and with the feeling of the free will from the part of the manipulated person. The manipulating action, by definition, has no intention to unveil to the victims the end purpose of it, even if it presupposes a reasonable action, in relation to which the victim sees no duality. The author reaches the conclusion that the nature of the software-human interactions is not favorable to digital well-being, at least until this moment.

If, prior to the digital era, the manipulation was performed through communication techniques and behavioral action from human to human (masses of people) and/or directly mediated, nowadays we benefit from digitalization techniques, which allow the transmission of information with an amazing speed, in immense quantity, in all the directions, from all the domains. The issue is, nowadays, to select information, which we have access to, sometimes swallowing information without criteria of quality and veridicity (informational obesity), affecting the judgment and the reasoning. The danger of the personal autonomy does not automatically come due to the development of the digital technology, but of the moral/immoral way it is valued/used. Subsequently, a careful surveillance of the human operators is undertaken regarding the purpose of the usage of digital technology, taking into account that it can influence both positively as well as negatively the psychological well-being.

Taking decisions is another aspect to analyze in this chapter, and it is related to the second factor of psychological well-being according to Ryff model, the control over the environment, which presupposes the taking of decisions. Taking decisions is an essential process in our daily life; we are taking decisions from the smaller ones, for example, which movie to watch or which product to buy, to bigger ones, which can change our lives, such as which career to choose. Each one of our decisions have an indirect or a direct influence on our psychological state of well-being and most of us submit a sustained effort in the process of taking decisions. Therefore, in order to help in the taking of decisions, in the last decades (Kim şi Eom, 2016), a large number of decision support systems (DSS) have been developed. These systems have the potential to facilitate the taking of decisions in our life and contribute to the magnifying of our psychological state of well-being. Despite this, there are also certain risks in the current designing of a DSS, which could lead to opposite effects. The majority of DSS uses specific criteria to offer recommendations to the users about what to do and what not to do. If we perceive the advice as being a satisfactory solution, a DSS can have a positive effect of our digital well-being. Despite this, especially for more complex situations, one cannot always guarantee that the resorting to decision support systems also represents a better solution.

The impact of technology on our psychological well-being shall continue to increase in the following years, as we integrate the digital systems more and more, in all the aspects of life.

There is a great potential for the digital technology to facilitate life and which can contribute to the improvement of our general welfare. Despite this, we must take into account the risks of this development, in order to make sure we shall not feel its opposite effect.

At the end of this chapter, I state that psychological well-being is far from being conceptualized with objective accuracy. Being understood as an internal, subjective state, it can be potentiated by multiple factors, personal (psychological), organizational, societal, and cultural, which make its evaluation difficult. One should keep in mind that material well-being does not necessarily trigger psychological well-being, but more the perception on one's own freedom of choice, the possibility to take decisions with regards to one's own life makes that the indicator of the perception of self-fulfillment to increase.

The well-being, in relation to digitalized technology, must be carefully perceived, because all the premises are created for the facilitation of the improvement of our psychological well-being or of the inner-outer harmony, as well as for abuses such as manipulation or the restraint or diminishing of the decision-making capacity.

References

Christopher Burr & Luciano Floridi (eds.), *Ethics of Digital Well-Being: A Multidisciplinary Perspective*. Springer, https://philpapers.org/archive/BURTEO-62.pdf

Diener, E. (1984). Subjective well-being. *Psychological Bulletin, 95*, 542–575. doi:10.1037/0033-2909.95.3.542, https://emmons.faculty.ucdavis.edu/wp-content/uploads/sites/90/2015/08/1985_1happiness-wealthy.pdf

Fischer, J. M., & Ravizza, M. (1998). *Responsibility and Control: A Theory of Moral Responsibility*. Cambridge University Press, New York;

Iluţ, P. (2015). *Dragoste, Familie şi Fericire. Spre o sociologie a seninătăţii*. Editura Polirom, Bucureşti;

King, V. (2016). *10 chei pentru traiul mai fericit: un manual practic pentru fericire*, Londra.

Landen, S. M., Wang, C. D. C. (2009). Adult attachment, work cohesion, coping, and psychological well-being of firefightersy. *Counselling psychology quarterly*, 23(2), 143–162. doi: 10.1080/09515071003776028

Papalia, D. E., Wendkos, O. S., & Feldman R. D. (2010). *The Human Development* (11th ed.). Bucharest: Trei;

Ryff, C. D., & Singer, B. (1998). The contours of positive human health. *Psychological Inquiry*, 9, 1–28. doi:10.1207/s15327965pli0901_1.

Salami, O. S. (2011). Personality and psychological wellbeing of adolescents: The moderating role of Emotional intelligence. *Social behavior and personality*, 39(6), 785–794.

Seligman, M. E. P. (2011). *Flourish – A New Understanding of Happiness and Well-Being – and How to Achieve Them*. London: Nicholas Brealey Publishing.

https://www.jisc.ac.uk/reports/digital-experience-insights-survey-2019-students-uk&usg#

https://www.researchgate.net/publication/307089973_Cultural_Variability_in_the_Link_Between_Environmental_Concern_and_Support_for_Environmental_Action

Gabriel-Constantin NICOLA

10 The Prosocial Behavior, Online Environment, and Well-Being

Abstract Once with the pandemic, the students were put in a position to change much of the way they related to school and the teaching-learning process. The reports, this difficult whole process, adaptive or on the contrary, have influenced their well-being and prosocial behavior.

Keywords: Prosocial behavior, well-being, online environment, students, school

The social contexts in which we live are varied. These refer to the set of circumstances in which an action, communication, relationship, etc. take place from two points of view as a spatio-temporal dimension and as a relational dimension. The two are in mutual influence – the context in which we carry out our activity, communication influences our meetings with peers – in formal spaces the meetings are of a certain type, in them informal of another type. We also react differently depending on the contexts in which we are regarding the motivation, the performance of a work task, the identity of those with whom they are, the type of interaction, the meanings given to the meeting, etc. Depending on our subjective perception of our social contexts, we have different types of reactions and ways of acting in them. In the last months, due to the pandemic, our social contexts have changed a lot and each of us has had to find adaptive resources to it. The context is the one that gives meaning to the person about the situations they will face when they are in that context. The whole context is the one that works as a filter for us and influences us; it even determines the social judgments and behaviors. The influence of the context is given by the nature of the conditions where it happens (nature, constraints, and finality of the situation) and secondly by the social dimension of the context. It, later, refers to two aspects: the ideological factor (social norms, the axiological side of the person) and the place that a person occupies in that social context and in society (related to the placement of the person in contexts, groups, society as a role, personal perception of others, etc.) (Curelaru, 2006).

The space of the student's class is constituted in a social representation for each of us. The difficulty given by the pandemic emphasized the fact that the student appropriates something that already exists – the social representation of the class – but also had to acquire something that did not exist, namely the functioning of the classroom context in the activity carried out entirely online. The student was suddenly asked to respond to how he organizes his inner discourse, activities and what processes preside over their rearrangement in the new conditions that occurred, so as to remain inserted in the context of the class and go through the school year until the end well. This perspective emphasizes the student's relationship to his own learning practices, his personal beliefs about who he is and what he can do in this context, how he responds to social demands, and how he uses them adaptively or not. Their own choices are given by the axiological side of the student, and this also guides his behavior both in groups and individually. The value dimension orients him to legitimize his beliefs, interests, relationships, and also the way he remains open to new acquisitions and transformations of his own person (Rad, Ignat et al., 2019).

With the school pandemic undergoing major changes, the most important of these was the relocation of the teaching-learning process to online space. Due to the sudden change and the difficulties inherent in a system unprepared for such a change, the students had to go through a crisis of adaptation to all of them. The crisis is a temporary disruption of the regulatory mechanisms of the person's or family's system, a disruption that can have internal and/or external causes. The crisis expresses in a very particular way the interdependence between psychic and social changes determined in the individual, and any change in the social area, because each person is a sum of constructs that are socially influenced and that determine the meaning of social experience (Barus-Michel, 2011).

Our mobilization to solve a difficult situation is better or less good depending on the complexity of the situation, the importance of the objective pursued, and thus we become more deeply involved in the action or have a superficial involvement in solving it. It is the direction that focuses us toward the proposed goal, and it is the finality that gives the measure of success or failure (Maier, Sîrbu, 2017).

The school and the family have always strived to establish lasting links and the reasons for this are: parents are legally responsible for their children's education, education is only a part of the child's education, and research highlights the influence of parental attitude on children's school results and social groups involved. In the school institution, they have the right to influence the way the educational processes take place. The school has an important role through the instructive-educational process, the knowledge and information provided, the continuous concern for the development of the students, and the development of the knowledge of one's own person for each student. However, all these overlap with the way in which the child was educated until entering school and is also still formed in the space of his family – training that is due to the family to which he belongs (Maier, Marian, 2015). Or in this context of the pandemic, the parents were also suddenly put in complex situations, not easy at all and so on – and the school and the parents collaborated less. Although it is worth noting the beneficial action of parents in the relationship with the school, it is less valued in our country.

Cultural Capital and Digital Capital

An important factor that influences school results is the cultural capital of the family. Bourdieu (1986) defines the concept of capital as a social relationship that produces effects in a social field (Grenfell 2007, p.56); in each social space, there are positions that individuals can occupy depending on the capital resources they have (Bourdieu, 1986). The author delimits three forms of capital: economic, social, and cultural.

Economic capital refers to income or possessions and is institutionalized through property rights.

Social capital is the sum of existing or potential resources that an individual or a group can have as part of a network of familiarity and recognition.

Cultural capital is the result of the interaction between education and culture that society values; it can take three forms: embedded capital, objectified capital, and institutionalized capital (Bourdieu, 1986).

McNamee and Miller (2009) define the concept of "cultural capital" as the set of norms, values, and lifestyles that can mediate the access to opportunities of individuals or groups of individuals (McNamee & Miller, 2009, p.79). This concept, seen from the perspective of the educational field, refers, in particular, to the advantages that some students have or can have in the educational system.

Researchers such as Reay (2005) and Miller (2009) have shown that students from the middle class adapt more easily to the school environment, compared to students from working-class families, precisely because they benefit from more cultural forms of diversified capital. Middle class parents have better experience and knowledge of how the education system works. The theoretical framework used in such studies is Bourdieu's (1973) theory of cultural reproduction according to which the ruling classes use the education system to transmit and reproduce their own culture.

We understand by objectified cultural capital the property of some objects such as writings of any kind, books, paintings, monuments, musical instruments, computer technology, etc. It is important that this type of capital is understood in relation to the incorporated capital as the latter is the one that provides the means to consume art and culture, to understand the codes and to use certain objects, etc. (Guan & Ploner, 2020).

Along with "cultural capital," "habitus" is an equally important component that we encounter in Bourdieu's theory. The position in the social field occupied by individuals is influenced not only by the available capital resources but also by the habitus (Bourdieu, 1986). Habitus is "a system of dispositions that gives the ability to think and act in specific ways" (Bourdieu, 1990, p.77). There are authors, such as Dumais (2002), who argue that there is a complementarity between cultural capital and habitus, namely between an individual's resources and their orientation toward the use of these resources. Social action must be understood as being generated by the two, together with the social field.

This concept has been extended in empirical research, the most commonly used being the class habitus (Bourdieu, 1984), but it has also been analyzed in relation to gender and race (Dumais, 2002; Reay, 2005), and from another perspective, the term "institutional" or "organizational habitus" was also used in order to analyze the effect of different schools on students' educational decisions (Reay, Crozier & Clayton, 2010).

Digital capital is a specific capital, which can be isolated and measured empirically (Ragnedda, Ruiu & Adde, 2020, p.79), and according to the definition of Guan and Ploner (2020), it is a component of cultural capital.

In this new situation given by the pandemic, students were confronted with the lack of digital capital related to school contexts and their adaptations were tested. The different situations of each one brought different dysfunctions at the level of each student, but also at the level of the class.

The prosocial behavior has the components: altruism, help, friendship, interpersonal attraction, and mutual respect. Among these components, studies show that resilience is associated with altruism, both for children and adults. One of the components of altruism is empathy and therefore the possibility of being understood by another. During this period, the dynamics of the students' classes were clearly observed and from the point of view of the prosocial behaviors encountered – for the classes in which the social behaviors were present, the dynamics took place differently than for the classes in which they were not present. Precisely from this perspective, one of the arguments of the teachers in the class was the stimulation of prosocial behaviors. A long-term flawed dynamic, the effects of social distancing, deficient relationships could all lead to absenteeism or even dropping out of school. And from here to social exclusion may be just one step (Badea, Constantin, 2002).

We are facing major challenges caused by the COVID 19 pandemic, and the digitalization of education can be a solution to make the approaches to the future more flexible. It is difficult to predict whether or not this technological challenge, seen as a short-term opportunity, will be able to become a threat (a risk) in the medium and long term (Ceobanu et al., 2020). Starting from the PISA assessment data, in the context of the SARS-CoV-2 pandemic, three dimensions are important in the analysis of the framework in which the transition to online learning takes place: internet access, the gap in the use of digital tools between students, the digital gap between schools, which refers to their ability to support learning in a digital context. The socio-economic status of students is negatively associated with each of these dimensions, so disadvantaged students have more limited access to the Internet, have lower skills and learn in schools with fewer digital resources. According to the analyses made by Moreno and Gortazar (2020), in Romania, 35 % of students who participated in PISA tests study in schools that have an online learning platform, a value that places Romania in the last part of the ranking of participating countries (Moreno & Gortazar, 2020).

Coates et al., in a 2004 study, anticipated that online learning usually proves to have lower educational efficiency than offline learning (Coates et al., 2004). These aspects are highlighted in recent Romanian studies but also in studies from abroad.

Other studies, such as that of Belo, Ferreira and Telan (2013), Samaha and Haiwi (2016), emphasize the direct relationship between device use and anxiety, stress, which is negatively reflected in satisfaction with life as a whole. There are also studies that look at the perspective of teachers, and they have noticed, regardless of the level at which they teach, that in the form of online learning they spend more time than in the traditional way for training and teaching and also that they manage much harder to motivate and to maintain students' interest in learning during class. Balance in the classroom refers to the image of the group that each student has about his class, to relationships, to group behaviors and to the relational dimension with teachers. In this way, it is found that the balance is at the intersection of several multirelational structures. In the pandemic, the dimension of the context was added to all this, which narrowed completely and had an impact on all the other dimensions that aimed at the balance of the student and the class in general. As part of the class, balance was also the climate of the student's class. The climate presupposes a collective attitude of the group toward the totality of the professional environment in which it takes place, an attitude that is given by the interaction of all the objective and subjective factors that participate in it. It has a certain stability and independence from the factors that created it but is not formed immediately after the onset of the action of certain determining factors, but over time (Cristea, 2015). The pandemic overlapped with a previous existing climate, of the class, which was not always adequate and the changes that occurred also changed the climate determinants of both the objective and the subjective.

To date, the online environment has not been an option for education in our country, and therefore has not been more than a source of information. Sometimes, and especially by young people, it is a form of play or socializing, so it is not associated with work but often with free time. With the pandemic, however, our business moved online and everything I thought about it changed considerably. The online has thus become a way of being – as work, socialization, relationships, as everything. Institutions, with reference to schools and universities, that understood this more quickly, were gaining ground and quickly found ways to act so that the workflow, learning, is not interrupted or lacking. The education remained online for more than two months, and at this time it is not known how it will be resumed in the new year in this way. Thus, it went from the reality face to face to the reality of the online environment, our reality thus changing its dimensions and the way it works. To the usual difficulties were added those related to the unusualness of virtual reality and also those related to our ability to adapt to it. We started looking for solutions, to try different platforms, to change what didn't seem to change too soon – the way we usually work, and this didn't happen because we wanted to but because we had to do it. All the searches brought changes, or all the stagnation made us think. By accepting the change, each of us managed to adapt to the new reality. It was necessary to manage different online platforms and we understood that e-learning platforms bring the online learning environment to our home and therefore closer to each of us. Even so, we humans are different in many ways and in the way we relate to devices. In terms of access to technology, some are digital natives and some are not, so progress in this regard has also been different. It was easier for students to access platforms, and for teachers it was not so easy. But for everyone it was a good time, but challenging through its conditions, to improve their digital performance and well-being in front of the computer and in relation to it. Over the challenges related to the strictly learning environment, fundamentally changed and passed online, also overlapped the difficulties of the pandemic period – multiple emotions of all kinds, the state at home, traffic restrictions, supply difficulties, all leading to overlap, at high levels of stressors in our lives. Our ability to adapt to new and ever-changing requirements is and will continue to be a key skill, and during this time, we have all had the opportunity to practice it. What helped the students during this period was the prosocial behavior they had. He mediated the class relations – those between the students and also those between the teachers. The ability of students to stay focused on proactive social dynamics, on its positive components, has led to a better adaptation to the new conditions but also to contribute to the adaptability of others, to be their support or model of action. Subjective well-being changed quite a bit during the state of emergency, but prosocial behavior also contributed to its recovery because it brought people almost into a supportive relational dynamic, which provided a good sense of construction and self-help. People in need thus had an end of the thread, even if virtual, to look for solutions or support. Students were able to relate to different teachers depending on the dynamics of the relationship in the new conditions and were able to identify other characteristics of them – such as empathy, the way they provide support, creativity, flexibility, and adaptability. The students' choices were influenced, among all others, by these new discoveries about online relationships. The systems in which we operate always bring us data about what needs to change in us and in our social dynamics (Hatos, 2019).

The greater the solidarity in a group, the more those who are part of the group make greater efforts to stay together, so in these new contexts the classes in which the students were more supportive worked much better (Mitrofan, 2003). In our social network we feel comfort and belonging and so we feel that anytime, whatever happens, we have someone close or someone who can offer us support, and this contributes to our own well-being. Not all membership groups have the same weight in our lives, and we do not value them all equally. The class is one of the groups but unfortunately not the most valued. The significant relational group is first of all our family and only then the other groups. Relationships in significant groups are for us a source of positive experiences or vice versa. The family is the group in which we grow and form and thus will have a great influence in our subsequent relationships and the space in which we will learn to relate to the world and life. In the groups in which we are socially immersed, we have different experiences, feelings of all kinds and this impacts our life throughout its existence. By adequately contributing to relational dynamics, by prosocial behavior, we create appropriate premises and developmental contexts. Our own life experiences make us access the world in one way or another, but as we experience the possibility of accepting ourselves, the ability to make sense of our actions, to enjoy results with our well-being. reaches a higher level. When our possibilities of acceptance are low, when those of choice are limited, our abilities to think in terms of solutions are limited and they misunderstand situations and social contexts and so our reactions will be inadequate and social dimensions lacking. Our disproportionate choices will affect our long-term prosocial and well-being behaviors and well-being. So, in conclusion, obtaining and maintaining well-being contributes to several factors in constant interconnection, namely cognitive, emotional, relational, and motivational factors.

References

Badea, V., & Constantin, M. E. (2002). În umbra societății. Incursiune în viața persoanelor fără adăpost, Editura Sper, București

Barus-Michel, J. (2011). Criza ca obiect al psihologiei clinice sociale, în *Psihosociologia crizei*, vol.coord. Barus-Michel, J., Neculau, A., Editura Trei, București

Belo, R., Ferreira, P., & Telang, R. (2010). The effects of broadband in schools: Evidence from Portugal. Available at SSRN 1636584.

Bourdieu, P. (1986). The forms of capital.

Bourdieu, P. (1990). Structures, habitus, practices. In *The logic of practice* (pp. 52–65). Cambridge: Polity.

Ceobanu, C., Cucoș, C., Istrate, O., & Pânișoară, I. O.(coord) (2020). Educația digitală. Iași. Polirom.

Coates, D., Humphreys, B. R., Kane, J., & Vachris, M. A. (2004). "No significant distance" between face-to-face and online instruction: Evidence from principles of economics. *Economics of Education Review*, *23*(5), 533–546.

Cristea, D. (2015). Tratat de psihologie socială, Editura Trei, București

Curelaru, M. (2006). Reprezentări sociale, Editura Colegiul Polirom, București

Dumais, S. A. (2002). Cultural capital, gender, and school success: The role of habitus. *Sociology of education*, 75(1), 44–68.

Grenfell, M. (2007). Language learner strategy research and modern foreign language teaching and learning. *Language Learning Journal*, *35*(1), 9–22.

Guan, S., & Ploner, J. (2020). The influence of cultural capital and mianzi (face) on mature students' orientation towards higher education in China. *Compare: A Journal of Comparative and International Education*, *50*(1), 1–17.

Hatos, A. (2019). Is using ICT at home good or bad for learning? A cross-country comparision of the impact of home use of ICT for entertainment and learning on Pisa 2015 Sience test results. doi:10.31219/osf.io/9dv5k.

Maier, R., & Sîrbu, M. (2017). Streamlining the work of social workers through the optimization of certain characteristics of emotional intelligence, Scientific Research and Education in the Air Force – AFASES 2017, Vol 1/ 2017, ISSN 2247 – 3173,

Maier, R.V., & Marian, A. (2015). Parteneriatul educaţional profesor – părinte, program de promovare a sănătăţii, Revista International Conference and Scientific Paper, AFASES 2015, mai 2015, vol I, ISSN –L 2247 – 3173.

McNamee, S. J., & Miller, R. K. (2009). *The meritocracy myth.* Washington, DC: Rowman & Littlefield.

Moreno, J. M., & Gortazar, L. (2020). Schools' Readiness for Digital Learning in the Eyes of Principals: An Analysis from PISA 2018 and Its Implications for the COVID19 (Coronavirus) Crisis Response. *Education for Development Blog, Washington, DC: The World Bank.*

Rad, D., Ignat, S., Maier, R. V., & Redeş, A. (2019). The dynamic relationship between humor and universalism as growth anxiety-free type of values, Revista Plus Education, Universitatea "A Vlaicu" din Arad, vol 22, nr.1, 2019, ISSN 1842-077X,

Ragnedda, M., Ruiu, M. L., & Addeo, F. (2020). Measuring digital capital: An empirical investigation. *New media & society, 22*(5), 793–816.

Reay, D., Crozier, G., & Clayton, J. (2010). 'Fitting in'or 'standing out': Working-class students in UK higher education. *British educational research journal, 36*(1), 107–124.

Reay, D., David, M. E., & Ball, S. J. (2005). *Degrees of choice: Class, race, gender and higher education.* Staffordshire, UK: Trentham Books.

Samaha, M., & Hawi, N. S. (2016). Relationships among smartphone addiction, stress, academic performance, and satisfaction with life. *Computers in Human Behavior, 57,* 321–325.

Swati MAURYA, Bulbul GUPTA, and Sapna JAIN

11 Study of Digital Well-Being Era on Society: Opportunities and Challenges

Abstract Digital well-being is frequently defined in terms of the skills that people require to prosperously make use of digital technologies. The appearance of digital professionals in designing online environments affects their social responsibility in encouraging or discouraging practices of well-being. The word "Digital" is used in our lives today, and people of every age group are spending more time with digital devices in daily life. This technological impact has many positive effects such as learning new knowledge and connecting with others from all over the world through using many apps. These days it is becoming necessary for the young generation to gain healthy habits and understand how to use the digital devices so that they fully develop their physical and social well-being. This technological impact has several positive effects in terms of learning new data and connecting with others from everywhere the globe. The social, personal, and professional life is affected by the way people handle the digital life. It has effects on relationships, health, and overall development of an individual. This chapter shall give an insight at the present situation of the advantages and disadvantages of digital life and digital well-being. The chapter shall discuss and analyze how digital well-being apps are useful for peoples in various scenarios and performed a survey on youths to identify what effect does it have on youngsters. The chapter shall provide in-depth analysis role of digital well-being in different fields such as education system, health care, and agriculture, which are the pillars of the society. The chapter shall discuss the detailed analysis of opportunities and challenges that are there in the field of education and health care by using case studies and digital well-being experiments, which can help the people in society to find a better balance with technology.

Keywords: Digital well-being, health care, education system, agricultural sector, opportunities, issues

Introduction

Digital well-being is frequently defined in terms of the skills that people require to prosperously make use of digital technologies. The appearance of digital professionals in designing online environments affects their social responsibility in encouraging or discouraging practices of well-being. The word "Digital" is used in our lives today, and people of every age group are spending more time with digital devices in daily life. This technological impact has many positive effects such as learning new knowledge and connecting with others from all over the world through using many apps. These days it is becoming necessary for the young generation to gain healthy habits and understand how to use the digital devices so that they fully develop their physical and social well-being. This technological impact has several positive effects in terms of learning new data and connecting with others from everywhere the globe. The social, personal, and professional life is affected by the way people handle the digital life .It has effects on relationships, health, and overall development of an individual. This chapter shall give an insight at the present situation of the advantages and disadvantages of digital life and digital well-being.

Digital life also brings and develops several negative impacts on people. The Internet revolution has caused several behavioral disorders like depression and inattentive behavior, which affect personal life. The attitude of the person get influenced from social communities online. Computer Engineers conducted a research in the Pew Research Centre to study the behavior analysis of people digital habits. This indicates that an individual can feel stressed out about the present access to anything they want, and the mood swings and distraction is so intense that they do not even worry about what time of the day. Moreover, consequences of information overload are impatience. A major connection to digital life can destroy communal relationships through less interactions with people. Entertainment time also sometimes causes a lack of relationship.

A study by California State University shows technology reduces the concentration of students and causes distraction. Through habits like checking Facebook every 15 minutes, it is hard for such students to focus on one thing for a longer period of time. Multitasking caused by technology is another portent that causes a negative impact on student's performance in class. Human nature will not modify, and that is why abuses will also exist in the future. Everything will be available on the Internet in the future, and that is why cyberterrorism will take advantage of that. Privacy will be minimized to a low level, which gives cyber-criminals the chance to attack in new ways. The digital well-being can contrivance and contrive private life and career through networking. A research project by the pew research Centre and Elon University examined the views of various technology experts, scholars, and health specialists on digital life, about how life will revamp in the coming years and the well-being that comes along with it. Innovation can be done via networking and all the information people can get from it. Such information makes it possible for people to develop new business ideas or just find an individual job via, for example, LinkedIn by summing up personal information on the platform, and job offers can be proposed.

The health care industry accretion has more benefits via digital development according to experts, which was surveyed by the Pew research institute that showed that the information regarding medical, safety, and health resources can be received within seconds, for example, medication for patients using digital platform. This is an important tool, which helped especially in the realm of elder care and pregnancy. The faster access to information enables hospitals to locate the patients within the hospital and information about prior illnesses and other health-related issues in which through the use of digital tools patients can receive help in a faster way as in case of a pregnant woman passing through a controlled process without any uncertainties. Digital well-being is also expanding the boundaries in the various structures of digitalization in agricultural, for example, internet of things, sensors, 3D printing for agriculture work, robotics, integration structure, universal connectivity, and artificial intelligence. Communal science researchers have newly started searching different form of digital agriculture in relative to farm management systems and food structure. There is scarcity on guidance of how this region of study is growing, and what are well-established. But as technology has grown, it is also impressive that the human lifestyle resembles both positive and negative aspects. Moreover, no suspect has been that technology has furnished product support and tools such as Google assistant, apps, and open-source code to make the correct balance of our lives and developed the accretion of digital well-being.

Another benefit is the use of efficient services. Digital life enables us to acquire online education at any point in time and almost everywhere. Information for research can be easily found through search engines like Google, which can provide thousands of results for a single question. Online platforms allow a faster, more efficient way to get purchases done with the added comfort of doing it from wherever you want. The best example for that is Amazon; for one, the purchase order can be done faster, and also the assortment of products is much bigger than in any stores that could exist coordination – organizing and booking trips, holidays or adventures, is easier than ever before. Involved people like family members can receive all the information for the journey and comparison portals ease tenacious searches on different pages and even avoid a drive to a travel agency. MIT Scientists prophesy the continuing enhancement of informational sharing. Devices will have more automation like actuator, which leads to the fact that more and more our life will be and all the decisions we make are with cooperating devices. The internet will be more commingled but more invisible as it is today, therefore the internet will be blend into all our background information. Across the world, technology has been evolved rapidly in a very less amount of time and enables individuals to interact with each other, and human beings can't envisage without digital technology.

Digital well-being is a term used by health researchers and health care equipment manufacturers to describe the notion that when humans interact with technology, the involvement should assist physical and mental health in a quantifiable way. The main goal of improving digital well-being in such a way to design technology that stimulates healthy use and proactively supports the individual to maintain a healthy lifestyle. Digital technologies develop the perimeters of data usable to people and raise human productivity but can also signify peril for individual's well-being. The cyberspace and the phone have rudimentary developed the way people connect with each other. This shows that online communal connection typically balance offline interactions. Authorities have also availed digital technologies to make public services more influent and efficient, and easy to access by users.

Digital transmissions, communal media, and smart phones have changed the step to school students and youngsters transmit, and growing attestation shows the advantages to learning consequences when digital pedagogic systems are used efficaciously. However, it is growing noticeably that the online place is not improved: cyber-bullying, over the sharing of privy data, can cause only main problems; young people also develop as a confident online learner. Also greater care exists about the penetrability of youngsters to being stimulated to express weak attitudes and actions, related to rejection and impatience, and the way to radicalization.

The Super Education Organization has a role to play for students to maintain their online life, both as a step of protecting their intimate well-being and also confirming that they have the digital suitably recommended for future career success. Through digital well-being, we will make our capacity to improve teaching students the critical thinking, and interpersonal transmission skills that they require to develop online.

Digital well-being has a fair objective: raise the efficiency of lecturers and teachers to coordinate digital education in a way that encourage the digital well-being of students. Via building teachers' efficiency, the structure and project work will build students' qualification and strength to maintain their connected computer time – from the extreme digital learning, delicately evaluate the media they create, and become self-reliant digital citizens.

Digital well-being is also expanding the boundaries in the various structures of digitalization in agriculture, for example, internet of things, sensors, 3D printing for agriculture work, robotics, integration structure, universal connectivity, and artificial intelligence. Communal science researchers have newly started searching different form of digital agriculture in relation to farm management systems and food structure. There is scarcity on guidance of how this region of study is growing, and what are well-established.

In digital well-being, there are major facilitators that provide digital agricultural variation. The three main keys are the adoption of internet networking and social structure among laborers, farmers, and horticultural enhancement; executive, rural population in the digital well-being skills; and a culture that sparks digital well-being and transformation. With the growth of high rate network connections and web-empower smart phones, many platforms have an important role to develop access to data for those in rural sections. Many small-scale workers in developing countries continue to isolate from digital well-being.

Organizing a "Digital Agriculture Ecosystem" needs a permissive environment for modernization of workers and farmers. Earlier, there is expanding funding and involvement in digital agriculture programs, and they are starting to bring international investors' attention. They usually have the benefit of digital learning and the efficiency for innovative modes. When digital well-being is unified in educational projects, they can also enhance an understanding of the handling of digital devices and the technique to create them.

Establishing of digital well-being technologies in agricultural areas can be a goal. Over the world, bucolic community is declining; and education, training, and service opportunities are limited. There is usually a shortage of framework, consisting of necessary IT framework, especially in isolated rural society. The expenditure combined with the IT framework presents an important role in a bucolic area where the percentage of scarcity is often high, mainly in least-developed countries.

Digitalization of the agricultural food organization contains the risk that the possible profit will be unfairly divided between urban and rural sections, in youngster population. Urban sector often have better developed "Digital Ecosystems" compared with the rural sector. Associated with the world tendency of middle and rich classes, establishing in cities, there is capability for digital well-being to inflame existing urban-rural disparities.

Nowadays, digital well-being plays a main role in the educational sector, in the health care sector, and in the agricultural sector, and all the three sectors are very important for an individual's well-being. In education sector, digital well-being gives a way to do the right things and helps to provide more knowledge to youngsters; mostly youngsters spend much time in social media, but they do not think that they waste their time in that; digital devices means we gain the same knowledge from that, the use of the device means healthy use and follow the work "Digital Well-Being." In agricultural sector, digital well-being provides best digital devices, so that farmers do their work healthy, complete their role day by day, and focus also on well-being. As we all know that our famers are very hardworking, because of the digital technology, farmers work harder, and all the digital devices are very helpful for the agricultural sector and famers as well for their digital well-being. In health care sector, digital well-being facilitates best technology for hospitals and for all health organizations. Our WHO also provides that information that is best for people and also focused on the human digital well-being. As we all know these days about COVID19 that is declared a pandemic disease by the WHO, doctors and health care organizations trying their best for fighting with this pandemic also try to focus on a person's well-being.

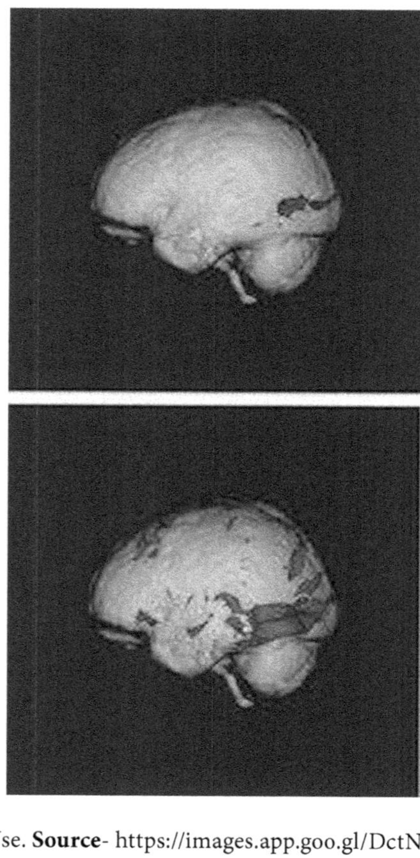

Fig. 1. Technology Use. **Source**- https://images.app.goo.gl/DctNFG4fWGbFVRPQA

Spaces of activation are indicated in blue and in red for the deactivation. Parts of the brain that were turned on more by internet searching than reading for people: (a) structure for using less internet and (b) structure for using more internet and additional activity in red space involved. These people may have determined to use the internet, and so were comprised with mental procedures involving.

Literature Review

Ms. Shika Dua et al. proposed a solution to overcome the issues and challenges of traditional education in the era of digital technologies. They have also deliberated about the imminent trends in the digital education system that will create a fantasized digital environment for the upcoming future generation. Discussed about factors for digital learning including primary factors and secondary factors. Primary factors consist of students, faculty, institutions, and technology whereas secondary factors include course, cost, society, and support. Authors analyzed that what are the problems faced by digital well-being at the time of digital learning.

G.N. Wikramanayake et al. examined how digital technologies influence on individuals within the field of education. The author explained the process of generation, creation, and acquisition of knowledge via technology, and such activities could be performed by tools like relational database management system (RDBMS) and electronic document management system (EDMS). RDBMS is a tool used for managing information in a system, manage primitive data like numbers and dates, and manages organizational data of the education system. EDMS applications emphasized on control of electronic documents; EDMS enables the process of managing documents effectively. Regarding the education system, the work is accomplished through an enhanced and more effective way known as e-learning. Also, describes how technology is used to access and apply such knowledge. The effects of technology will be discussed, in general, with the help of some examples.

Sarah Diefenbach et al. researcher mentioned about the opportunities and challenges in the period of digital technology design from a knowledge base perspective with theoretical and practical contributions. They primarily targeted on the accountable role of technology as a digital well-being improvement tool and to present a fruitful frame for various disciplines involved in positive technology. Explore each side that is first, investigating digital well-being technology as a form of "therapeutic interaction," emphasized on the requirements for sensible design solutions in the emerging dialogue between technology and user. Second, a stronger thought of the bitter-sweet ambivalence of modification, utilizing (positive) scientific discipline interventions to full impact. Targeted on the bitter-sweet feeling of modification, as well as potential relapses and risks of self-threat. Therefore, technology-mediated interventions tailored from (positive) psychology will have a positive impact.

Marco Gui *et al.* introduced a problem faced by digital well-being in the era of digital technologies and how we can resolve that problem. Along with they showed how its side effects lead individuals to a hazardous situation. This chapter considered the impacts of digital technology on a well being and what is "good" in the digital environment. From the chapter, it is concluded that the framework of digital skills is not thinking about the ability to deal with communication superabundance and explained all concepts of "digital well-being." Concerning some characteristics of digital well-being such as the economic exploitation of human attention, the overabundance of possible choices, the convergence of various activities in the same device, and the easiness to switch from one focus to another.

Christopher Burr *et al.* represented a review of the literature on the ethical issues concerning digital well-being. Review paper mainly focused on major factors that are related to social domains like social development, governance, education, media, entertainment, and health care. Hence, the conclusion symbolized that represented some questions, offered some remarks related to the key finding of the review paper. They examined and then present a brief review of digital well-being, the role of digital technologies in the health care industry; major challenges like privacy and security of patients' information; and open questions like "Who is accountable for health care?" "How do ensure equal access to digital health services?" "How can we make sure that the intelligibility of automated decisions?" Introduced methodologies and different barriers concerning accessibility.

Alexandra Kitson *et al.* targeted on hoe technologies can support via the experiences of self-transcendence. Implement the definitions of digital well-being and the way it correlates with and sometimes as a result of self-transcendence. Also delivered a brief review of subjective well-being means how a person thinks they are doing in life, is the integration of positive moods, the inadequacy of negative thoughts, and life gratification. Many researchers have used subjective well-being steps that have displayed substantial validity via attestation associated with biological markers, self-report, and neuroimaging. The researcher has explained that technologies like VR have the capability of evoking awe due to their impressive properties and the ability to show people impossible.

John McAlaney *et al.* analyzed the impacts of many personal and major factors on the acceptance and rejection of the online peer support group as a process to develop well-being, how it influences others, and derives both positive and negative aspects. From a case study, it is concluded that individuals besides such type of groups to be purpose-driven and discard their instantiations as ordinary social communication. Online peer groups would need to think as a purpose-driven gathering as a special type of social network.

Role of Digital Well-Being in the Field of Education

It is supposed for educators, for example, teachers, lecturers, trainers, and skilled developers fascinated by advancing their understanding of digital well-being education and exploring new ways to develop the digital well-being of their students. It shows outcome as associate innovative, inventive, and participative approaches to digital well-being education, as well as media accomplishment, digital citizenship, and significant thinking, and sets out the challenges, risks, opportunities, and future directions for digital well-being education.

The opportunities area unit has seen because of the sweetening of moral structure for a digital society. As digital well-being in an exceedingly digital syndicate, there's a requirement to be cognizant of laws, threats to private info, and the way the digital expertise impacts our psychological state similarly to physical health. We tend to all get to be knowledgeable of the way to respond ethically in an exceedingly digital syndicate. As a lecturer, they need to be cognizant of the impact of their selections on students and teach ethics and on-line etiquette.

Digital well-being plays a significant role in the field of education. Typically education is self-contained on many sources like school, colleges, teachers, and print media. The learners can access the information sources by matriculating themselves in schools and colleges. Before the digital period, delivery of information among people was not possible and even those accessed were unable to perceive current information regarding the context. Everyone wants to know about the situation as it happens and when it happens, and nowadays the world leads our mindset to knowledgeable world via the digital well-being. Thus, education becomes the highest priority. Digital technologies provide many opportunities for learning and become an integral part of our life.

If we see from the perspective of digital well-being, these days' young people are getting indulged in technical things in the field of education, which provides many opportunities to youth and it helps in their development. Such types of opportunities are:

- Superintendent
- Standardized test developer
- Guidance counsellor
- Career counsellor
- Education consultant
- Child life specialist
- Camp director
- Coordinator
- Researcher
- Lobbyist
- Textbook author or editor
- Blogger
- Educator
- Corporate trainer
- Health educator
- Teaching abroad

Young people, being a digital native, can become their educators. And it was seen that youths know more about technical things and quite familiar with it than their family members or elders, teaching them how to access digital devices including tablets, I-pad, PowerPoint, word, etc. or how to send text and capture pictures. This reversal of roles seems in the field of education also. Young people know that some educators do not have the digital skills and inclination as they do. Then they teach them and help those who are less aware of digital technology. However, for the young people, this does not make the role of educator small whereas it establishes a strong between the teacher and the student. They see their educator as a guide or a mentor who always directs his students in the right direction.

Challenges Faced by Digital Well-Being in the Field of Education

We exist in a digital environment where every individual of all ages uses the internet to establish a connection, for effective communication, delve, and learn via digital devices. And it is ascertained that educators in higher institutions emphasized the well-being of their students in the digital world. An education institution knows the importance of digital literacy for society but only 20–25 % of students are taught by the digitally confident educator. The digital attainment of educators is needed notably within the space of digital well-being.

Nowadays, education institutions have become aware of the aftermaths of digital overburden on the psychological state as well as the physical state of an individual student. From the perspective of digital well-being, there are numerous challenges befalling for different stakeholders within the context of education. In this section, we will discuss all those four groups:

1. Resistance to change: Every improvement has two sides, leading to the development, and others are related to some challenges with some of the enhancement of this development. Another challenge faced by digital well-being in the field of education is unaccustomed of employees toward technology; managers must need to handle this. Usually, people oppose changes even if the changes make the current situation superior to the earlier situation. They cannot believe that a technology-based learning program as a conversation with an instructor would be helpful.
   To surmount these challenges some steps can be taken out:
   - Refresher benefit: Characteristics of multimedia allows making the material high fascinating and easier to allude. This privilege the accomplishment of learning within a less amount of time.
   - Communication: Among students, effective communication gives deep knowledge and enables them to accept learning via digital devices.
2. Learner motivation: The next challenge is how we can keep our students motivated for a long time to complete the course. This is a common challenge that employees did not work properly; they may not explore the material. Appealing and incentives are the methodologies to overcome these challenges.
   - Incentive: Fostering of the courses and certification provides employees an embodied aim.
   - Appealing: One of the best process is to motivate participants to ensure the digital learning course that is provided must be visible and appealing to the eye; this makes digital learning more effective and attractive.
3. Technological skills of learners: The digital learning implementation will be dependent upon the computer literacy of employees using it. The puissance of learners to pierce and interact with the course material dictates the utility he will get out of the program. To overcome this resistance some measures can be taken:

- Help when required: This is the responsibility of the educator to make sure that whenever a student faces any problem then digital learners facilitators must be available and make them feel they are supported in the program. Technical support must be accessible by participants such as live-chats, doubt section, auto-help buttons, emails, etc.

4. Evaluating effectiveness: Another challenge of digital learning is identifying the course whether the course intension is being affected or not. In the absence how can an employer tell if the implementation of learning is achieving its goal?
   Solution:
   It is important to know how many employees use digital learning programs, how much time they spend on it, but, above that, it is more important to know that performance acquires new knowledge. If they display the skills and information gleaned from digital learning programs in their work, then the digital learning program in their work and the digital learning implementation have been effective.
5. Learning and education providers: According to a fund will be affected due to the insufficiency of the political system and political will, to raise the costs of learning and that of education providers. It is also emphasized that how we could be upgraded teacher's continuing professional development (CPD), and this does not include the technical skills, and it is not mandatory to upskill every educator. Educators are not methodically well prepared to deal with the technology; due to this a challenge has been betiding. Some people on the other side felt that there may be high demand but lack of supply from the training provider due to poor internet connection. In an online class, the educator is unable to deliver information due to some technical issues.

Role of Digital Well-Being in the Health Care

In the health care industry, digital opportunities are a positive aspect of a health care system that influences eulogistic impact on others. Block chain health records, artificial intelligence (AI), and telemedicine that allow medical devices are examples of digital transformation in the health care sector. Lamentably, the health care and pharmaceutical industry retreat in the back at the time of implementing digital strategies. From a recent study, it is analyzed that only 7 % of peers said they had gone digital as compared to the other fifteen company industry. Every individual is grateful for this opportunity or transformation of technology, such as virtual reality tools, wearable devices, telehealth, and 5G technologies. Facilities are provided to the people as soon as possible and also who need it in the very shortest time, and this saves a lot of time.

Nowadays, our changing lifestyle has become a major reason for an unhealthy person. Every individual can easily access the food (energy) but have little opportunity to spend it. Acquiring only food is not only a source for getting a healthy lifestyle, but it also requires some more effort. Staying healthy now needs some more exertion that is indirectly related to involve in working or by obtaining food. Concerning good health, this became a requirement to make conscious decisions about work, food, play, and other activities. The burden of lifestyle-related illness devour almost 70 % of health care budgets in western economies, and the accurate value of these budgets is set to rise rapidly because

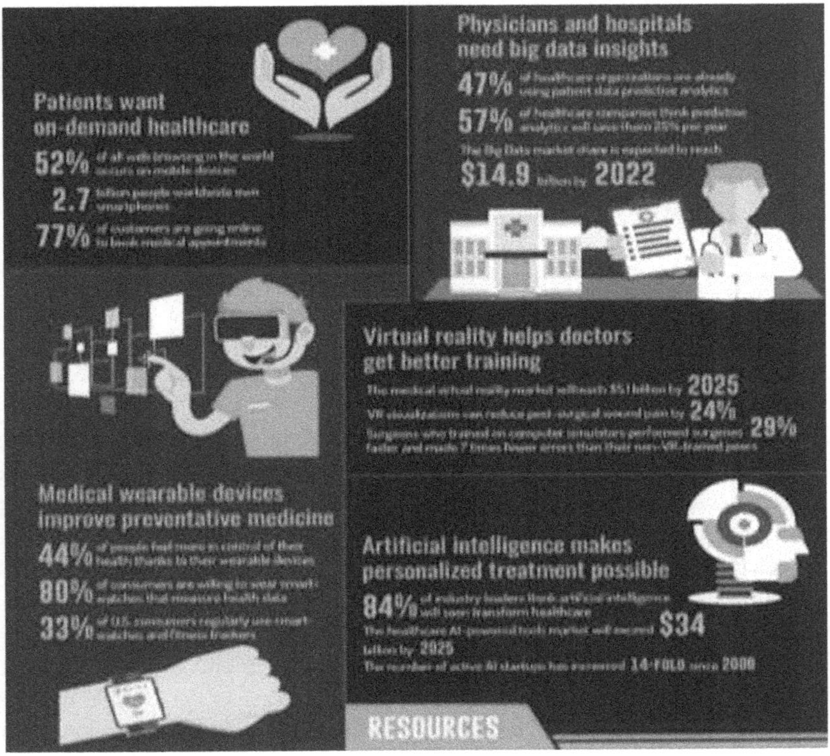

Fig. 2. Digital Health Opportunities. **Sources:** https://digitalauthority.me/wp-content/uploads/2017/11/digital-transfromation-infographic.jpg

of the aging population in many of these countries. With health care budgets at breaking point already, clearly, there is a requirement for another way. The promise of Digital Health to alter higher self-care and stop or table the event of significant malady appears to supply the way out of a tough state of affairs.

Opportunities

Whenever we discuss "on-demand," then it leads our mind toward consumers who want things at a time, at their convenience, and wherever they happen to be. The health care industry is piercing into the period of digital innovation, as patients depend on "on-demand" health care due to their busy schedules. Within the consideration of content marketing, mobile plays a major role. In content marketing, one of the most important things is that we have to determine where our targeted customers come together and reach them on their platform that is a mobile device. A recent study shows that around 77 % of citizens of the U.S. own a Smartphone, and four billion peoples are dependent on the internet.

According to DMN3, consumers are going online for acquiring medical services due to the following reasons:

- 47 % of research doctors
- 38 % of research hospitals and medical facilities
- 77 % book medical appointments

1. Big data in health care:

Big data is a summation of information about a business via formats like online transactions, e-commerce, financial transactions, and social media, and identifies patterns. Big data resembles an opportunity that delivers many services such as lower rate of medication errors: Through patient record analysis, the computer code will flag any inconsistencies between a patient's health and drug prescriptions, alerting health professionals and patients once there's a possible risk of a drugs error.

Facilitating preventing care: A huge range of persons entering into the emergency room are recurring patients also known as "frequent flyers." Big data analysis helps us to identify these peoples and implement deterrent plans to keep them from returning. High accurate staffing: Big data's predictive analysis could help hospitals, as well as clinics, also compute future admission rates, which helps these facilities allocate the proper staff to deal with patients. It saves a lot of money and when a facility is understaffed then it decreases emergency room wait times.

2. Development of wearable medical devices:

Another opportunity within the time of digital health care is doctors can easily gather their patient information or their health-related information from medical devices such as wearable devices. Nowadays in the digital era, patients and doctors both are emphasized on maintenance and prevention and demanding about their reports. As output, health care companies are being farseeing by investing in wearable technology that can give time-to-time monitoring of high-risk patients to identify the probability of a major health event. From a recent study, it is prognosticated that the wearable device market reaches more than $27 million by 2023. The list of some common devices:

- Heart rate sensors
- Exercise trackers
- Sweat meters
- Oximeters
- Fitness watches

From a study, it is found that health apps in saving money and wearable devices could save the U.S. health care system close to $7 billion per year.

3. Artificial intelligence:

AI is quite simply a digital transformation trend in health care. AI shows the abstract of medical innovation, and industry players are eager to invest millions on it. The health care AI-powered tools market is anticipated to exceed $34 billion by 2025, which implies this technology will shape almost all aspects of the industry.

Virtual health assistants and chat bots are examples of AI-based technology that patients are becoming sociable with. Chat bots can fill a huge number of roles from customer service representatives to diagnostic tools and even therapists. Their contrivance is being recapitulated into large investments. The positive aspect of AI can be notified in the field of health care like genomics, precision medicine, medical imaging, and drug discovery. For example, earlier cancer patients used to receive cookie-cutter treatments with more failures. But now these patients have access to personalized therapies tailored to their genetic makeup and lifestyle due to AI's sophisticated pattern.

Here, an issue arises that what AI-powered computer programs do for oncology, in a nutshell, is to investigate thousands of pathology images of different cancers to deliver exact diagnosis and predicting all possibilities of anti-drug combinations. And, in medical imaging diagnostics, this technology helps radiologists spot details that escape the human eye. Machine learning algorithms are utilized by pharmaceutical and biotechnological companies to list the drug development cycle.

4. Predictive health care:

Previously, we have discussed how big data could provide health care companies. Another factor is the transformation of digital technologies in health care. It is portending what disease and illness will become major issues in the coming years. Whatever information we get from big data and other marketing sources is useful in the development of health care companies. For example, we could hire an analyst to investigate keyword activity across social media channels and on major search engines to identify the most common searches for medical conditions, illnesses, and general health. The analyst could then develop a predictive model that might anticipate where and when the following big health scare will occur, and the way our company can brace oneself for that event.

Challenges in the Field of Health Care

The digital transformation of the health care industry can radically ameliorate the ability of doctors, hospitals, and organizations to treat patients and help them live longer healthier lives. This section has aim to focus on what are the challenges in the era of digital health care.

1. Data processing:

In the health care industry, processing and analysis of data become one of the major challenges. Part of the problem is because of the sheer amount of information that hospitals, clinics, and health professionals collect. Without robust AI systems that can investigate information or data, it is difficult for organizations to provide better and more personalized care to patients. Another challenge is that the process of collecting and synchronizing data. With the expansion of telemedicine, doctor visits are happening across many channels making it harder for health professionals to update patients' health records. As an output, it will be important for the health care industry to form an avenue to record for both patients' in-person and virtual visits.

2. Cyber security:

This challenge comes in almost every industry, and health care is no different. Organizations should be very attentive about cyber threats, which can be very expensive. As an example, a study by IBM displayed that health care organizations had the very best costs related to data breaches, which were thrice higher as compared to other industries. Taking the appropriate steps to strengthen these areas is important to the security of the health care industry. Apart from this, adopting IoMT and the digitalization of the industries are all aspiring to be an attack. Concerning security, IoMT devices become the reason.

3. Digital user experience:

Whenever it comes to technology, the end-user must be taken into account to produce the product and services that are easy to access. Designing products such as mobile application, a connected heart monitor, or service that perform their function properly and are user-friendly is a challenge. In the health care industry, this is very necessary since many products will be used by both patients and medical professionals. A comfortless or poorly designed IoMT device, for example, can smudge a patient's experience. Besides, if the flexibility and usability become difficult then it will also limit the overall willingness of medical professionals to use or prescribe the device to other patients. The ability for technology to produce more improvements to the health care industry will highly rely on its overall quality.

Role of Digital Well-Being in the Field of Agriculture

Digital well-being in agriculture used communal media podium related to digital technology to enhance human well-being. The interested farmers work and distribute videos describing the perfect management training that worker can use for enhanced productivity. Data are acknowledged as worker trust other farmers because all are earning a liveliness related situations. Mobile cash is a different interference under digital well-being that changes the paper money. Mobile cash is secure and takes less time to transfer and also helps for human well-being. Digital well-being has become a game changer for the agriculture sector; many mobile apps have become a field that makes agriculture sector simple. Some apps give information to farmers on present weather for days to come; agriculture helper advice in a time of growing, and to be used fertilizers.

Large trading companies, leading information technology sectors, and organizations have also involved in agriculture sector, and the environment for technology improves well-being of farmers. *E-Choupal of* Indian Tobacco Companies a digital platform gives service to the farmers of over 3500 villages, and farmers have the capacity to manage food grain department and changes. *Trringo*, a mobile app for farmers helps to rent motors using digital device and to help workers using the machine, and it is helpful for farmer well-being. Concept of Custom brings in the agriculture launched over this app, and all these apps are very helpful for poor farmers and workers who have only paid their rent and are not able to spend large money for buying other farm machinery. Tax Collected at Source, India's top Information Technology firm, offer visual and audio developers to farmers using smart phones through its *mKRISHI* services. Stellapps app is used to enhance milk production. Ekgaon Technologies village for network, offers services to farmers, and women using mobile transmission to enhance the sustainable improvement of small farmers. Digital well-being is very helpful for those farmers who are not able to do farming because of some reasons. All these apps are helpful for agricultural work and enhance the level of the work and health of farmers. Digital well-being plays vital role in the agriculture sector. Thus the positive change and effective change in agriculture sector by improvements and advancement in technology and in agricultural applications. Farmers have access to data of everything that they want to know and improve in digital platforms.

Challenges Faced by Digital Well-Being in the Field of Agriculture

Digital agriculture use software and hardware systems that understand their atmosphere through best devices, provide multifunction, and take the move that decreases the chances of gaining a distinct goal. There are challenges that digital well-being faces for agricultural digitization:

1. Secure expected value
   We all know that technology becomes costly day by day because of the enhancement in the features. In technology, adding new features is easy, but the time and money it takes is very tough; rather than focusing on the amount that this technology is proposed to increase the feature, focus on the well-being also.
2. Put the infrastructure for efficient data
   Another issue that digital well-being faces is the import of information that is offered; it is all about positioning the structural hardware and software

devices correctly. Manage and provide the data concept to other digital systems. It is very helpful for farmers and their well-being.

3. Associate the right people and expertise
   For this, software engineers and information scientists are needed. For developing the agriculture sector, food scientists are very important. They are helpful for farmers and their well-being, business development, and organizations. Typically, involvement of scientists from different backgrounds is important for understanding many of the problems.
4. Convenience for people to pay the bill
   In the digital agriculture program, focuses on agricultural budget system will be important to be developed, but it is also very helpful for the farmers working in the field. All the stage of the project digital device mainly takes high cost. But farmers will not be able to buy and pay the bills of costly technology. This is the biggest challenge for the digital well-being in agricultural sector.

Many digital agriculture organizations are enhancing technology for helping farmers and their well-being, but it is also a big challenge for digital well-being and agriculture sector for improving productivity.

Study Analysis

Impact of Technology on Health Sector

From the research, we have analyzed how digital technologies influence digital well-being or in the health care sector. Typically, there are so many technologies that impact a patient's health in both aspects that are positive and negative. Concerning the performance of digital technologies in the health care sector, these technologies perform very well from the perspective of an advantage as shown in Figs. 1, 2, 3. However, as we know that everything has pros and cons technologies also have some bad and good impacts on individual health. Moreover, this graph indicates how much technologies affect digital well-being in terms of percentage. Around 30 % of big data impacts a person and wearable devices we are using in our daily routine like Jawbone UP, Fit Bit Flex, Samsung Gear 2, Google Glass, GOQii, etc. affect our body. Meanwhile artificial intelligence, robotics, and cloud on which we are dependent also influence our lives.

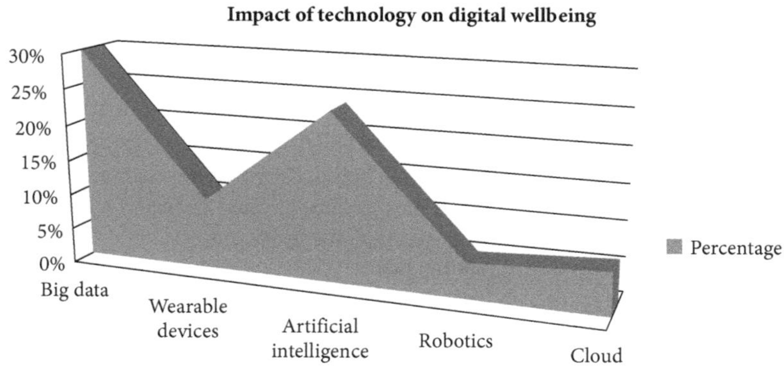

Fig. 3. Health Sector Analysis

Impact of Technologies on Students (Different Age Groups) in the Education Sector

In the education sector, we have examined that nowadays technologies have a great impact on students but the effect of technology varies on different ages such as teenagers and youths are influenced more by technology as in Fig. 4 .

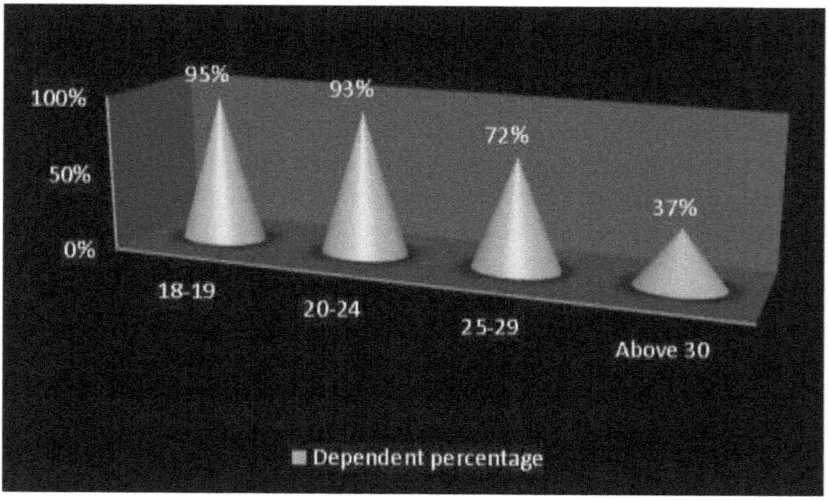

Fig. 4. Education Sector Analysis

Due to the development of technology, many things become possible, which was not in previous eras, and technology makes our life too easy. Technology is a source through which a student can get more knowledge, experience, and skills. But besides that, technology resembles a bad behavior toward student health in the education sector. The above graph indicates that almost 95 % of students use social media including LinkedIn, Twitter, Instagram, etc. which is a part of technology. Hence, it impacts on the students of age group between18 and 19 mainly. Apart from that, persons whose ages are between 20 and 24 are also impacted by digital technologies in their academic period. And it was seen that people whose age is more than 30 are also affected by technology.

Impact of Digital Apps on Digital Well-Being in the Field of Agriculture

In today's period, technology is progressing not only in the field of education or health but also in other areas like agriculture. Many of the farmers work was done using a lot of time and resources, but technology has solved it for a long time. There are many digital apps, due to which the problems of farmers have improved. If we have seen from the aspect of influence, it would have a good effect on farmers as in Fig. 5 . This is what we showed in this graph: because of each app, there is a good impact on people and these apps are agriApp, IFFCO Kisan app, Farmerbee, and Agri media video app.

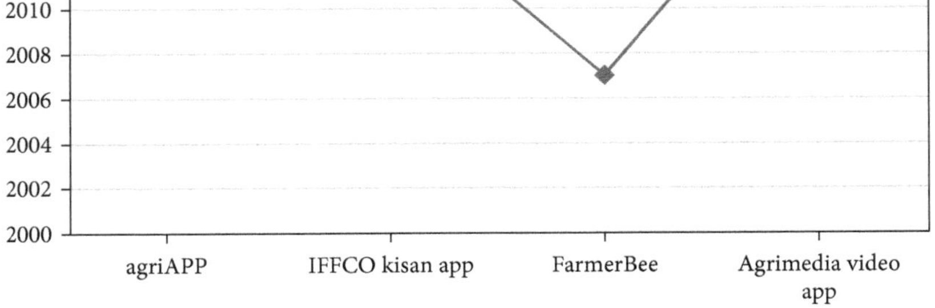

Fig. 5. Agriculture Sector Analysis

Conclusion

It is clear that we need to change and improve our thinking about digital well-being and use digital devices and technology in the right way in all the sectors. Digital well-being play the crucial role in the education system, in the health care system and the agricultural sector. As we all know that both technology and well-being are important for human life, communal sector not only focuses on the digital devices but also focuses on the health care. In this chapter, digital well-being in health care gives a way how to use screen and mobile phones and enhancement of well-being with technology. Well-being means being healthy and comfortable with the proper use of technology. Opportunities and challenges on digital well-being in the health care system and education system improve an individual's knowledge because it gives way to face the problems and enhance knowledge about digital system. Although there are positive and negative effects of digital well-being on human health, it indicates how to use technology in the right way and what should people avoid for healthy health. Inequality digital conversion has a greater impact on persons with lower levels of education and abilities, and from its advantages may benefit just a few. Lastly, we wanted to mention that digital well-being is more important for future development of human well-being, especially in the education system, health care system, and agricultural sector.

Discussion Questions

1. Define the digital well-being?
2. What are the positive and negative effects of digital well-being on human health?
3. Do you think that excessive use of social media affects human health?
4. Is digital well-being beneficial for education sector?
5. What is the role of the High Education Organization in the education sector?
6. How dangerous is the sleeping disorder for kids? What are the precautions to be taken for the sleep disorder?
7. What are the most important sectors nowadays in digital well-being? Explain in brief.
8. What are the right skills required for digital well-being?
9. What is the role of digital well-being in the education system?
10. What are the challenges faced by digital well-being in the field of education system?

11. What is the role of digital well-being in the health care sector?
12. What are the challenges faced by digital well-being in the field of health care sector?
13. What is the role of digital well-being in agriculture sector?
14. What are the challenges faced by digital well-being in the field of agriculture sector?
15. What is the healthy use of digital devices? And how youngsters follow the work "Digital Well-Being" correctly?
16. How much are digital devices useful in agriculture sector and for the farmer well-being?
17. How education system enhances digital well-being for students?
18. What are the major opportunities of digital well-being in health care?
19. How digital communication changed the step to school students?
20. Why digital well-being is more important for future development?

Key Terms

Digital: Digital means the representation of data in the form of binary that is 0 and 1. It is an electronic technology that produces, stores, and processes information in terms of two states called positive and non-positive.
Digital Well-Being: Considering the effect of technologies and digital services on an individual's physical, emotional, and mental health.
Cyberspace: Cyberspace refers to the virtual computer world, and more specifically, is an electronic medium used to form a global computer network to facilitate online communication.
Therapeutic interaction: It is a process of communication that emphasized on advancing the physical and emotional well-being of a patient.
Chat bots: It is a part of software application that simulates human conversation via voice command and text chats.
Oximeter: An instrument for measuring the proportion of oxygenated hemoglobin in the blood.
Cyber security: Cyber security is the practice of defending computers, servers, mobile devices, electronic systems, networks, and data from damage, failure of hardware, attacks, and unauthorized access.
Genomics: Genomics is an interdisciplinary field of biology focusing on the structure, function, evolution, mapping, and editing of genomes.
IoMT: The Internet of Medical Things (**IoMT**) is the accumulation of medical devices and applications that link to health care IT sector via online computer networks.

References

A. A. Lijadi, "Theoretical Foundations to Outline Human Well-Being: Metaanalytic Literature Review for Defining Empowered Life Years," no. February, 2018.

A. Gaggioli, "Digital Wellbeing: Considering Self-Transcendence Digital Wellbeing : Considering," no. May, pp. 0–4, 2019.

A. M. Ronchi and A. M. Ronchi, "Well-Being in the Digital Age," *e-Citizens*, no. March, pp. 23–41, 2019, doi: 10.1007/978-3-030-00746-1_3.

A. Maccagnan, S. Wren-Lewis, H. Brown, and T. Taylor, "Wellbeing and Society: Towards Quantification of the Co-benefits of Wellbeing," *Soc. Indic. Res.*, vol. 141, no. 1, pp. 217–243, 2019, doi: 10.1007/s11205-017-1826-7.

C. Burr, J. Morley, M. Taddeo, and L. Floridi, "Digital Psychiatry: Ethical Risks and Opportunities for Public Health and Well-Being," *SSRN Electron. J.*, vol. 1, no. 1, pp. 21–33, 2019, doi: 10.2139/ssrn.3477978.

C. Burr, M. Taddeo, and L. Floridi, "The Ethics of Digital Well-Being: A Thematic Review," *SSRN Electron. J.*, Jan. 2019, doi: 10.2139/ssrn.3338441.

C. Burr, M. Taddeo, and L. Floridi, *The Ethics of Digital Well-Being: A Thematic Review*, no. 0123456789. Springer Netherlands, 2020.

C. D. Ryff, "Psychological Well-Being Revisited: Advances in the Science and Practice of Eudaimonia," *Psychother. Psychosom.*, vol. 83, no. 1, pp. 10–28, 2013, doi: 10.1159/000353263.

C. M. Pulido, L. C. Mara, V. Ionescu, and T. Sordé-Martí, "Social Impact of Psychological Research on Well-Being Shared in Social Media," *Front. Psychol.*, vol. 11, no. February, pp. 1–12, 2020, doi: 10.3389/fpsyg.2020.00135.

D. Gasper, *Discussion Paper No . 2004 / 06 Human Well-being: Concepts and Conceptualizations*, no. May. 2004.

D. Teghe and K. Rendell, "Social Wellbeing: A Literature Review," *Sch. Soc. Work Welf. Stud.*, vol. 10, no. August 2005, 2005, doi: 10.13140/RG.2.2.28891.26406.

E. C. W. Ng and A. T. Fisher, "Understanding Well-Being in Multi-Levels: A Review," *Heal. Cult. Soc.*, vol. 5, no. 1, pp. 308–323, 2013, doi: 10.5195/hcs.2013.142.

E. Diener, S. Oishi, and L. Tay, "Advances in Subjective Well-Being Research," *Nat. Hum. Behav.*, vol. 2, no. 4, pp. 253–260, 2018, doi: 10.1038/s41562-018-0307-6.

F. Burchi and C. Gnesi, "A Review of the Literature on Well-Being in Italy: A Human Development Perspective," *Forum Soc. Econ.*, vol. 45, no. 2–3, pp. 170–190, 2016, doi: 10.1080/07360932.2014.995197.

H. Moilanen, S. Äyrämö, S. Jauhiainen, M. Kankaanranta, and C. C. Chiou, "Collecting and Using Students' Digital Well-Being Data in Multidisciplinary Teaching," *Educ. Res. Int.*, vol. 2018, 2018, doi: 10.1155/2018/3012079.

https://seismic.com/company/blog/5-challenges-of-digital-transformation-in-healthcare/

https://www.frontiersin.org/articles/10.3389/fpsyg.2018.00331/full

https://www.frontiersin.org/articles/10.3389/fpsyg.2018.00331/full

https://medical-technology.nridigital.com/medical_technology_mar19/connected_medical_devices_what_challenges_as_digital_healthcare_is_normalised

https://seismic.com/company/blog/5-challenges-of-digital-transformation-in-healthcare/

https://www.a-connect.com/knowledge/opportunities-and-challenges-in-digital-health-2017/

https://www.healthcareguy.com/2014/10/26/health-it-and-digital-health-job-opportunities-qualifications-and-certification-benefits/

https://www.mckinsey.com/business-functions/mckinsey-digital/our-insights/four-keys-to-successful-digital-transformations-in-healthcare

https://www.medicalnewstoday.com/articles/317022#More-connectivity-in-the-future

https://www.robotlab.com/blog/6-technology-challenges-education-is-facing

https://www2.stardust-testing.com/en/the-digital-transformation-trends-and-challenges-in-healthcare

J. Mcalaney, M. Aldhayan, B. Almourad, and S. Cham, "Predictors of Acceptance and Rejection of Online Peer Support Groups as a Digital Wellbeing Tool Predictors of Acceptance and Rejection of Online Peer Support Groups as a Digital Wellbeing Tool Digital media including social networks, gaming and online s," no. January, 2020.

M. Gui, M. Fasoli, and R. Carradore, "Digital Well-Being. Developing a New Theoretical Tool for Media Literacy Research," *Ital. J. Sociol. Educ.*, vol. 9, no. 1, pp. 155–173, 2017.

N. M. Trendov, S. Varas, and M. Zeng, "Digital Technologies in Agriculture and Rural Areas," *Brief. Pap. FAO*, p. 26, 2019.

N. N. Surtaeva, "Social Well-Being Research Problems in Modern World," no. December, pp. 393–399, 2017, doi: 10.15405/epsbs.2017.07.02.50.

P. Anand, "2016 UNDP Human Development Report: Happiness, well-being and human development: The case for subjective measures [Background Paper]," 2016.

P. Howard-Jones, "The Impact of Digital Technologies on Human Wellbeing," *Atlantic*, p. 98, 2011.

S. Grand-Clement, A. Devaux, J. Belanger, and C. Manville, "Digital Learning: Education and Skills in the Digital Age," *Digit. Learn. Educ. Ski. Digit. age*, 2017.

U. H. Ufz, "Human Well-Being. In: Potschin, M. and K. Jax (eds.): OpenNESS Ecosystem Services Reference Book. EC FP7 Grant Agreement no. 308428.," *Available via www.openness- Proj.*, vol. 1, pp. 1–6, 2016.

U. Varshney and C. K. Chang, "Smart Health and Well-Being," *Computer (Long. Beach. Calif).*, vol. 49, no. 11, pp. 11–13, 2016, doi: 10.1109/MC.2016.351.

Aurelian STOICA

12 Rumors and Gossip in the Online World: Social Influence Processes as Challenges to the Digital Well-Being

Abstract: In the past decade, our entire society changed massively due to a rapid immersion into the digital world. The growing portfolio of mobile applications, virtual reality devices, augmented reality software, messaging and VoIP services, and social media platforms, with the support of artificial intelligence, analytics, and high-performance computing infrastructures, engaged billions of citizens into a matrix of both learning opportunities and digital challenges and risks. Although many studies focused on underlining the benefits of the new technologies in terms of an increased access to information and a stronger connection with peers, this is only one side of the changes we encounter. This chapter approaches current challenges for the digital well-being due to the people's exposure to social influence in the digital world, with focus on gossip and rumors transmitted online. Such processes induce a significant negative impact for the involved audiences not only in the face-to-face interactions, but even in a stronger manner in exchanges mediated by social media sites (SNS) and instant messaging platforms. The study pleads for strategies to attain digital well-being in order to eliminate education and information gaps, consolidate skills, and create a culture of trust and support between users/citizens and the expanding technology.

Keywords: Digital well-being, new technologies, social influence, online gossip, online rumors

The general concept of well-being faced many challenges over time in the significant theoretical attempts of defining it. We generally understand these days well-being as the state of happiness, good health, social integration, and professional enrichment. *Oxford English Dictionary* defines well-being simply as the state of being comfortable, healthy, or happy. More than 50 years ago, Norman M. Bradburn focused on explaining the well-being through constructs such as positive affect and negative affect and positioned happiness – seen as an "adjustment to one's environment" – as a central pillar of his theory (Bradburn, N.M., 1969). Happiness, or the psychological state of well-being, is defined in this view as the balance between the two mentioned affects. Philosophical perspectives reviewed well-being theories based on the Hedonic (achieving a balance of pleasure over pain) and Eudaimonic (related to the ethics and practice of a good life) dimensions of happiness, underlining well-being's narrowing role in terms of resources for engagement (Tesar, M. & Peters, M.A., 2019). It is relevant to mention that, as a core pillar of the well-being decades studies, happiness has also been correlated by other researchers with the broader notion of social competence, especially through the assertiveness component (Argyle, M. & Lu, L., 1990).

Criticizing Bradburn's idealization of happiness as outcome variable, other researchers came with a wider perspective that detailed specific well-being dimensions such as self-acceptance, positive relationships with others, autonomy, environmental mastery, purpose in life, and personal growth (Ryff, C.D., 1989). The multidimensional model of psychological well-being has been further theoretically reviewed by Carol Ryff and Corey Keyes in a new study that confirmed the superiority of the 6 factors model based on confirmatory factor analyses (Ryff, C.D. & Keyes, C.L.M., 1995). Starting from Dan Brock's three main philosophical approaches, defining quality of life in terms of normative ideals, satisfaction of preferences, and experience of individuals (Brock, D. 1989), new studies drove the well-being research toward the concepts of pleasant and unpleasant moods and emotions and life satisfaction (Diener, E. & Suh, E.M., 1997). Another classical approach explaining well-being is the dynamic equilibrium theory, developed by Bruce Headey and Alex Wearing. The authors concluded that "people arrive at an equilibrium state in which their present life is viewed as being almost as satisfying as the best life they could aspire to, the life they feel they deserve and the best previous period of their life. Their present life is regarded as considerably better than the worst previous period of their life and then the life of the average person in the country" (Headey, B. W. & Wearing, A. J., 1992).

A more recent study aiming at structuring the key theories and efforts made in order to review the well-being field explained that past theoretical approaches were focused mainly on dimensions of the phenomenon, rather than the definition (Dodge et al., 2012). Same authors proposed a new interpretation of the concept, as "the balance point between an individual's resource pool (Psychological, Social, Physical) and the challenges faced (Psychological, Social, Physical)."

Human evolution is interfering in modern times with the ICT development, radically affecting our relationships with the others and with the entire world. We therefore agree with and place this study's approach into Luciano Floridi's paradigm stating that while in the prehistory phase, there were no ICT, in the history phase, social and individual well-being relate to the ICT, and in the hyperhistory phase social and individual well-being will heavily depend on the ICT (Floridi, L., 2014). The evolution in the current technological environment requires adequate skills and capabilities, at such level that ICTs (and subsequently the expertise to successfully manage them) are already seen fundamental to the individual well-being and the citizens welfare (Thorseth, M., 2014).

As a result, traditional well-being shifts nowadays to a technological level concept: digital well-being, defined by some authors as the capabilities and skills needed in order to successfully master the new technologies. The findings of the data governance report issued by the British Academy and the Royal Society (2017) placed at the top of principles guiding the development of system architectures the promotion of human flourishing. Jisc (a provider of digital solutions for UK education and research) structured a comprehensive digital capabilities framework composed of 6 main areas: ICT digital proficiency, information, data, and media literacies (critical use); digital creation, problem solving, and innovation (creative production); digital communication, collaboration, and participation (participation); digital learning and development (development); and digital identity and well-being (self-actualizing).

In this approach, digital well-being is considered to be: "the capacity to look after personal health, safety, relationships and work-life balance in digital settings; to use digital tools in pursuit of personal goals (e.g., health and fitness) and to participate in social and community activities; to act safely and responsibly in digital environments; to negotiate and resolve conflict; to manage digital workload, overload and distraction; to act with concern for the human and natural environment when using digital tools. An understanding of the benefits and risks of digital participation in relation to health and wellbeing outcomes" (Jisc, 2018). It is therefore a complete 360 degrees vision, starting from the inner core with the individual perspective and integrating in the wider circles the social and environmental variables. It is a far more comprehensive approach compared to the studies that focus only on the smartphone apps designed to break the device addiction in order to achieve digital well-being (Roffarello, A.M., De Russis, Luigi, 2019).

The new technologies environment permeated our societies more and more powerful with each available innovation. Wearable devices, public online services, smart applications, mobile Internet, and social media platforms shaped the communication environment with unprecedented speed and impact. The user placed in the middle of this technical flow is faced both with opportunities to connect and inform, and, at the same time, with the challenges and risks associated with massive amounts of overcommunication. Important tech companies like Google launched organized initiatives to assess online behaviors and protect users from excessive notifications and aggressive pushes from equipment's operation systems and apps. However, this is not going to be an easy task, as system engineers from software companies are motivated financially and professionally to invent apps that trigger repeated reactions from the users.

The overwhelming visual input, excessive multi-tasking, and overconsumption of news are not at all solved with the increase of digital skills, beginning to represent serious challenges and menaces. Digital well-being becomes a state where individual digital skills are not enough: community must also be involved through norms and values in order to ensure its members comfort and satisfaction (Gui, M., Fasoli M. & Carradore, R., 2017). The finding is important because tech supporters advocated previously the direction of skill development as the main strategy to facilitate digital immersion. Gui and his colleagues proposed a new dimension of the digital well-being to the 6 main categories previously selected by other researchers (Iordache, C., Mariën, I. and Baelden, D., 2017): the ability to manage side effects derived from the immense quantity of information.

As the avalanche of stimuli, notifications and data overwhelm the user's capacity to deal with such massive amounts of information, some tech giants already structure different philosophies when developing applications. Google is such a case. With its 2018 Digital Well-Being initiative, the company aims to help humans shape a better relationship with technology by setting the main values to guide them through a matrix of algorithms and apps. It is taking back control over machines, as the digital is not something magic, like a black box, but a result of the modern society that is metaphorically "pressing us for time," through machine-mediated communication (Wajcman, J., 2015).

A different view approaches the online platforms as producers of societal structures, by shaping an environment of services, information, and people around each user: The Big 5 of Tech (Apple, Amazon, Alphabet-Google, Microsoft, and Facebook) exert influence on how societies are organized through the platform ecosystem (van Dijck et al., 2018). Those authors organize Big 5 applications in 4 key domains: News, Education, Health & Fitness, and Urban Transport. Predictive algorithms and advertising policies built by platform owners set content trends and bring key topics in front of the news feed. As more and more people (in 2016, half of the population in US and Europe) use social media for news purpose, institutions and private organizations disrupt the original scope and influence algorithms and features to spread rumors, conspiracies, and disinformation. In the past decade, a significant shift happened, as tech companies switched from hardware business to services model. Big 5 opened their business for software-based models, engaging users in participative environments and boosting online education. Millions of people pass now exams in massive open online courses organized on education platforms synced with Big 5. Opportunities for learning are at unprecedented levels, and people can decide for free, open courses or paid, recognized certificates.

Digital well-being aims at strengthening education through integration of online technologies in the process of teaching and learning. A strong education is a key pillar for a healthy digital well-being. Recent studies on children indicate that digital well-being implies forms of education and support in the use of Internet that are more complex than just providing hardware equipment and making users aware of online perils like inappropriate content or misinformation (Nansen et al., 2011). As education stands as main solution, we agree with the views underlining that digital coping skills are required in order for users to manage the digital overabundance and side effects derived from their digital involvement (Büchi et al., 2019). We already see a good progress with the advancements of the researches that are able to make predictions for the satisfaction with life (a general well-being indicator) of the Facebook users, based on the assessment of the language people use on social media (Schwartz et al., 2016).

In a recent Erasmus project – Digital Wellbeing Educators (DWE) – designed to develop the digital literacy of educators in HE sectors to successfully address digital education and increase the digital skills of the European students, participating partners identified 9 key challenges to digital well-being, as follows:

1. Distractibility/Finding Balance (cyber loafing); 2. Haven for misconduct (cyberbullying, cybersecurity); 3. Alienated relationships; 4. Overconsumption of devices and technologies; 5. Psychological implications (24/7 availability stress, lack of empathy, and lack of confidence in using technologies); 6. Physical implications; 7. Unethical attention seeking (addictive design of technology); 8. Echo chambers, stereotypes, and fake news; 9. Democracy challenges (promoting social inequalities, radicalization, and identity management) (Royo et al., 2019). The findings are important as they confirm that the digital dimension of well-being is far more extensive than overabundance of apps, addictive user behavior, and healthy balance between real life activities and virtual presence. The point no. 8, regarding echo chambers, stereotypes, and fake news, is especially relevant for this study, as we focus on the social influence phenomena such as gossip and rumors, that are currently spreading online as communication shifts nowadays from face-to-face to machine mediated. As an Australian report issued in 2017 found in a research on young people, common apps like Snapchat, Facebook, and Instagram are used these days to learn things, find

friends, find out important stuff, keep in touch with friends, and to gossip (Gwinner, K., Melrose, P. and Moffatt, A., 2017).

The Organisation for Economic Co-operation and Development is also positioning growth and well-being at the core of its policy strategy. Digital transformation is defined as the sum of the economic and societal effects of digitization and digitalization, while the digital ecosystem contains key technologies such as Internet of Things, 5G Networks, Cloud computing, Big data, Artificial intelligence, Blockchain, and Computing power (OECD, 2019a). The framework proposed by OECD experts for governmental digital transformation policy includes the following policy modules placed around growth and well-being: (1) access, (2) use, (3) innovation, (4) jobs, (5) trust, (6) society, and (7) market openness. For every society, digital transformation is a complex process that encapsulates both benefits and growing opportunities as well as challenges and risks. It has a clear role to enrich communication, improve education, boost health care sector, but, at the same time, in parallel with the facilitated online communication, there are challenges like cyberbullying, spread of disinformation, and loss of jobs due to automation.

The importance of the digital transformation for the human well-being in terms of opportunities and challenges has determined OECD to perform an extensive analysis focused on that specific topic. In the era of Internet, mobile devices, and access to various online platforms, even the well-being concept suffered significant updates. Individual well-being consists of eleven dimensions grouped in two main sets. One set is the quality of life, which is composed of health, work-life balance, education and skills, social connections, civic engagement and governance, environmental quality, personal security, and subjective well-being. Another main set is represented by material conditions, groups income and wealth, jobs and earnings, and housing (OECD, 2019b).

Opportunities target each of those above dimensions, from the creation of digital resources to improved education, access to employment, better health services, improved government service delivery, and safety of transactions. Correspondent risks expose gaps in Internet use, lack of digital skills, job polarization, mental health effects, spread of disinformation, and security incidents. Disinformation distribution is perceived here as a method to undermine trust in governments and official information channels, as there are online platforms that offer streams of news replacing traditional media. The dimensions were further detailed by OECD experts so that a total number of 33 indicators describe opportunities and challenges. Most of the indicators are grouped in the education and skills dimensions (digital skills, digital skills gap, digital resources at school, teacher ICT skills risk, and online courses), jobs and earnings (employment in information industries, online job search, jobs at risk of automation, lower extended job strain associated with computer-intense jobs, job stress associated with computer-intense jobs), and governance and civic engagement (people expressing opinions online, individuals interacting with public authorities online, availability of open government data, individuals excluded from e-government services due to lack of skills, and exposure to disinformation).

Internet and equipment like mobile phones, tablets, or PCs are necessary but not sufficient for the individual growth and development in the digital ecosystem. Digital skills and communication abilities become more and more important in order to successfully navigate in the new structures shaping our social organization. Individuals play the role of basic units of the network society, viewed as a social formation with an infrastructure of social and media networks defining its organization on all levels, based on information that is processed and exchanged (van Dick, J., 1991/2006). The network society follows the mass society – social formation with an infrastructure of groups, organizations, and communities, having as basic units the collectivities. In a similar perspective, the network is considered a set of interconnected nodes having also the valence of a new social morphology in the society. The information technology empowers the networks with the capability to expand throughout the entire social structure (Castells, M. 2009).

The place of collectivities in the social matrix is subsequently substituted in the digital era by the individual as an interconnection link between different networks. As van Dijk put it, computer networks and telephony fuel and multiply the spread of rumor, fashions, gossip, and news in traditional social networks. And this was before the social media platforms dominance in the communication field. But with the rise of such tools the speed of spreading mis and disinformation has grown exponentially. It is relevant to consider the number of online platforms monthly active users for the first trimester of 2020: Facebook – 2,5 billion, YouTube – 2 billion, WhatsApp – 2 billion, Facebook Messenger – 1,3 billion, WeChat – 1,165 billion, and Instagram – 1 billion (Statista, 2020). As a study on rumor circulation on Twitter demonstrated, a message originated from any node of this platform can reach an average number of 45,6 million users in just 8 rounds of communication (Doerr, B., Fouz, M. and Friedrich, T., 2012). It is a proof that speed and organic reach are two key dimensions of today's online platforms that should be taken into consideration by the governmental strategists in charge with public communication.

If new technologies impact so many people worldwide and drive so many benefits in all sectors, an important question arises regarding their main role for specific social categories. An Italian research report on digital well-being in high schools had relevant conclusions for the education sector. The test for measuring awareness and competence in the use of digital technologies had findings confirming distress among teenagers (3,659 students in 171 classes) due to smartphone usage (Gui et al., 2018). On the information & literacy side, the report stated that students were more skilled in communicating using chats and social media than selecting and validating information. For UK children present in the social networking world, "being able to talk to friends" and "keeping up to date with gossip" were also the first two preferences (Swist, T., Collin, P., McCormack, J. & Third, A., 2015).

Two main dimensions were profiled by the Italian research authors as an urgency in the education strategy: the smartphone overuse and the search for and evaluation of information online. Many studies approached the first dimension to demonstrate the existence of a challenge to the user's digital well-being, we therefore propose to focus on the second one, which is linked to the side of social media platforms reflecting the process of online diffusion of social influence components such as gossip and rumor. Those components are living modules of the daily communication in the cyber environment and are massively influencing the way we understand critical pieces of reality, react to them, and adapt our behavior. Some of the social influence processes generate reactions such as increase of anxiety and panic at individual level and even more complex social reactions at group level. We consider the social influence processes in the online world to have an impact on the overall digital well-being at least as important as the information overabundance or the smartphone overuse.

As communication mediated by the social media sites grows exponentially, some authors questioned why false messages have a more significant impact in diffusion compared to the real news. A key finding linked the false news circulation to the novelty degree and the emotional responses of the users: false information was linked to fear, disgust, and surprise in replies, while true stories were connected to anticipation, sadness, joy, and trust. The study concluded that this foundation ensured a diffusion of 126,000 rumors on Twitter, spread by 3 million people between 2006 and 2017, that was farther, faster, deeper, and broader than the circulation of true stories (Vosoughi, S., Roy, D., & Aral, S., 2018). Numerous studies (as resumed in Kim, H., 2014) demonstrated the benefits people obtain using social networking sites (in particular) and mobile Internet (in general). Strengthening personal communication, reducing physical distance, and enabling social support are just a few examples of the advantages brought by the digital technology for the psychological well-being.

At the same time, social support operationalized on Facebook does not significantly relate to an improved life satisfaction, underlining the limitations that modern tools still have. Access to useful and relevant information is an integral part of the digital well-being framework, and this is done extensively these days through social networking sites. But when intentional or accidental spread of unverified information happen through the same channels, especially during crisis or natural disasters, this is a point where we foresee effects on the user well-being itself. Two forms of the damages that rumors can induce to people are reputation loss and financial loss (Ahsan, M., Kumari, M., & Sharma, T.P., 2019); we consider those two areas important dimensions that influence directly the individual well-being.

Starting with World War II, researchers interested in rumors carefully assessed their effects, especially focusing on the negative ones. As some of them found already in the 40s, negative statements ("bogy rumors") were more numerous than the wishful thinking ("pipe dream rumors"), alerting war officials to structure preventive measures (Allport, G.W. & Postman, L., 1947). As ambiguity of the context and importance for the audience were the key variables in their rumor formula, the concept was frequently associated with false information, although a kernel of truth is still present in the message. At that time, a recommendation proposed by the rumor specialists was to replace rumors with actual news, and tales with facts. Same tactic is tried also when we encounter rumors in modern social media, and we suggest to the impacted audiences to rely on official and mainstream news, but also to check verifiable facts about the story from trusted sources. Rumor's main functions are to make sense of reality in ambiguous contexts and to manage threats to welfare through a better preparation and response to the situation (DiFonzo, N., & Bordia, P. 2007a). In a prior study, the authors approached close to the fact-finding and the relationship-building motivations the self-enhancement factor, which is maintaining a positive image of own self and favoring versions that match one's view of the world and the position of the in-group (Bordia, P., & DiFonzo, N., 2004).

But are rumors solid enough factors to determine violent social upraises, so that we can perceive them as threats to people's general well-being? When rumors are targeting members of external groups and they mix with other determinants such as stress conditions, social structure, political climate, and hostile belief system, we are in a point where those contextual features support the process of determining the rumors themes (Knopf, T.A., 1975). Knopf criticized Allport and Postman psychological approach – that just establishes a relation between riots and inciting rumors without clearly investigating it – explaining that the social situation itself plays a role in rumor creation, and group behavior is more important compared to the individual when researching the process. More recently, unrests in the United Kingdom confirmed the powerful role that new technologies (Twitter, BlackBerry Messenger) have, on one side, in spreading news about collective violence acts during protests and, on the other side, in encouraging the participants to engage in looting behavior (Solomos, J., 2011). With modern Twitter hashtags campaign, current social media network accentuates such determinants, and we witness that similar protests like the ones in the 60s are repeated with significant effects in 2020's US.

Belief in the truth is one core condition for the rumors to influence the social ecosystem, as DiFonzo and Bordia underlined. As an effect, consumers change their behavior, economic organizations are impacted, racial tensions arise, clashes between opposing groups generate violence and, ultimately, fatalities. Rumor is a social influence process, with dimensions such as abovementioned sense-making of the situation, uncertainty explanation, and management of the external threats, but it is also a propaganda facilitator, when intentional spread is found in malicious campaigns – political elections, wars, and consumer market decisions (DiFonzo, N., & Bordia, P. 2007b). When rumors emerge on a race and religion foundation, they have powerful effects, as demonstrated by the 2002 violent clashes between Hindu and Muslims in the Gujarat State in India, when more than one thousand people lost their lives due to violent riots fueled and accelerated by rumors. As the collectors of the rumors described, for three months people were deprived of sleep and not able to perform regular house tasks due to climate induced by rumors about the opposing religious group (Kakar, S., 2004).

Compared to the rumor, DiFonzo and Bordia (2007a) consider that functions of the gossip are building, structuring, and maintaining the social network. While rumor is focused on providing an understanding of an ambiguous situation or event, gossip is most frequently seen as an evaluative discussion about persons which are not present in the communication. As a result, gossip represents a social exchange process based on individual anxieties that is oriented toward the elimination of an existent discomfort (Rosnow, R. L., & Fine, G. A., 1976). But when malicious gossip is directed toward a member of the group, it has a significant disruptive potential affecting the harmony and cohesion of the group (Stirling, R.B., 1956). Both gossip and rumor have known significant advancements in terms of impact and importance as the transmission channels incorporated mass-media. With the developments of the present technologies, this progress is becoming even bigger. In the modern times, gossip is encouraged and endorsed by the social media sites and messaging platforms and can be easily transformed into an offensive flow of communication, like cyberbullying, which is a profoundly negative phenomenon for the digital well-being. As a social process, gossip is also used in the workplace in order to gain internal influence, by affecting and changing attitudes and opinions about others. At the same time, gossip is interesting for its particular function of emotional release, when people use it to reduce stress and anxiety in organizations (Grosser et al., 2012).

Studies focused on the spread of gossip on the social networking sites (SNS) demonstrated that, contrary to other models, it has the potential to change the SNS structure itself, because it can damage some relationships while it endorses others in the communication process (Shaw, A. K., Tsvetkova, M., & Daneshvar, R., 2011). Therefore, we can approach the SNS not just as news platforms with a unidirectional impact toward the audience, but also as flexible and modellable structures. If such phenomena like rumors and gossip can impact the SNS at their turn, the changes are going to be reflected back in the way SNS influence the audience. It's a spiral movement, in which a social process emerges from direct communication, transposes into SNS environment, finally impacting back the users and their behavior.

As instant messaging platforms like WhatsApp have been used lately in some countries (like Brazil and India) to spread false rumors and misinformation in the election campaigns (Melo et al., 2019; Reis et al., 2020), it is relevant to perceive their role for the digital well-being. Because the platform allows public groups to be created and the access is granted with a simple invite link, its potential to harm both the physical and mental health of users – in the process of unverified or fake information circulation – increased exponentially. WhatsApp is especially encouraging the spread of online rumors and gossip due to its structure of communication in groups. People tend to act in a less critical manner in the platform's closed groups because they feel secure to openly share rumors, conspiracies, and gossip about others, under the protection of an encrypted umbrella that shields their online exchanges. It is us, in the group, freely communicating about the outside hostile and dangerous world (Davies, William, 2020).

Facebook posts and WhatsApp messages not only deliver disinformation to broad audiences, but in some cases the effects are extremely violent. In India, online messages incited mobs in several regions of the country, that escalated into deadly lynchings against strangers or people of different religious confession, with a significant number of victims (Arun, C., 2019). Other studies also consider that WhatsApp is a channel for news communication and rumors spreading (text or image) to an available broad audience, the latter conducing to social unrest and violence (Garimella, K. & Eckles, D., 2020).

Other forms in which individual well-being is threatened by rumors or gossip with the help of social media are the medical topics. As studies underlined, AIDS denialists acting to block governmental policies in the African public health sector exacerbated the number of actual victims by circulating statements implying that HIV is harmless and the medical drugs cause the disease (Zollo, F. & Quattrociocchi, W., 2018).

Analysis on 2016 US presidential campaign revealed a complex foreign mechanism of disinformation working to influence online American audiences, mainly on Facebook and Twitter. False rumors spread on social media incited a man to fire a rifle inside the Comet Ping Pong restaurant in Washington DC, where he was convinced he would find trafficked children in underground tunnels (Fisher, M., Cox, J.W. & Hermann, P., 2016). The rumors on this scandal named Pizzagate pointed Democrat Party leaders (one of them was Hillary Clinton) as allegedly being involved in the story, but in the end it was proven an absolutely false scenario. Other false rumors posted on Facebook pages, destined for Texas public in US, gathered in opposing protests two different large groups in the same place, in the same time, with the objective to generate clashes (Pamment et al., 2018). This is an example of a spiral process that threatens well-being both in the online world and the physical space, numerous evidences proving that the interferences between the two sectors were induced by foreign actions aimed to divide and influence large areas of the US society.

Those actions bring to the discussion the misleading intention of such actions that use social influence processes to attain their intended purpose. Internet allowed vast amounts of information to be published on a multitude of communication platforms, but the frontier between unverified information and misinformation is very thin; the latter is considered to impact productivity and decision-making (Koohang, A., & Weiss, E., 2003). Studies warned about the dangerous consequences of false rumors circulation during emergency situations like natural disasters or terrorist attacks. In such contexts, when citizens rely upon social media platforms in finding latest news and updates, the spread of false rumors (rumor as an unverified news encapsulates both the kernel of truth and the false information) can harm citizens' well-being (Zubiaga et al., 2015). During crisis, affected communities share misinformation through social media in the sense making process, unverified information standing out as a practical tool used by people to cope with the uncertainty and tension of the context (Huang et al., 2015).

Considering the negative impact rumors have on people, researchers are incentivized to find and develop new tools and applications for data mining in social media. Such attempts have been increasing in the last years, and we consider useful the structure of the process provided to guide those efforts by a group of experts. It is composed of four main stages: rumor detection, rumor tracking, stance classification (supporting, denying, querying, and commenting), and veracity classification (true, false, unverified) (Zubiaga et al., 2018). Others focused on developing a socio-technological approach that encourages a crowd-sourced critical thinking aiming to stop the spread of false rumors in social media during natural disasters, like the Great East Japan Earthquake from March 11, 2011 (Tanaka, Y., Sakamoto, Y. & Matsuka, T., 2013).

Despite their role as anxiety and stress relievers, rumors and gossip transmitted through digital technologies in online environments have a negative impact on people's mental health, physical safety, and digital well-being. Governments should assess more precisely the effects of digital transformation, not only in terms of the benefits, but also in terms of the challenges we will face from now on in this cyber ecosystem. Education of digital skills, increase of media literacy, stronger framework for online exchanges, better policies for tech suppliers, and a trusted official communication are just some examples of measures that should be on top of every national digital strategy. And it will still not be enough, if we don't apply individually a critical stance toward online information easily shared by ambiguous sources, without confirmation or validation from recognizable voices, whose integrity and reputation are already known to the public.

References

Ahsan, Mohammad, Kumari, Madhu, and Sharma, T. P. (2019). Rumors detection, verification and controlling mechanisms in online social networks: A survey. *Online Social Networks and Media* 14(November 2019): 100050. doi:10.1016/j.osnem.2019.100050.

Allport, Gordon W., and Postman, Leo. (1947). *The psychology of rumor.* New York: Henry Holt Company.

Argyle, Michael, and Lu, Luo. (1990). Happiness and social skills. *Personality and Individual Differences* 11(12): 1255–1261. doi:10.1016/0191-8869(90)90152-H.

Arun, Chinmayi. (2019). On Whatsapp, rumours, and lynchings. *Economic and political weekly* 54(6): 30–35.

Bordia, Prashant, and DiFonzo, Nicholas. (2004). Psychological motivations in rumor spread. In G. A. Fine, V. Campion-Vincent, and C. Heath (Eds.), *Rumor Mills: The social impact of rumor and legend*. New Jersey: Transaction Publishers.

Bradburn, Norman M. (1969). *The structure of psychological wellbeing*. Chicago: Aldine Publishing Company.

British Academy and Royal Society. (2017). *Data management and use: Governance in the 21st century*. https://royalsociety.org/~/media/policy/projects/data-governance/data-management-governance.pdf

Brock, Dan. (1989). Quality of Life in Health Care and Medical Ethics. Wider Working Paper. World Institute for Development Economics Research of the United Nations University. https://www.wider.unu.edu/sites/default/files/WP66.pdf

Büchi, Moritz, Festic, Noemi, and Latzer, Michael. (2019). Digital overuse and subjective wellbeing in a digitized society. *Social Media + Society*, October-December 2019: 1–12. doi:10.1177%2F2056305119886031.

Castells, Manuel. [1996] (2009). *The rise of the network society. Information age: Economy, society, and culture*, Vol. 1, 2nd edn. New Jersey, US: Wiley-Blackwell

Davies, Williams. (2020). *What's wrong with WhatsApp*. https://www.theguardian.com/technology/2020/jul/02/whatsapp-groups-conspiracy-theories-disinformation-democracy

Diener, Ed, and Suh, Eunkook M. (1997). Measuring quality of life: Economic, social, and subjective indicators. *Social Indicators Research*, *40*(1–2): 189–216. doi:10.1023/ A:1006859511756.

DiFonzo, Nicholas, and Bordia, Prashant. (2007a). *Rumor psychology: Social and organizational approaches*. Washington, DC: American Psychological Association.

DiFonzo, Nicholas, and Bordia, Prashant. (2007b). Rumors influence: Toward a dynamic social impact theory of rumor. In A. R. Pratkanis (Ed.), *Frontiers of social psychology. The science of social influence: Advances and future progress* (pp. 271–295). London, UK: Psychology Press

Dodge, Rachel, Daly, Annette P., Huyton, Jan, and Sanders, Lalage Dorothy (2012). The challenge of defining wellbeing. *International Journal of Wellbeing*, *2*(3): 222–235. doi:10.5502/ijw.v2i3.4.

Doerr, Benjamin, Fouz, Mahmoud, and Friedrich, Tobias. (2012). Why rumors spread so quickly in social networks. *Communications of the ACM*. June 2012, 55(6): 70–75.

Fisher, Marc, Cox, John Woodrow, and Hermann, Peter. (2016). *Pizzagate: From rumor, to hashtag, to gunfire in D.C.* Washington Post, December 6, 2016.

Floridi, Luciano (Ed.) (2014). *The onlife manifesto. Being human in a hyperconnected era*. Oxford: Springer.

Garimella, Kiran, and Eckles, Dean. (2020). Images and Misinformation in Political Groups: Evidence from WhatsApp in India. Preprint. DOI: arxiv-2005.09784.

Grosser, Travis J., Lopez-Kidwell, Virginie, Labianca, Giuseppe (Joe), and Ellwardt, Lea. (2012). Hearing it through the grapevine: Positive and negative workplace gossip. *Organizational Dynamics,* 41(1), January–March 2012: 52–61.

Gui, Marco, Fasoli, Marco and Carradore, Roberto. (2017). "Digital Wellbeing". Developing a new theoretical tool for media literacy research. *Italian Journal of Sociology of Education*, 9(1), 155–173. doi:10.14658/pupj-ijse-2017-1-8.

Gui, Marco, Gerosa, Tiziano, Garavaglia, Andrea, Petti, Livia, and Fasoli, Marco. (2018). *Digital Wellbeing. Validation of a Digital Media Education Proposal in High Schools.* Research Report: https://ecrea.eu/page-18206/7277306

Gwinner, K., Melrose, P. and Moffatt, A. (2017). *Digital wellbeing, youth engagement consultation project: Technical report.* Brisbane, Australia. Kids Helpline, and Brisbane Youth Service. https://eprints.qut.edu.au/view/person/Gwinner,_Karleen.html

Headey, Bruce W., and Wearing, Alex J. (1992). *Understanding happiness: A theory of subjective wellbeing.* Melbourne: Longman Cheshire.

Huang, Y. Linlin, Starbird, Kate, Orand, Mania, Stanek, Stephanie A., and Pedersen, Heather T. (2015). Connected through crisis: Emotional proximity and the spread of misinformation online. *Collaborating Around Crisis. CSCW 2015.* March 14–18, 2015, Vancouver, BC, Canada.

Iordache, Cătălina, Mariën, Ilse, and Baelden, Dorien (2017). Developing digital skills and competences: A quick-scan analysis of 13 digital literacy models. *Italian Journal of Sociology of Education*, 9(1), 6–30. doi:10.14658/pupj-ijse-2017-1-2.

Jisc. (2018). *Jisc digital capabilities framework: The six elements defined.* http://repository.jisc.ac.uk /7278/1/ BDCP-DC-Framework-Individual-6E-110319.pdf

Kakar, Sudhir. (2004). Rumors and religious riots. In G. A. Fine, V. Campion-Vincent, and C. Heath (Eds.), *Rumor Mills: The social impact of rumor and legend*. New Jersey: Transaction Publishers.

Kim, Heewon. (2014). Enacted social support on social media and subjective wellbeing. *International Journal of Communication* 8 (2014): 2340–2342, 1932–8036/20140005, pp. 2201–2221.

Koohang, Alex, and Weiss, Edward. (2003). Misinformation: Toward creating a prevention framework. *Information Science*, 3, 109–115.

Knopf, Terry Ann. (1975). *Rumors, race, and riots*. Piscataway, NJ: Transaction Publishers.

Melo, Philipe de Freitas, Coimbra Vieira, Carolina, Garimella, Kiran, Vaz de Melo, Pedro O. S., and Benevenuto, Fabrício. (2019). *Can WhatsApp Counter Misinformation by Limiting Message Forwarding?* https://arxiv.org/abs/1909.08740

Nansen, Bjorn, Chakraborty, Kabita, Gibbs, Lisa, MacDougall, Colin, and Vetere, Frank. (2011). Children and digital wellbeing in Australia: Online regulation, conduct and competence. *Journal of Children and Media*. doi:10.1080/17482798.2011.619548.

OECD (2019a). *Going digital: Shaping policies, improving lives*. Paris: OECD Publishing. doi:10.1787/9789264312012-en.

OECD (2019b). *How's life in the digital age? Opportunities and risks of the digital transformation for people's wellbeing*. Paris: OECD Publishing. doi:10.1787/9789264311800-en.

Pamment, James, Nothhaft, Howard, Agardh-Twetman, Henrik, and Fjällhed, Alicia. (2018). *Countering information influence activities: The state of the art*. Department of Strategic Communication, Lund University.

Rebecca Birch Stirling. (1956). Some psychological mechanisms operative in gossip. *Social Forces* 34(3), March 1956: 262–267. doi:10.2307/2574050.

Reis, Julio C. S., Melo, Philipe, Garimellaz, Kiran, Almeida, Jussara M., Ecklesz, Dean, and Benevenuto, Fabrício. (2020). A dataset of fact-checked images shared on WhatsApp during the Brazilian and Indian elections. *Proceedings of the International AAAI Conference on Web and Social Media* 14(1): 903–908. Retrieved from https://aaai.org/ojs/index.php/ICWSM/article/view/7356.

Roffarello, Alberto Monge, and De Russis, Luigi. (2019). The race towards digital wellbeing: Issues and opportunities. In *CHI conference on human factors in computing systems proceedings (CHI 2019)*, May 4–9, 2019, Glasgow, Scotland UK. New York, NY, USA: ACM, 14 pages. doi:10.1145/3290605.3300616.

Rosnow, Ralf L., and Fine, Gary Alan. (1976). *Rumor and gossip: The social psychology of hearsay*. New York: Elsevier.

Royo, Carme, Sime, Julie-Ann, Themelis, Chryssa, and Sicilia, Miguel Angel. (2019). Digital wellbeing education – a compendium of innovative practices. *Eucen Studies – Journal of University Lifelong Learning* 3(01), 13–18.

Ryff, Carol D. (1989). Happiness is everything, or is it? Explorations on the meaning of psychological wellbeing. *Journal of Personality and Social Psychology*, 57, 1069–1081. doi:10.1037/0022-3514.57.6.1069.

Ryff, Carol D., & Keyes, Corey Lee M. (1995). The structure of psychological wellbeing revisited. *Journal of Personality and Social Psychology* 69(4), 719–727. doi:10.1037/0022-3514.69.4.719.

Schwartz, H. Andrew, Sap, Maarten, Kern, Margaret L., Eichstaedt, Johannes C., Kapelner, Adam, Agrawal, Megha, Blanco, Eduardo, Dziurzynski, Lukasz, Park, Gregory, Stillwell, David, Kosinski, Michal, Seligman, Martin E. P., and Ungar, Lyle H. (2016). Predicting individual wellbeing through the language of social media. *Conference: Pacific Symposium on Biocomputing.* doi:10.1142/9789814749411_0047.

Shaw, Allison K., Tsvetkova, Milena, and Daneshvar, Roozbeh. (2011). The effect of gossip on social networks. *Journal Complexity* 16(4), 39–47.

Solomos, John. (2011). Race, rumours and riots: Past, present and future. *Sociological Research Online* 16(4): 20 http://www.socresonline.org.uk/16/4/20.html

Statista. (2020). https://www.statista.com/statistics/272014/global-social-networks-ranked-by-number-of-users/

Swist, Teresa, Collin, Philippa, McCormack, Jane, and Third, Amanda. (2015). Social media and the wellbeing of children and young people: A literature review. doi: 10.13140/RG.2.1.3296.6885.

Tanaka, Yuko, Sakamoto, Yasuaki, and Matsuka, Toshihiko. (2013). Toward a social-technological system that inactivates false rumors through the critical thinking of crowds. *46th Hawaii international conference on system sciences.* pp. 649–658.

Tesar, Marek and Peters, Michael A. (2019). Heralding ideas of wellbeing: A philosophical perspective. *Educational Philosophy and Theory.* doi:10.1080/00131857.2019.1696731.

Thorseth, May. (2014). On tolerance and fictitious publics. In L. Floridi (Eds.), *The onlife manifesto. Being human in a hyperconnected era.* Oxford: Springer.

van Dijck, José, Poell, Thomas, Waal, Martijn de. (2018). *The platform society. Public values in a connective world.* New York: Oxford University Press.

van Dijk, Jan A. G. M. [1991] (2006). *The network society. Social aspects of new media.* London: SAGE Publications.

Vosoughi, Soroush, Roy, Deb, and Aral, Sinan. (2018). The spread of true and false news online. *Science* 359: 1146–1151.

Wajcman, Judy. (2015). *Pressed for time. The acceleration of life in digital capitalism*. Chicago and London: The University of Chicago Press.

Zollo, Fabiana, and Quattrociocchi, Walter. (2018). Misinformation spreading on Facebook. In Sune Lehmann and Yong-Yeol Ahn (Eds.), *Complex spreading phenomena in social systems. Influence and contagion in real-world social networks* (pp. 177–196). Cham, Switzerland: Springer.

Zubiaga, Arkaitz, Liakata, Maria, Procter, Rob, Bontcheva, Kalina, and Tolmie, Peter. (2015). Towards detecting rumours in social media. *Conference paper: AAAI 2015 workshop on AI for cities.*

Zubiaga, Arkaitz, Aker, Ahmet, Bontcheva, Kalina, Liakata, Maria, and Procter, Rob. (2018). Detection and resolution of rumors in social media: A survey. *ACM Computing Surveys* 51, 2, Article 32 (February 2018), 36 pages. doi:10.1145/3161603.

Editha Margareta COȘARBĂ and Henrietta TORKOS

13 Developing Digital Well-Being Skills through New Education Types in Primary Schools

Abstract: This chapter presents a brief study on the contribution of school subjects within the new education types in the development of digital well-being skills in primary school. The theoretical frame enhances two main directions: the value of new education types in the Romanian national curricula in primary schools and their correct use in order to develop skills of pupils regarding digital well-being. There has been made an analysis of the way in which the curricula support and motivate the use of some school subjects in primary school, in order to develop digital skills of pupils, necessary in the twenty-first century education. It establishes the main guidance regarding digital instruments meant to be used within the classrooms and eventual safety methods in the digital area. It also contains a research on the use of digital instruments in the instructive educational practice of primary school teachers within Arad County and the rate in which some new educations contribute to the development of healthy use of information and communication technology (ICT) in the classroom and outside of it. The main instrument used was the questionnaire applied to a number of 98 primary school teachers within educational institutions from Arad County. The preliminary results show that pupils are not sufficiently supervised while using ICT in schools, neither motivated sufficiently to use digital resources during lessons.

Keywords: Digital, skills, online, classroom

Introduction

To think of education as one for change was a signal given in 1926 by W.H. Kilpatrik, but the one who raised the issue of such an education was Gaston Bergher: "The specificity of our world is that it is changing faster and faster and that it puts us in front of original, even unpredictable situations", he wrote, wanting to emphasize the fact that the emphasis is falling primarily on human training in education. It is an education that ensures, above all, a behavior open to change and an attitude that gives and provides the use of innovative behavioral techniques.

The projection of the future and the redefinition of a healthy society depend to a large extent on this conscious and active involvement, and the development in a world of globalization, as a result of intensifying interdependencies between peoples, presupposes and involves social modernization ensuring competitiveness with developed states world. "Contemporary society leads its existence in a world of openness, when tomorrow it is necessary to know more and differently than today, to be able to do something we have never done before when we learned to do something" (Niculescu, 2006).

Curricular reform involves a set of innovative changes at the macro and micro educational levels that can ensure the necessary interdependencies between the instructive-educational contents, the teaching and learning strategies, and the evaluation strategies of the educational activity. The complex and integrated nature of some processes – issues such as globalization, migration, interculturality, environmental protection, information explosion, poverty, and also local conflicts, demands an educational approach adapted to the constantly changing society.

The individual of the society of the future thus needs to be well equipped in a world where the speed, complexity, and depth with which change takes place produce real "shocks." From the competence of a country springs the force of its development, and this competence is in man, in the way he actively and efficiently responds to the need for education. The quantitative and qualitative evolution of education, the effectiveness with which the school fulfills its social mission, is decisive for the future of any society in which it operates (Marinescu, 2013). Learning acquires new values. Depending on the requirements of the mentioned ideals, the type of human formation is outlined to be able to "know" and especially to want to "become," according to the new needs and configurations of the future society. On this basis, starting from the x-ray of the society in which we live, the educational ideal of the time and the world in which we live is outlined, so that today's and tomorrow's generations adapt to the new living conditions, to the new tasks, at the same time, finding their place, role, and purpose, developing their personality and enriching their personal life.

Students must acquire strategic skills and competencies to cope with the uncertainties and continuous changes of today's world, knowledge, and skills wider than those provided by previous specializations. First, among them, skills to learn how to learn, problem-solving skills, assessment skills.

Theoretical Foundation

School success is given by the student's ability to "perform" in various structures and disciplinary contexts, while success in personal, professional, and social life is given by the ability to get out of the disciplinary approach and by the ability to make connections and rapid transfers leading to the effective resolution of the concrete problems they face. In recent years, there has been a broadening of attention and concerns from focusing on the formalized institutionalized structure of education – schooling – to the broader learning process. This takes place not only in schools, but also in contemporary societies outside of school. Families, community, and media are learning environments. Culture, considered the main gain of humanity to be transmitted through education, has greatly expanded its significance and, in addition, has changed its accents, from academic culture to oral and audio-visual culture, from the predominance of monoculturalism toward intercultural openness.

The Computerized Educational System in Romania – Historical Landmarks

Socio-economic changes, accelerated scientific development, and the expansion of the use of modern technology tools lead to the need to develop specific skills to be able to actively participate in social life to use the tools of the information society.

Current trends in countries with developed economies have shown that education and the development of human potential are and should be seen as priorities of national strategies and policies in the social, economic, and technological fields. Education becomes a main tool of the development of modern societies and is considered as a premise for economic and technological changes (Cristea, 2008).

A specific objective of European programs is to integrate individuals into the information society in terms of knowledge, motivation, and skills, as a tool to strengthen labor market awareness and improve the adaptability of the workforce.

The effectiveness of these issues will change the pace of change and determine the extent to which the practice of information and communication technology (ICT) learning becomes either fundamental to a new educational paradigm applicable at all levels of the education system or a viable complementary version of existing model. The challenges imposed by building the knowledge-based society, in the perspective of using new technologies, have a direct impact on the education and teaching systems, determining specific developments in legislation, management, material base, curriculum, and educational structure.

As early as 2001, a report from the European Commission – Directorate-General for Education and Culture – states that "the incorporation of information and communication technologies into European education systems is a process that will have major implications for the organization of learning and teaching methods in the long run." This sector has become an educational priority, and all European Union countries are working to include ICT in the school curriculum and in teacher training programs.

The knowledge society has imposed the use of information and communication technologies as a reference point for fundamental changes in education systems, and the challenges were initially outlined in three major directions, starting with the summits in Lisbon and Feira: equipping schools, training teachers, and providing the necessary resources. Subsequently, combining with other priority directions, such as quality assurance in education, lifelong learning, and professionalization of teaching (Commission of the European Communities, 2001).

The increase of the performances of the Romanian education system with the support of information and communication technologies was declared in 1998 a priority objective by the Ministry of Education and Research. The SEI-Computerized Educational System program consists of a set of projects and activities aimed at implementing information and communication technologies in pre-university education and increasing the access of students and teachers to modern technologies and the Internet.

The SEI project has been running since 2001 by the Ministry of Education and Research, being organized in four implementation phases. The pilot phase (2001) aimed at equipping 120 computer laboratories, being supplemented during the projects ADLIC (Computerized Admission in High Schools) and Evalman (Computerized Assessment of textbooks). Also during this period, in this first phase, the foundations of the SEI educational portal (portal.edu.ro) were laid. The second phase was carried out in the period 2002–2003 and consisted of the computerization of 1,100 high schools, the initiation of 15,000 teachers in the use of computers, the development of multimedia educational content. The third phase, January-August 2004, aimed at equipping another 290 laboratories, guaranteeing the information of the 1,510 high schools in Romania, the development of 350 multimedia lessons. In the fourth phase, started in December 2004, the computerization of 3,300 primary and secondary schools, the elaboration of 1,400 lessons in electronic format, and the initiation of 20,000 teachers were foreseen.

The impact of information technology on school education is remarkable, and it seems that this development will lead to position effects, the computer introduced in education is an "information enhancer" (Levy, 1995).

Recent Perspectives

In recent decades, modern man is identified by the presence of new types of problems, which are imposed both by their serious and pressing character, and by their regional and universal dimensions. Such problems are continuous deterioration of the environment (both terrestrial and marine), deterioration of the atmosphere, limitation of natural resources, the rampant nature of population growth in some areas, etc. Contemporary life is characterized by a series of mutations: the amplification and unpredictability of economic and socio-political changes, the intensification of changes in the sphere of professions, and the amplification of the interdependencies between the social macrosystem and its components. New education should not be seen only as a source of renewal and reconstruction of content that derives from the traditional dimensions of education. It is the merit of the Romanian school regarding the preoccupations for the problem of the new educations, which coincided with the preoccupations from the western world. In a high-tech society, we should look at new education not as isolated dimensions, but in their multiple systemic relationships and from the perspective of the future effect (Marinescu, 2013).

The ability to master modern technologies intellectually, politically, and socially is one of the major challenges of modern man in this century. The new educations in the order of their appearance would be:

- Environmental education (or ecological education);
- Population education (or demographic education);
- Nutritional education;
- Education for new technology and progress;
- Education toward the media;
- Education for peace and cooperation;
- Education for democracy and human rights;
- Modern health education;
- Modern economic and domestic education;
- Education for free time;
- Education for a new international order;
- Education with an international vocation;
- Education for a quality life;
- Intercultural education, etc.

According to Butnari, the main competencies that can be developed by studying these new forms of education are as follows:

- Manifestation of a solidary, tolerant, and civic spiritual openness in relation to others, by respecting fundamental right of man, in the context of general human and national values;
- Cooperative and collaborative resolution of interpersonal conflicts;
- Managing one's own human development (personal and professional) starting from the premise of positive and necessary adaptation to current changes;
- Constructive capitalization of the information taken from the media, in the context of general human values and national values;
- Efficient management of one's free time in the sense of training and personal development;
- Designing a healthy lifestyle from a biological, psychological, and social point of view;
- Active participation in projects of community interest in order to make the ecological, sanitary-public, and demographic environment more efficient and a family;
- Elaboration of business plans in the sectors of the national economy;
- Capitalization of various psycho-pedagogical and demographic strategies, etc., in order to create a solid family, based on integral moral principles (Butnari, 2017).

Today, more than ever, in a society characterized by an accelerated dynamic of structural changes, but also of the depth of these changes, of the placement of man in the context of these "technological outbursts," constantly raises new tasks for education, which must be to face them. All over the world, due to the many achievements, there is a growing feeling of insecurity and anxiety, observing how under our eyes in the "file of human nature" there is more change than we can digest. The use of technologies implies a degree of civilization, and the advantages of civilization do not require demonstrations, once the products of the technological revolution are part of our environment (Marcu and Marinescu, 2011).

Through the computer and virtual networks, each person can get in touch with other people, with other ways of thinking and targeting things. The information system is additive, cumulative, and multidirectional, each additional connection adds the new, opens other interpretive keys, and regenerates the collective intelligence (Michel, 1999).

The insertion of ICT in the educational activity has a strong impact on the didactic strategies and on the development of some forms of organization of the training that are not possible with the help of the traditional methods and means. The act of learning is no longer considered to be the effect of the teacher's efforts, but the fruit of the student's interactions with the learner, with the computer, with the mobile phone, and with the information sources provided (Internet, online collaborative learning environments, etc.). Among the advantages of learning and benefiting from ICT insertion, we mention the following (Pisău et al. 2019):

- Stimulating the capacity for innovative learning, adaptable to conditions of rapid social change;
- Consideration of learning from the point of view of the subsequent use of the acquired knowledge;
- Individualization of learning and increasing the efficiency of conscious acquisition of knowledge through immediate appreciation of students' responses;
- Achieving interdisciplinary, interactive, and student-centered learning, using heuristic methods;
- Developing the creativity of students who learn using specific educational software;
- Reducing learning time and raising the quality of learning;
- Increasing the interest and motivation of learners;
- Ensuring access to information;
- Creating interactive representations;
- Ensuring the tactical and strategic support of the educational process;
- Diagnosis and correction of errors;
- Ensuring the management of activities.

Specific Skills and Competencies of Teachers in Relation to Information Technologies

As they adapt to new teaching methods and means, teachers are forced to acquire new skills and abilities related to the methodology of disciplines, in an integrated self-training approach, involving: multimedia resource management to achieve learning objectives, software design educational on pedagogical theoretical bases, and rethinking the teaching-learning-evaluation activities from the perspective of human-computer interaction.

The skills of information technologies required of teachers can be classified into the following categories (Cristea, 2008):

- Basic operations: without asking teachers to become experts in the use of the computer, a number of skills and abilities can be listed that allow them to manipulate the computer to perform basic operations in training activities assisted by new technologies: the proper use of various components and peripherals of the computer, the use of information storage media, and customization of the work environment under a widely used operating system.
- Information technology: teachers are increasingly placed in the situation of manipulating information for documentation, preparing the new lesson, presenting information, developing tests, assessment tests, on-line collaboration activities with other teachers at distance, etc. These activities are associated with specific skills and competences in the use of information technology: to locate information, to select the appropriate applications and software, to organize materials, to analyze the relevance of information, and to present it appropriately through the minimal use of information.
- Evaluation of the educational software: in the context of the computerization strategy of the Romanian education, the lessons on electronic support start to become a usual tool of the teacher who wants to give an extra quality to the teaching-learning-evaluation process. This involves the ability to select multimedia materials and e-lessons in accordance with the learning objectives, respectively, the ability to assess the relevance of an electronic material for an educational situation.
- Pedagogical aspects of the use of new technologies in training: the role of new technologies in learning, and of educational software in particular, varies from providing access to information and knowledge to facilitating the understanding of phenomena, individualized training, etc. In order to be able to effectively use various applications in electronic format in teaching, along with technological initiation in computer use, teachers need a pedagogical introduction appropriate to the new requirements: curriculum design with computer technology component, development of lesson plans starting from learning objectives, elaboration of interactive didactic strategies that include educational objects in electronic format.

Methodology

Through the questionnaire-based survey method, the study centralizes and analyzes the individual experience of 98 teachers in relation to the implementation of new education in pre-university education through the use of information technologies.

The questionnaire, the researchers' own conception, includes questions related two areas of interest: one of them regarding new education types and the other one regarding ITC and its use in primary schools from Arad County.

Of the 21 items of the questionnaire, 5 represent identification variables, 15 items give teachers the opportunity to select answer options, giving the possibility to perform a clear and relevant statistical analysis.

Among the reference questions, we mention: *Do you know which are the disciplines within the new educations?, How often do you use digital means in the classroom to facilitate the instructive-educational process?, How often do you organize activities that include the use of information technologies for the group you work with?, How would you assess your level of confidence in information technology in the development of transversal skills and life skills? How would you assess your level of confidence in the effectiveness of the use of digital elements and information technology in terms of information assimilation and learning content?*

Out of the total number of surveyed teachers, 36 % carry out their instructive-educational activity in rural areas, and 64 % in urban areas.

Compared to the age category of the teachers who completed the questionnaire, there was a significant variation, so 9 % of teachers are aged between 19 and 25 years, 20 % are aged between 26 and 35 years, 34 % are ages between 36 and 45 years, 28 % between 46 and 55 years, and 9 % between 56 and 61 years.

Identifying the form of employment in the Romanian education system of the surveyed teachers, we found that 56.9 % have concluded employment contracts with the educational units in which they work indefinitely, 33.7 % have as a form of employment a determined period, and 9.4 % are employed by the hourly payment.

Regarding the item that refers to the seniority in education, we can conclude that 23.6 % of the teachers who completed the questionnaire are less than 5 years old, 30.3 % carry out their teaching activity in education of 6 to 10 years, 27 % have a seniority in education between 11 and 20 years, and 19.1 % have a seniority of over 20 years in education.

At the first question, which analyzes the knowledge about new education types, primary school teachers answered in the following way:

The results show that the participants at the present study admit that their knowledge on the new education types is at small extent (47.7 %). Only a small number of teachers say they know nothing about new education types and a similar number admit knowing about this concept at a total basic.

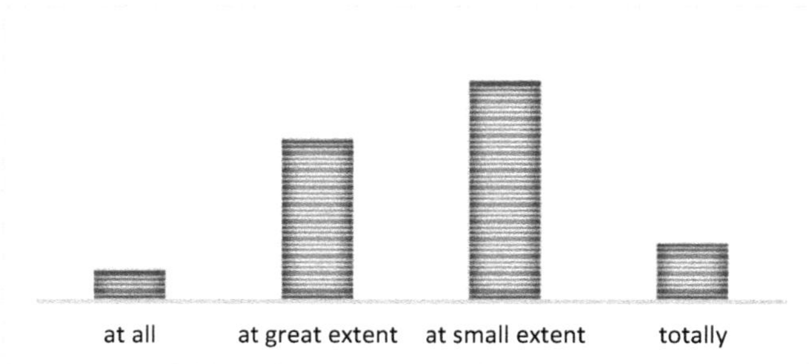

Graphic 1. Primary school teacher's knowledge of new education types

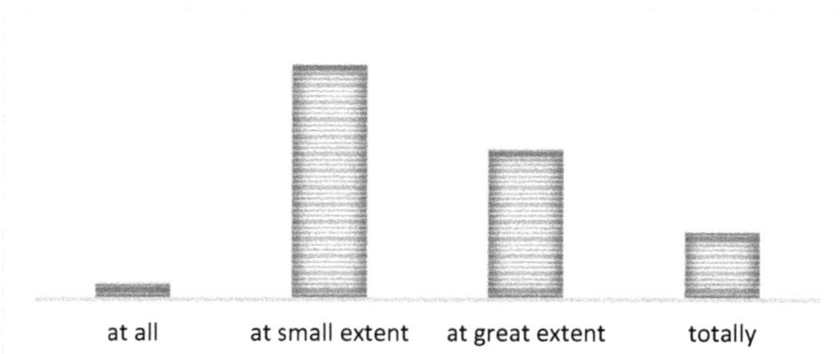

Graphic 2. Primary school teacher's knowledge of ICT

The other element in the structure of the questionnaire, was the knowledge of ITC instruments. The answers were structured as it follows:

As there can be seen, the results are distributed in a similar way as the one of the analysis of knowledge on new education types. This can show a positive correlation between the use of new education types in the instructive process in primary schools and the use of ICT.

The present study was concerned about the place that ICT gets in the mentality and culture of the participants. The results are presented in the following graph:

As the results show, 38.9 % of the respondents, believe that ICT is the totality of the digital means used in the educational process. Only 14.4 % of the participants, think that ICT is a subject within the new education types.

Tab. 1. Positive correlations between the knowledge of new education types and ICT concept familiarity

Independent Samples Test

		Levine's Test for Equality of Variances		t-test for Equality of Means						
									95 % Confidence Interval of the Difference	
		F	Sig.	t	df	Sig. (2-tailed)	Mean Difference	Std. Error Difference	Lower	Upper
TOTALFOPOST	Equal variances assumed	7,605	,010	8,920	31	**,000**	6,089	,683	4,697	7,481
	Equal variances not assumed			9,433	25,991	**,000**	6,089	,646	4,762	7,416

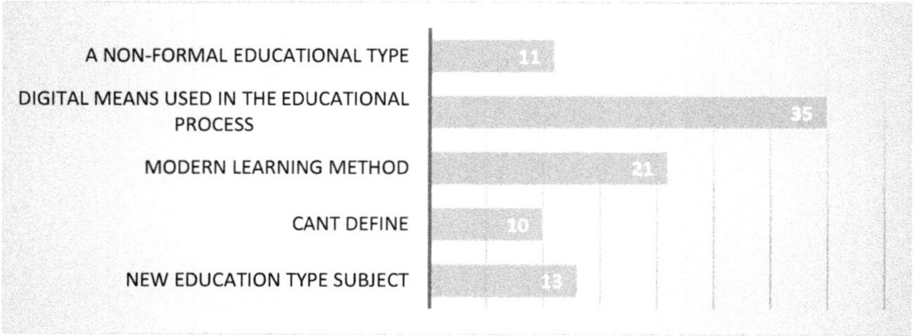

Graphic 3. Primary school teachers answer regarding the definition of ICT

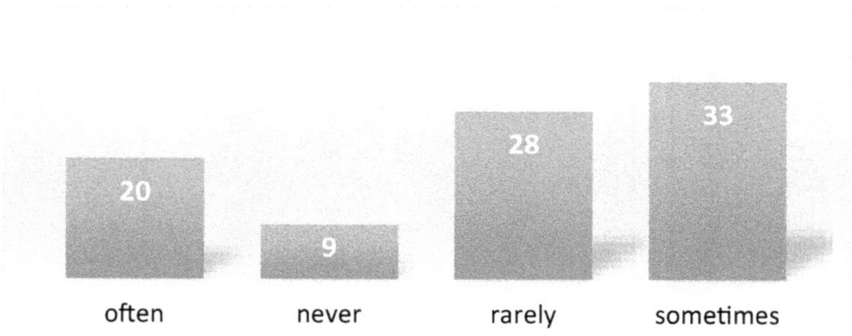

Graphic 4. The rate of ICT instruments use in primary schools from Arad county, in order the facilitate the instructive-educational process

The next question of interest of the present study was the rate in which teachers use ICT at class, in their educational routines, because the answer at this question can also show the interest they show in the digital well-being of their pupils. The results are presented as it follows:

As the results show, most of the participants answered that they rarely use ICT instruments in order to facilitate the instructive educational process in their classes (31.1 %). There were only 9 respondents that never use ICT in class in order to ease the learning process.

Tab. 2. Positive correlations between time of using ICT in class and the development of some transversal competencies

Independent Samples Test										
		Levene's Test for Equality of Variances		t-test for Equality of Means						
									95 % Confidence Interval of the Difference	
		F	Sig.	t	df	Sig. (2-tailed)	Mean Difference	Std. Error Difference	Lower	Upper
TOTALICT	Equal variances assumed	1,257	,271	13,784	31	**,000**	5,989	,434	5,103	6,875
	Equal variances not assumed			13,933	30,835	**,000**	5,989	,430	5,112	6,866
TOTALICTCOMP	Equal variances assumed	,952	,337	11,325	31	**,000**	8,333	,736	6,833	9,834
	Equal variances not assumed			10,921	23,587	**,000**	8,333	,763	6,757	9,910

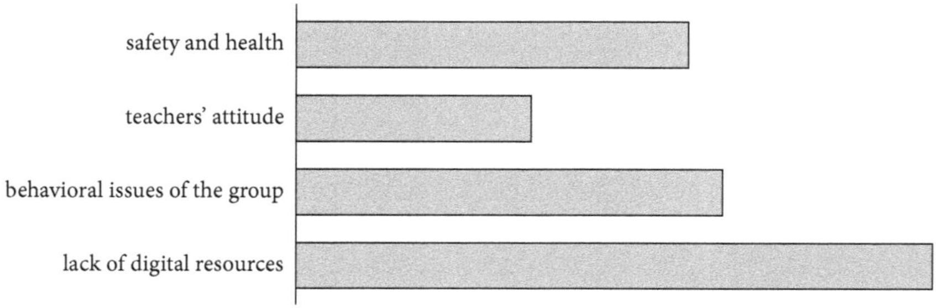

Graphic 5. The influences in decision making regarding introduction of ICT

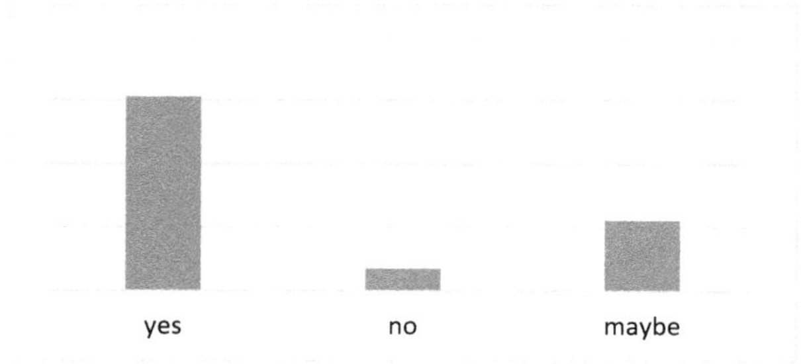

Graphic 6. Primary school teachers as organizer of activities that contain ICT elements at their own classes

The answers from this question are positively correlated to the answers of the following questions:

- the weekly time teachers allow pupils to spend using ICT instruments;
- the rate of organization of activities that involve the use of ICT;
- the trust in using ICT in classes in order to develop some competences.

Another interesting question of the present study was whether primary school teachers that have participated in the research are influenced by some elements in their decisions regarding the introduction of ICT elements in their daily routine, and which of these have the greatest influence on this issue. The results are presented as follows:

As it can be seen in Graphic 5, teachers use ICT the least, because of the lack of digital and technological resources. This is unfortunately still a problem in some schools. There have been some positive correlations between the area of

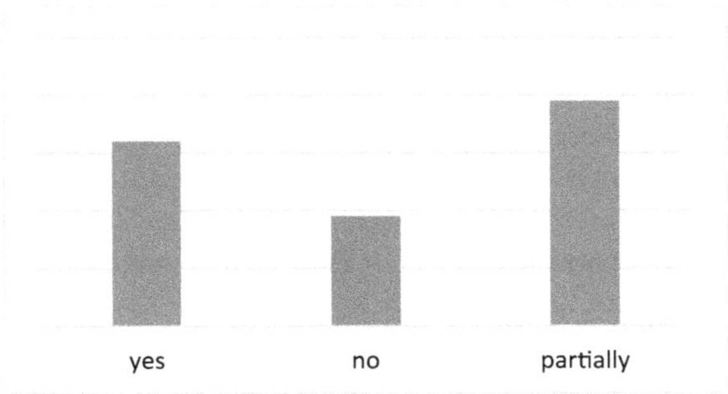

Graphic 7. The access to digital and technological instruments of primary school teachers in the classes they work in

practice and the answer to this question, considering the fact that most of the respondents that have checked this answer work in the rural area.

The second reason for not using ICT in primary school teachers weekly routine of those who participated in the present study is "behavioral issues of the group," meaning that teachers refuse to allow the usage of ICT in classes or during school time because they fear of not being able to control the group. "Safety and health" was the choice of 37.8 % of the respondents, which is still a big number when thinking of the number of time studies show pupils spend in front of digital gadgets. The attitude of teachers was the answer of only a number of 20 teachers, which is also concerning, considering the fact that teachers' choice influences a lot the use of different elements in the learning process.

The other question that was subject of analysis is if primary school teachers from Arad County, who participated in the present study, believe that teachers from class can organize learning through the use of ICT themselves or if specialized teachers are needed for it. The answers were in majority: yes, teachers from class can themselves organize learning activities without the need of specialized teachers in this matter. Only 7.8 % of the respondents think that they can't organize this ICT-related activities for their class. There is a correlation between those who have answered this and those who do not believe that ICT in class can develop certain competencies and also those who are not interested in using it in order to ease the learning process.

The last question that we have considered at great importance regarding the complementarity of new education types and the use of ICT in primary schools from Arad County was whether teachers have or not have access to ICT instruments.

The results show that most of the participants have only partial access to the digital and ICT resources in the classes they work in, which is the main reason for not using ICT as part of new education types in the daily teaching-learning process. Twenty-one percent of the subjects have declared that they do not have access to ICT instruments at all, even if some of the participants said that they would use it if they would have it at their disposal.

A number of 32 primary school teachers have answered that they have access to ICT instruments at the classes they work in, and they were also the ones that have declared to trust in the benefits of it and use it as often as they can, in order to ease the educational process and mostly in order to develop lifelong abilities in their pupils life.

Conclusions

This brief research has shown the strong connections between new educational types and the use of ICT in the desire to offer healthy digital environments for primary school pupils. The respondents have shown interest in the introduction and exploitation of ICT as a new education type in primary schools, as great tools of offering qualitative education. The results have shown that there is an increased interest in learning more about digital safety and the use of ICT instruments among the respondents.

Most of the primary school teachers that have completed the questionnaire admit they have got into contact with both analyzed concepts through classes or pedagogical committees, (37.8 %) and a number of 33 respondents say they have gotten into contact with the concepts from the internet. This shows that there is a need of courses for teachers in order to raise awareness regarding this issue. Ten percent of the respondents have said that they have never heard of new education types nor ICT use in class and the same percentage said that they have found out about this subject from TV. Only 5 % of the respondents admit reading about this topic in a specialty magazine or books.

These results show that there is plenty of space to be filled in regarding this topic, which have motivated us to do some more research on this subject and also to work on practical ways to introduce the benefits of ICT use as new education type in primary schools from Arad County.

References

Butnari, N. (2017), Noile educaţii. Suport de curs, Editura Universităţii de Stat, Moldova

Commission of the European Communities. 2001. The concrete future objectives of education system. Brussels

Cristea, S. (2008), Curriculum pedagogic, Editura Didactică şi Pedagogică

European Comission, Directorate-General for Education and Culture. Basic Indicators on the Incorporation of ICT into European Education System. Facts and figures. 2000/01 Annual Report

Legea învăţământului nr. 84/24.07.1995, actualizată până la data de 25.06.2003

Levy, P. (1995), *Qu'est-ce le virtuel?*, Editions La Decouverte, Paris

Marcu, V., Marinescu, M. (2011), Implementarea tehnologiilor în educaţie sau educaţia tehnologică, https://vdocuments.mx/implementarea-tehnologiilor-in-educatie-sau-educatia-tehnologica.html

Marinescu, M. (2013), Noile educaţii în societatea cunoaşterii, Editura Pro Universitaria, Bucureşti

Michel, J. (1999), *Nouvelles approches de la formationa par les mouvelles technologies et le multimedia. La demarche de l'ecole nationale des ponts et chaussees*, Communication faite au colloqe organmise par Le Journal du Multimedia a Paris

Niculescu, R. M. (2006), Dramă şi metaforă în educaţie, Editura Univers Trans. Braşov

Pisău, C., Cătănescu, G., Dragomir, R., Dragomir, C., Soare, T., Burlacu-Călinoiu, R. (2019), *Integrarea noilor tehnologii în educaţie. Ghid metodic pentru profesori*, Editura Casa Corpului didactic, Prahova

Egerău Anca MANUELA

14 Challenges and Possibilities Regarding the Integration of Health Education Models for Digital Well-Being in Preschool and Primary School

Abstract The modern education area has lately been invaded with new social requirements. One of them is the preoccupation of educational institutions in providing instruction in the safe use of digital instruments. Mostly, it is desired to create proper teaching-learning situations in order to motivate safety in the digital area. This chapter presents the theoretical bases of health education and its contribution in the maintenance of digital well-being. Also, it sets the frame of digital safety in the preschool and primary school environment. The brief research is based on the use of health education between teachers that have different qualifications from pre- and primary schools, within Arad county. The main instrument used is the questionnaire. There have been 112 participants from 15 preschools and primary schools from Arad county. The subjects have expressed their opinions regarding the use of health education in their daily practice in connection with the use of digital technology. The preliminary results have shown that the participants do not offer sufficient instruction to their pupils regarding health education, nor time or methods to develop competencies that would lead to safe digital use.

Keywords: Digital, challenges, models, health education

Introduction

In recent years, there has been a broadening of attention and concerns from focusing on the formalized institutionalized structure of education – schooling – to the broader learning process. This no longer takes place only in schools, but in fact most learning seems to take place in contemporary societies outside of school. Families, community, and media are learning environments. Culture, considered the main gain of humanity to be transmitted through education, has greatly expanded its significance and, in addition, has changed its accents, from academic culture to oral and audio-visual culture, from the predominance of monoculturalism toward intercultural openness. Learning, therefore, is no longer just the prerogative of pupils and students, being concentrated as an activity, especially in the first part of life; the evolution and characteristics of contemporary society have led to the assertion and necessity of the idea of lifelong learning.

The interdisciplinary approach emerged as a reaction to the disintegration of the modern intellectual space with the aim of preserving the global character of the intellect. Interdisciplinarity identifies a component of the environment for the organization of knowledge and involves the development of a system of knowledge at the intersection of several areas of knowledge and skills to use this knowledge for new acquisitions to solve complex problem situations.

Theoretical Foundation

The introduction of transdisciplinary topics as a separate discipline solves the problem of different approaches given to the same topic in different study objects, but it is necessary to identify a "free space" in the curriculum, which should be assigned to the new study object. The introduction of a new discipline also has a number of legal implications (its validation by decision makers). Another problem is that of selecting the topics that will become new objects of study in the school curriculum (number, criteria, and arguments). At the same time, the introduction of new disciplines consumes from that space through which schools can create their own profile or affect the time budget of other disciplines. Therefore, the reactions of the actors involved will not always be favorable. From the perspective of curricular development, it is necessary to build a new curriculum; it is about the development of the theoretical and methodological framework, as well as about curricular support materials for students, for teachers, and for professional training activities. It is important to note that integrated topics do not focus primarily on practicing specific skills or accumulating knowledge. The emphasis is mainly on the application of knowledge and skills acquired in new situations.

The aims of integrated topics usually consider the support that needs to be given to students to understand how the knowledge and skills they acquire can be combined to complete a task, to discover a solution or to understand and explain a situation (Cucoş, 2006).

Recent Perspectives

Health is the process in which all aspects of a person's life work together in an integrated way. No aspect of life works in isolation. Body, mind, spirit, family, community, country, workplace, education, and beliefs are all interrelated. The way in which these aspects interact contributes to the enrichment of a person's life, which helps to determine the uniqueness of the person and his health. Health includes more than just the smooth running of the body. It also involves mental-emotional, intellectual, and social relationships, as well as spiritual values. From a modern point of view, health has several dimensions – emotional, intellectual, physical, social, and spiritual, each of which contributes to the well-being of a person.

Health promotion is the process that gives individuals and communities the opportunity to increase their control over the determinants of health and, thus, to improve their health. A unifying concept for those who recognize the fundamental need to change both lifestyle and living conditions health promotion is a strategy of mediation between the individual and the environment, combining personal choice with social responsibility and aiming to ensure a future better health (WHO-EURO, Health Promotion Glossary, 1989). Health promotion is a term that involves a multidimensional approach to improving health, which includes education activities, activities to promote behavioral and lifestyle changes, policies, and legislation.

The World Health Organization (WHO) emphasizes (1986) that health is far too important to be left to health practitioners alone; education and policy-making must be central to the development of health at the individual, community, and national levels. This model presents 3 distinct spheres of activity, but which, at the same time, overlap: health education, health protection, and disease prevention.

From a modern point of view, health has several dimensions – emotional, intellectual, physical, social, and spiritual, each of which contributes to a person's well-being. Of these, in this study, we will focus on those elements that are related to health in the online environment.

- Emotional health includes understanding emotions and knowing how to solve everyday problems, stress and the ability to study, work or perform activities efficiently and in a good mood. The quality of a person's health reflects a person's emotions, his feelings towards himself, and toward other people. While they are important in themselves, emotions influence physical health. Some researchers have argued that strength of character can help strengthen the immune system against the harmful effects of stress. This force is defined as having an optimistic way of assuming in approaching life, in viewing problems, including illness as a challenge that can be manipulated.
- Intellectual health – The intellect, an important aspect of the mental plan that contributes to the development of important decisions, plays a crucial role in the health and well-being of the individual. Even if the intellectual capacity

varies from individual to individual, all individuals are able to learn how to acquire and evaluate their information, how to choose between alternatives, and how to make decisions on different types of issues, including health. Intellectual health is sometimes included in emotional health as part of mental health. However, although closely intertwined with emotions, intellectual thinking differs from it. Emotions can alter a person's ability to think, and confused thinking can exacerbate problems. However, the relationship between the emotional and the intellect does not overlap.

- Social health refers to the ability to fulfill the role of life, such as the role of son or daughter, parent, spouse, and friend, close or citizen, in an efficient and comfortable way, with pleasure, without disturbing the climate of social ecology, protecting of others. Each of these roles involves different responsibilities and risks. All require effective communication such as "give and take," because healthy relationships never go in one direction. Fulfilling human needs for love, intimacy, and belonging is an important factor in achieving social health. People who are deprived of these needs can develop behaviors that can threaten their health and good mood, thus entering the sphere of anomie, deviance, and social pathology.

The dimensions of health form a whole – each has an effect on the others. All these distinct dimensions work together to ensure the efficiency of the functions and thus ensure comfort. The cultivation of a certain dimension entails the development of the other dimensions. Similarly, the neglect of a single dimension can have severe consequences for overall health and good mood. To maintain health, we must pay attention to the five dimensions, identifying the links between them and trying to keep them in balance so that they ensure optimum (Lungu, 2009).

Health education is a safe path, through which the notions reach the preschool child as rules or norms that will penetrate deeply into the daily way of life. We can consider health education as a component of general education, a branch of human culture, one of the foundations of health, with a role in influencing the modern way of life, in achieving generations that have a sanogenic behavior. The general culture, including the culture of health, is formed by the general instruction of the population in the continuous set of generations. Health education is part of the cultural life of each country, so the organization and propagation of the notions of health care, sanogenesis, does not belong exclusively to the health sector but to other sectors such as education, civic organizations, church, various associations, productive units, state or private commercial units, all having certain responsibilities in this respect.

Health education involves acceptability, mutual respect, information, means for learning different sanogenic habits, cooperation of recipients, it is also a human right and an obligation of society, embodied in an annual school analytical program integrated into the curriculum of all levels of education, since kindergarten level (based on the educational message of health culture, exemplary images and practical demonstrations in the form of games adapted to the child's age) (Bursuc, 2005).

After the family, kindergarten and school are the child's first life experience in society. This institution places it in a new framework through its size and content. Within the group, the preschool child lives the first experience of life in the community, other than the family. Placing the child in kindergarten thus inaugurates the expansion of his/her existential universe, which takes place in the vicinity of a new director, that of the educator, who consolidates, retouches, or corrects the profile acquired in the family. In today's society, the role of kindergarten as an institution for preparing the child for social integration is overwhelming, especially in the context in which the role of the family from this point of view is diminishing more and more. The current environment and way of life, especially for the child, have invested the kindergarten with new values along with those of social integration and informational training for the school, namely those related to monitoring, evaluation, and development of psychomotor skills and physical capacity, as well as those related by stimulating its global growth and development (Butnari, 2017).

In order to connect the new education types with the digital well-being, after the analysis of health education, we would like to present some recent perspectives on the digital well-being in schools.

Over the last 15 years, the concept of "digital skills" has continuously broadened following the development of new digital technologies and applications. Also, we have witnessed to a theoretical expansion of what is considered "media literacy." In the 80s and 90s, digital skills were mainly referred to as technical skills, needed to work with computer hardware and software (Van Dijk, 2005).

In schools, information and communication technologies are widely seen as enhancing learning, this hope fueling their rapid diffusion and adoption throughout developed societies. But they are not yet so embedded in the social practices of everyday life as to be taken for granted, with schools proving slower to change their lesson plans than they were to fit computers in the classroom (Livingstone, 2011). There has to be a constant preoccupation of teachers, for this issue, in order to maintain digital safety in the preschool and primary school environment. The rules and elements presented above, which are connected with health education as part of new education types, apply to digital well-being too.

Research Design

The present research was based on the method of survey. The main instrument used was the questionnaire. This instrument was applied, with the purpose of collecting data regarding the opinions, knowledge, and experiences of the teachers from Arad county regarding the concept of new education types, based on the health education in connection with digital health and well-being in the online area. The participants were in a number of 112 preschool and primary school teachers from 15 preschools and primary schools from Arad County.

Objectives of the Study

The main objective of the study was to find out how new education types support health education in the online area, and if health education combined with other kinds of subjects within the new education types can give sufficient base to the digital use within preschools and primary schools. The subjects, have expressed their opinions regarding the use of health education in their daily practice in connection with the use of digital technology.

Research Questions

1. Is the formal educational system from Arad county concerned with the use of new educational types and so with the proper use of health education even in the digital area?
2. What kind of freedom and preparation instruments do teachers from these two specialties have in order to offer quality health education in preschools and primary schools from Arad County, even in the digital area?

Research Findings

The results of the analysis were introduced in the statistical program in order to analyze the results. The finding of the research shows the following (Tab. 1):

Tab. 1. Distribution of participants from preschool and primary schools within Arad County

Level	Participants
Preschool	52
Primary school	60

Therefore, following the processing of the collected statistical data, the following were observed:

1. 52 preschool teachers answered the questionnaire;
2. 60 primary school teachers answered the questionnaire;
3. The average age of the respondents is 42 years; the minimum age is 22 years and the maximum age of the respondents is 51 years.

The next variable to be analyzed is the rate in which preschool and primary school teachers use new education types, especially, health education. The answers show that in preschool they use it less than in primary school, as only some of the curricular make it mandatory.

We were interested in the level of familiarity with the concept of health education as part of new education types, and the answers appear in the following diagram:

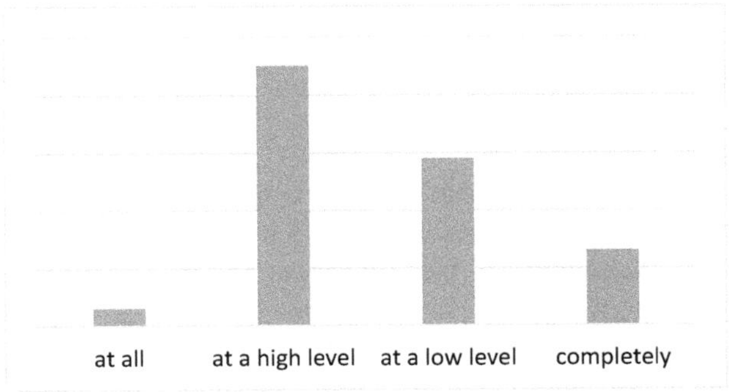

Diagram 1. Level of familiarity with the concepts

Another variable to be analyzed would be the way in which respondents came into contact with this concept. The results show that most of the preschool

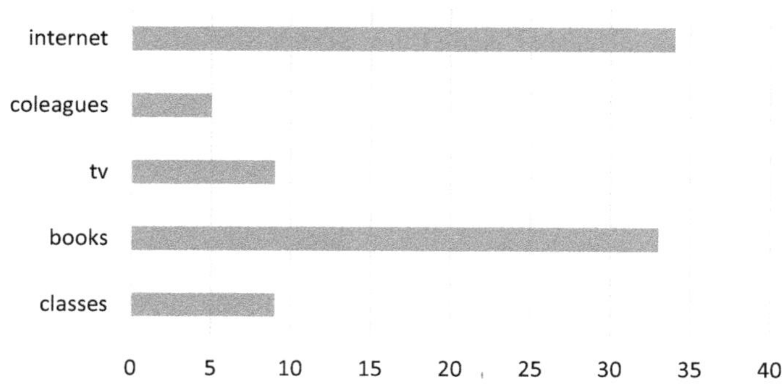

Diagram 2. Ways of getting familiar with the concepts

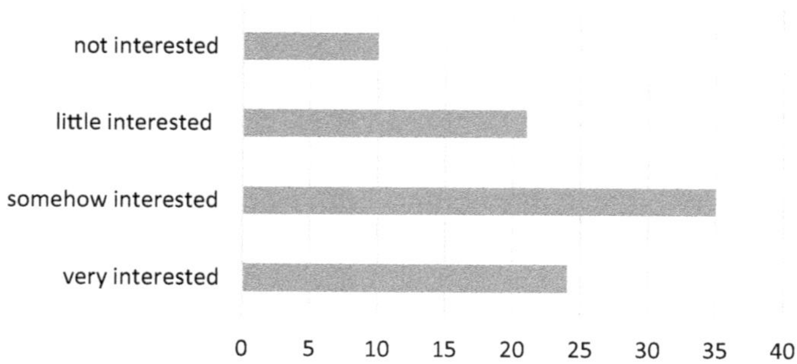

Diagram 3. Rate of interest in personal training regarding health education and digital health education

and primary school teachers that have participated in the research have got into contact with both the concepts through internet and through books. Unfortunately, classes and TV have the same answers, and hearing about it from colleagues got the least answers. We consider that classes, and pedagogical meetings should be more concerned about this topic.

The following variable measured the interest to participate at personal training courses in this regard. More than half of the respondent's state that they are interested in personal training activities that concern health education and digital health education. They are closely followed by almost 40 % of pre-school and primary school teachers who declare that they are very interested in personal development in this direction. This result must be a motivating engine

Tab. 2. Positive correlations between the use of new education types and the desire to learn more and practice with the group and classes elements regarding digital health

Independent Samples Test										
		Levine's Test for Equality of Variances		t-test for Equality of Means						
									95 % Confidence Interval of the Difference	
		F	Sig.	t	df	Sig. (2-tailed)	Mean Difference	Std. Error Difference	Lower	Upper
TOTALNE&DW	Equal variances assumed	7,605	,010	8,920	31	**,000**	6,089	,683	4,697	7,481
	Equal variances not assumed			9,433	25,991	**,000**	6,089	,646	4,762	7,416

for the educational managers, who can use the handiest way to approach the outdoor topic, under the aegis of pedagogical circles.

The findings of this study show that there is a significant positive correlation between the use of new education types and the desire to learn more and practice with the group and classes elements regarding digital health (Tab. 2).

Conclusions

This study has showed that in preschools and primary schools that have participated in the present research, from Arad County, teachers are preoccupied in knowing more about health education and learning new ways to combine in with digital technology elements, in order to create health education in the digital area. Many areas still need to provide extra classes to get to a better knowledge on this topic. We recommend school managements to introduce training sessions for teachers in order to get more theoretical information and practical advice on how to correctly combine health education with digital health education. We are thrilled to observe that teachers that have knowledge on this topic also use it regularly in the instructive educational routine. Also, teachers who answered not knowing enough on the topic presented desire to learn more and to find out practical ways to implement in their classes. We have also noticed that age influences the use of new education types, especially health education. Teachers over 45 years old are less preoccupied in digital health of their classes, while teachers younger than 30 years old are less interested in health education and more interested in digital health education and the correct use of digital instruments during school and at home too.

The present study is useful both in the theoretical frame set of the topic as in the practical one, in the area in which the research was done. We wish to implement the findings in other areas too, and on different age groups and specialties.

References

Bursuc, B. (2005), Educație pentru sănătate, Cluj-Napoca

Butnari, N. (2017), Noile educații. Suport de curs, Univ. de Stat din Moldova, Fac. de Psihologie şi Ştiințe ale Educației, Dep. Ştiințe ale Educației. – Chişinău

Cucoş, C. (2006), Pedagogie, Ediția a II-a, Polirom, Iaşi

Livingstone, S. (2011), Risks and safety on the Internet: The perspective of European children: Full findings and policy implications from the EU Kids Online survey of 9–16 year olds and their parents in 25 countries, EU Kids Online, London

Lungu, V. (2009), Educaţia prospectivă şi problematica contemporană. În: Didactica Pro. Revistă de teorie şi practică educaţională, nr. 4 (56)

Van Dijk, J., A., G., M., (2005), The Deepening Divide: Inequality in the Information Society, Ed. Sage, London

World Health Organization, (1989), Health Promotion Glossary, Geneva: WHO

Cornelia Evelina BALAȘ and Daniela NEAȚA

15 The Role of Extracurricular Activities in Children's Personal Development and Well-Being

Abstract: The chapter presents a research in which educational workshops were used, ensuring the active, free, creative, and personal involvement of each student. Educators benefited from an optimal framework, learning to communicate assertively and to overcome the blockages that appeared within the activities. At present, the balance is tilting from informative to formative, from quantity to the quality of knowledge, forcing the school to prepare and train new generations of young people with skills adapted to the new needs of today's society.

Keywords: Extracurricular activities, children's personal development, well-being

1. The Importance and Premises of Research

The proposed topic for research is topical, trying to find solutions in the formation and development of children's life skills. They highlight the level of development of the student and his emotional intelligence in close connection with social and thinking skills. The success in a competitive society depends on socio-emotional skills, i.e. self-confidence, personal autonomy, and managing social relationships.

Children's personality is different, both temperamental, characteristical, and aptitudinal. Every child is unique and has his own needs, desires, and emotions. His method of responding to life will be determined by how he is treated and the experiences he has in his relationships with others from his school, family, and social retinue. The school must provide him with educational contexts, which will prepare him for a harmonious evolution. The creative style of the students will be stimulated to develop their self-confidence and self-esteem, communicate in an expressive and clear manner, and know each other as well as possible.

The intertwining of formal education with the nonformal one lays the foundations for the complete evolution of young schoolchildren. Extracurricular activities are based on a learning style designed to identify and develop the socio-emotional skills and competencies of each student; they support creativity, so that students will have the opportunity to identify their personal branding, to be aware of their values that will support them in their personal development. Sometimes, we are put in the situation of looking at ourselves from the outside and describing, assessing, and also self-evaluating ourselves.

The instructive-educational methods applied in the workshops for young schoolchildren contribute both to the process of nonformal education and to the promotion of socio-emotional development of the students involved in the project, by supporting a culture based on values and sustainable moral, ethics principles.

2. The Purpose of the Research

An education based on emotional intelligence is a complex process of actions that helps create a balance in students' lives. Socio-emotional development is important not only for school results but also for a successful life. The ability to cope with emotions results in better performance at school and in interpersonal relationships, thanks to a better management of emotions.

The current research aims to demonstrate the link between the participation of young students in extracurricular activities and their benefits on socio-emotional development, but also the opportunity to discover personal talents. Extracurricular activities, which complement the curricular education, offer a holistic education through discovery, by taking on roles and by developing team spirit and effective communication.

3. The Research Hypothesis and Objectives

Based on the scientific, psycho-pedagogical arguments presented in the first part of the research, I set out to highlight the role of socio-emotional intellect in the personal development of young schoolchildren. We know the cases of brilliant students, in terms of school performance, that exceed the successes of their colleagues, but who later in adult life fail to capitalize on their potential, due to a lack of social skills. There is also the reverse case, when modest students, from an intellectual point of view, demonstrate a better social adaptation to different contexts, thus being considered successful people.

3.1 The Research Hypothesis

An education based on emotional intelligence creates a balance in our daily actions. Children need a positive environment that offers them countless opportunities for knowledge and self-knowledge. Emotional intelligence is closely related to awareness and control of one's emotions, to his inner motivation to evolve, to empathy and social skills, that is, the ability to create positive relationships, to cooperate and collaborate, to capture attention and manage conflicts.

Children need emotional intelligence in order to succeed in life, to gain confidence in themselves, to get to know each other better, to turn their negative emotions into positive ones, to know how to manage their emotions when they are angry, upset, tired, sad.

As a result, **the hypothesis** pursued during the proposed research is:

If we organize and carry out thematic extracurricular activities within the *Socio-emotional development workshops* intervention program, **then** there will be a significant progress in the level of socio-emotional skills needed for the personal development of the young student.

The specific hypotheses established take into account that through the achievement of some socio-emotional extracurricular activities, progress will be observed regarding:

- developing the self-concept;
- recognition, expression, and self-control of emotions;
- increasing school performance;
- developing interpersonal communication skills.

3.2 The Research Objectives

The experimental approach that I proposed, started from the following objectives, established in congruence with the theme of the chapter, which will represent directions of action in the designed investigative intervention:

- Knowledge of the psycho-intellectual and creative abilities of the students participating in the research: group sensitivity and emotional intelligence of each student;
- Designing and carrying out a module of extracurricular activities, by conducting a number of ten workshops, to stimulate the personal development of the young student: communication skills, emotional intelligence, time management, relationship skills, financial education, and personal branding;
- Offering students a set of tools and work models that increase their school performance in the activities carried out every day in school;
- Improving the awareness of one's personality through instructive-educational methods;

- Checking the degree to which personality stimulation strategies have positively influenced its level;
- Monitoring and recording the progress during and at the end of the applied research.

4. The Research Methodology

In order to verify the hypotheses and achieve the research objectives, we used several investigative methods such as:

- test for emotional intelligence (children's version, adapted by M. Roco);
- observation;
- conversation;
- the pedagogical experiment;
- analysis of the activity products.

To interpret the results we used graphic methods: histogram and areolar diagram.

4.1 The Method of Observation

With the help of this method one can detect the temperamental manifestations expressed in emotional feelings. It allows us to appreciate the typological manifestations in the child's activity. Thus, in the face of difficulties, children may have inappropriate behavior due to lack of self-control, and display emotional and verbal reactions sometimes manifested in explosive forms. In the face of failure, dissatisfaction reactions can occur, outbursts of anger expressed in a violent way.

Throughout the study, I used the pedagogical observation, through which I followed the students' receptivity to the proposed tasks, the level in which they were involved in solving the exercises and finding ingenious solutions, how they made gains through their own thinking effort.

4.2 The Method of the Didactic Experiment

To test the hypothesis, systematic observations were made on the socio-emotional behavior of the young students involved. It is a method that is based on the intervention of the researcher in the development of the studied aspects. Unlike the observation, where the phenomena are studied in their normal course of development, the experiment involves a change of variables, in order to notice the results on other variable aspects. The experiment is defined as a provoked observation.

4.3 The Research Variables

The independent variable was represented by the systematic application of the *Socio-emotional development workshops* intervention program during a school year, with the frequent use of games held in extracurricular activities.
As ***the dependent variable***, we set the students' personal development through the formation of social skills (following rules, social relationships, and pro-social behavior) and emotional skills (recognition, expression, and management of emotions).

5. The Sample and Its Characteristics

In order to demonstrate the importance of nonformal education in the development of students' personality, the study was conducted during a school year, on a single sample of 15 students (girls and boys), representing the third grade, from Mănăştur Secondary School, Arad County. The participants in the research are homogeneous in age (9–10 years), level of education, and nationality (8 Romanians and 7 Roma). The level of mental development of students is heterogeneous; among them are children who come from family backgrounds with few openings to education and knowledge.

In the investigative approach we started from the fact that there are cognitive, emotional, and volitional differences between students. These differences must be known in order for the learning process to be carried out in the most flexible way possible. We made observations at different times on the entire class of students, so that the data collected could be compared, during and at the end of the research.

5.1 The Place and Period of the Research

The research took place at Mănăştur Secondary School, outside of class hours.

5.2 The Research Period

The action research took place between September 10, 2018 and June 14, 2019.

- The pre-experimental stage: September 10, 2018 – October 30, 2018;
- The stage of the formative experiment: November 1, 2018 – April 30, 2019;
- The post-experimental stage: May 2, 2019 – June 14, 2019.

5.3 The Pre-Experimental Stage

The pre-experimental stage is a very complex stage, prior to the experimental intervention. We carried out actions of systematic observation of young students, observing and noting a list of inappropriate behaviors, arranging each of them according to frequency, duration, latency, and intensity.

To check the level of emotional intelligence of students we applied a test designed for children, adapted by Mihaela Roco. Students will have to choose from the test the answers that best describe their reaction in certain situations.

5.3.1 Test for Emotional Intelligence (Children's Version) – Pretest

The analytical table reflects the students' results at the test for determining emotional intelligence.

Name and Sur-name	**Items**										**Total Points**
	1	**2**	**3**	**4**	**5**	**6**	**7**	**8**	**9**	**10**	
A.I.I.	20	20	-	-	-	5	-	-	20	-	65
C.A.	20	20				20	20				80
D.T.	20	20		20	20	20		20		20	140
L.C.N.	20			20	20		20			20	100
M.I.T.	20			20		5				20	65
P.E.M.	20	20		20				20		20	100
P.R.C.	20	20	20		20	5	20	20	20		145
R.G.M.	20	20		20	20	20		20	5		125
R.L.	20	20	20			20	20		5	20	125
S.A.	20	20	20		20	5		20	20	20	145
S.M	20	20		20	20	20		20		20	140
T.P	20	20	20	20		20	20		5	20	145
T.M.	20		20			5				20	65
V.A	20	20		20	20				20	20	120
U.S.	20	20	20	20	20	20		20	20		160

Test results: above average –1; medium – 10; below average – 4

Improving emotional intelligence can be achieved by learning and practicing its dimensions. Compared to cognitive intelligence, which tends to reach a high level in adolescence, remain constant in adulthood, and then begins to decline in the old age, emotional intelligence develops with age and lived experiences. By managing their own emotions, students can control their anger and tolerate frustrations, thus being able to express their feelings without aggression. Learning and practicing empathy helps the student to listen to those around him and to be able to look at a problem from their point of view.

Children will adopt a pro-social attitude and will integrate more easily into the group. If he has an above average emotional IQ, the student will be able to motivate himself, master his impulses and persevere for his goals. Emotional intelligence promotes creativity, productivity, and flexibility, making it easier to solve problems.

A fundamental characteristic of emotional intelligence is the management of emotions that occur especially during assessment tests, because anxiety and depression have a devastating impact on the clarity of the mind. Anxiety before tests interferes with logical thinking and the memory needed for effective learning.

Students who know how to control their emotions can turn anxiety into a more thorough preparation, in order to obtain better results. Stimulating the creative capacity of the young student is the key factor in education and depends on the personality of the teacher and students, but also on the socio-affective climate in which they work.

5.4 The Stage of the Formative Experiment

During this stage we implemented an educational intervention program, organizing socio-emotional development workshops. The specific objectives of the program are:

➢ **For the development of emotional skills:**

- To identify one's own emotions and those of other colleagues, as well as their causes, in various contexts, based on the verbal/nonverbal component;
- To communicate assertively;
- To develop emotional identification and self-regulation strategies.

➢ **For the development of social skills:**

- To initiate adaptive, collaborative relationships in social groups;
- To manage conflictual relationships;

- To accept the differences of opinion of those around;
- To provide and request feedback.

5.5 Intervention Program "Socio-Emotional Development Workshops"

Socio-emotional development means promoting constructive behaviors, the acquisition of socio-cultural values, which will generate a decrease in aggression, in negative emotions in schoolchildren. These educational workshops aim to increase interest in school activities, learning and involvement in extracurricular activities, and constantly monitoring the progress made.

The educational workshops will take place in an interactive atmosphere, conducive to communication, open to the development of proactive and creative attitudes. We have developed work strategies to make extracurricular activities attractive to students, as they learn to push their limits.

During the learning activities, the children had freedom of expression. The exercises were of the self-knowledge and inter-knowledge kind. Then the students experienced what it means to be included in a group and accepted by it, for the purpose of welding the group. The activities were organized through games of attention, communication, socialization, stimulation of imagination, and creativity. The original and competitive spirit of the class appeared.

5.6 Workshop 1 Theme: Society and Its Challenges

The human is a social being who needs to be with others. By interacting with them, the individual discovers the values and rules of social coexistence, becoming an integral part of society.

***The objectives of the workshop*:**

- To identify the essential elements of society;
- To establish the problems that society faces;
- To identify the role and social status.

***Description of activities*:**

- Brainstorming, starting with the question "How can I change society?"

5.7 Workshop 2 Theme: Be an Effective Communicator!

Verbal and nonverbal communication is an essential component of everyday life. Whether we go to school, give a speech, have a discussion with our colleagues, or are in a situation that requires a lot of self-control, communication is the factor on which our entire success sometimes depends on. Thus, the way a person behaves: words, gestures and facial expressions, outfit, the way he shakes your hand, the smile, and the look are important aspects that give you details about his personality.

The objectives of the workshop:

- to develop verbal, nonverbal communication skills, for a better relationship in personal and professional life;
- to develop practical language skills for a solid communication base;
- to learn techniques for an efficient presentation, which makes the verb "to speak" to become the verb "to communicate";
- to learn interactive listening techniques;
- to develop emotions management skills by experiencing the practice of positive thinking;

Description of activities

1. How to introduce myself correctly!

The keynote address should be interesting.

- Game – "The ball of feelings"

2. First meeting, first impression!
   We will realize that any friendship, love, or simple relationship starts with "let me introduce...." We will learn about how much we can lose from a poor start impression or how hard it is to change the first impression we made.

- Game – "How others see us and. . . how we see ourselves."

3. Learn to master verbal communication!
   We will define the purpose of verbal communication and its importance in everyday life.

- Role-playing game: "Best meeting!"

4. Experiencing the practice of positive thinking.
   According to the triangle of thoughts-facts-feelings, positive thinking has a decisive role in our actions.

- Role-playing game: – "The maze of mirrors."

5. The interactive listening cycle.
   We will understand the concept and importance of interactive listening.

- Game – "We build the world together!"

6. How to overcome our emotions?
   We will present some of the techniques used in reducing and managing emotions. We will also learn to turn disruptive emotions into constructive emotions.

- Game – "No emotions!"

7. Assertive communication
1. Game – "Guess me"

   Objective: to convey messages through nonverbal communication
   Duration: 50 min
   Materials: sheets of paper, pen
   Methods and techniques: observation, heuristic conversation, and explanation
   Activity description: Students place the chairs in a semicircle. Before starting the game, the group leader explains the importance of using the body as a means of communication and to avoid discrepancies in the transmission of messages. Each student presents a specific situation from the following, through which one can learn to express one's own identity:
   - attracting attention;
   - communication of fatigue;
   - manifestation of affection;
   - expressing anger;
   - communication of impatience.

   Each participant will express a need through body language, facial expressions, and eye contact. The group will have to acknowledge what their colleague said, writing on a piece of paper the name and emotion conveyed. At the end, the students will verbally express what they felt when performing the exercise.
   Each will check their notes to see if they have correctly identified the emotion perceived visually.

5.8 Workshop 3 Theme: Personal Branding

"It doesn't matter how you see yourself ... It matter how others see you!"

In a competitive and ever-changing society, the personal brand is a promise to society and to ourselves. The personal brand has become a certificate of quality of the actions we take, giving us the opportunity to build our own image. It is a long-term investment.

The objectives of the workshop:

- to identify the mechanisms of the personal branding process;
- to identify personal values;
- to develop social skills, to easily establish relationships with colleagues in the school environment, but also outside it, relations of cooperation, collaboration, communication;
- to understand that sustainable business success is built on personal authenticity.

Activity description:

1. Personal introspection: talent, passion, and values

- "Values" exercise adapted from Peter Senge and Robert Dilt

2. Building your own successful brand

- SWOT analysis (personal characteristics: strengths, weaknesses, development opportunities, and risks that may arise in the way of the proposed objective)

3. Be the change you want to see in the world!

- Exercise: "A thorny issue"

4. Personal Branding – Who am I?

- Exercise "Johari Window" – a tool for understanding and knowing your personality

5. Strengths and weaknesses

- **Game – "Magicbox"**

  Objective: Following this activity, students will be able to understand that the human specificity is the appropriate combination of qualities and defects.
  Resources: a spacious room
  Steps:

- Students are told they have access to a magic box where they can find any quality they want and think they need;

- This box is also willing to receive human traits that the participants consider they have and that they want to get rid of;
- Finally, each participant shares with the group how he or she feels and thinks now that he/she has received what he/she wanted and discarded what was bad or superfluous.

5.9 Workshop 4 Theme: Be a Good Mediator

In this workshop, children will develop their mediation skills in resolving conflicts, and also persuasive and decision-making skills.

The objectives of the workshop:

- to develop negotiation skills, obtained on the basis of consensus;
- to improve their ability to influence, through empathy;
- to develop communication skills in conflict situations.

Description of activities:

1. How to get creative and deal with conflicts

Conflict means opposition, disagreement between two or more parties.

- Game – "Express yourself, if you can"

2. Emergence of conflicts and ways to resolve them
   When discussing a situation, there are also divergences of opinion based on their own interests, on the type of personality, culture, education, and environment. We will learn negotiation techniques for reaching an acceptable agreement.

- Role-play game – The negotiator

3. The winning negotiation strategy
   In a negotiation, we must adopt a win-win strategy. Children will learn about the exchange of comparable value and about partnerships based on respect and trust.

- Game – The successful juniors

4. Effective negotiations tactics

   We will develop our negotiation skills, keeping conflicting discussions under control through negotiation techniques.

- Exercise: Bazaar Tactics

5.10 Workshop 5 Theme: Real Time Management

We all know how valuable time is, that's why we don't want to waste it, but to capitalize on it in an efficient way.

The objectives of the workshop:

- to develop their skills to prioritize activities to achieve maximum results;
- to learn time management techniques in order to obtain benefits;
- to understand the importance of strategies to set long- , medium- , and short-term goals;
- to make the most of their time outside of school hours.

Description of activities:

1. Time and its importance!
   Students will learn why to manage their time and what are the effects of wasting it.
   Flipchart **exercise** "**Time Thieves**" – Advantages and Disadvantages.
   The children will be divided into two groups. They need to identify the causes of the loss of time accompanied by solutions. The team that identifies the most realistic solutions wins.
2. **Routine, Urgency, Importance!** – Key elements in time management.
   Students will learn how to prioritize their tasks according to their importance.

- **Exercises:** Matrix of priorities (urgent, non-urgent, important, and non-important); The Pareto principle.

3. Be SMART!
   Students will learn methods of planning daily activities and how assessment at the end of the day helps us.

- Exercise: Pomodoro Technique

4. To do list!

   Students will learn about the list of priorities, an effective way to manage time.

- Exercise: Brainstorming

5.11 Workshop 6 Theme: "Any Problem Can Become an Opportunity"

"I have enough money for the rest of my life if I don't buy anything." – Jackie Mason

The objectives of the workshop:

- to acquire skills, abilities, and knowledge, which will lead them to manage their own finances;
- to form capacities to develop a business plan;
- to identify the link between Financial IQ and Emotional IQ;
- to understand and accept that financial independence is learned from school in order to have a successful business in the future.

Description of activities:

1. The financially independent ones do not work for money!

   Students will learn how to approach the subject of money, related to their behavior, attitude, and thinking.

- Role-play

2. The financial alphabet

- Exercise: Barter

3. See for yourself about your business!
   What is it and why do we need a personal budget?
   We will learn what a budget is and what impact it has on our personal as well as professional lives.

- Brainstorming

4. What am I? Needs or desires?
   We will learn about Maslow's pyramid and the importance of setting goals

- Brainstorming: classification of personal goals related to Maslow's pyramid

5. Resource analysis – Where the money comes from?

   We will learn the difference between income and expenses, in order to have a clear picture of our own finances.

- Brainstorming: weekly list: income/expenses.

5.12 Workshop 7 Theme: Leadership

"To straighten the world, we must first straighten our nation; to straighten the nation, we must first straighten our family; in order to strengthen the family, we must first cultivate our personal lives; we must first straighten our own hearts" – Confucius

The objectives of the workshop:

- to understand and accept that people are different in their qualities and characteristics;
- to identify what qualities you need to have to gain the leading position;
- to understand the concept of "teamwork";
- to understand the importance of goals, values, and vision in personal life;
- to identify the four types of skills: IQ, EQ, VQ; and PQ, and to make performance.

Description of activities:

1 . Self-knowledge. Are you a lider?

We will discover ourselves as identities by writing our personal story, following the model "who I was and why, who I am and why, who I want to become and why".

- Individual exercises: My story

2. The qualities of a leader
We will learn and become aware of the qualities that a leader must have.

- Case study

3. Leadership: IQ, EQ, VQ, PQ.
We will learn about the skills needed to reach the top of the pyramid:

- IQ ability – intelligence coefficient;
- EQ ability – coefficient of emotional intelligence;
- VQ ability – vitality coefficient;
- PQ ability – political coefficient.
- Skills testing

4. The power of feedback!

We will learn what is and what is not feedback, and what is its power.

- Role-play games

5.13 Workshop 8 Theme: "Talk about the Key Points of Your Personality"

The objectives of the workshop:

- to develop the attitude of collaboration, assertiveness, and integrity;

- to appreciate diversity and respect;
- to develop skills to manage stress and frustration;
- to develop the capacity to be tolerant and empathetic;
- to develop the ability to communicate functionally.

Description of activities: This workshop gives students the opportunity to get to know each other better in relationships with others, but also with themselves, to create a positive self-image. During the activities, the "Johari Window" will be used as a working method. This is an imaginary window open to us and the world. It is a model of personal development, which supports self-knowledge and self-assessment, from their perspective, but also from those around them. The subjects will go through the four quadrants, namely:

Arena – „I know and you know"	Dead angle – „I don't know, but the others know"
Facade –„I know, but the others don't know"	Unknown – „I don't know and neither do the others"

Arena has information known to everyone, and its size shows the quality of relationships.

The dead angle or *blind spot* contains information known to others but unknown to you. These are other people's opinions about you, but they don't tell you directly.

Facade represents the area of information known only to you: goals, objectives, future plans, and emotional state. To protect this information we put on a facade.

The unknown represents the feelings, the abilities that we have not yet discovered. Sometimes these qualities appear in certain life situations, without both ourselves and others knowing that we have them.

5.14 Workshop 9 Theme: Poster with People

***The objectives of the workshop*:** To learn that people have different qualities and characteristics.

Description of activities: Each student will receive a poster. They will have to draw pictures according to the tasks in the figure for 15 minutes. At the end, everyone will share what they drew with their colleagues. The conclusion is that people have different but changing qualities and we cannot categorize them by a single quality.

Something you like to do — Something you don't like to do
Something special for you — Something you're good at

The children enthusiastically received the making of this poster.

5.15 The Post-Experimental Stage

At this stage we analyzed the effects of interventions on children's behaviors in extracurricular activities. The same emotional intelligence test was applied again (Appendix 1) and the results were as follows:

Name and Surname	Items										Total Points
	1	2	3	4	5	6	7	8	9	10	
A.I.I.	20	20	-	-	-	5	-	5	20	-	65
C.A.	20	20				20	20		20		100
D.T.	20	20		20	20	20		20	20	20	160
L.C.N.	20			20	20		20	5		20	105
M.I.T.	20			20		5			5	20	70
P.E.M.	20	20		20			20	20		20	120
P.R.C.	20	20	20		20	5	20	20	20	20	165
R.G.M.	20	20		20	20	20		20	5		125
R.L.	20	20	20		20	20	20		5	20	145
S.A.	20	20	20		20	5	20	20	20	20	165
S.M	20	20		20	20	20		20	20	20	160
T.P	20	20	20	20		20	20	20	5	20	165
T.M.	20		20			5			5	20	70
V.A	20	20		20	20	5			20	20	125
U.S.	20	20	20	20	20	20	20	20	20	20	200

Test results:

- Below average – 3; Medium – 6; Above average – 5; Exceptional – 1

6. The Research Results and Their Interpretation

The results of the extracurricular activities carried out within the "Socio-emotional development workshops" intervention program demonstrated their effectiveness in improving communication and collaboration skills, the spirit of initiative and emulation. Each member of the class had the opportunity to express his opinion freely, thus gaining self-confidence and developing a sense of belonging to the group. The difference between pretest and posttest was observed regarding the level of development of social and emotional skills in children.

Thus, it is necessary to diversify and differentiate the objectives, contents, methods, and techniques, the different ways of learning, due to the unique personalities, based on different intelligences.

The harmonization of emotional intelligence with intellectual intelligence is an important goal to be achieved in the education of students, necessary for an easy integration into the labor market. Knowledge was more easily assimilated by combining formal classroom activities with nonformal ones.

The differences of opinions and interests, which generated misunderstandings and tensions, were resolved peacefully within the group. The young students accepted and respected the different opinions of their colleagues and tried to understand them, empathizing with them.

7. Conclusions

This chapter aimed to investigate the impact of extracurricular activities on the personal development of the young students and their effectiveness on the socio-emotional development of the child. Structured contexts were provided by using rules within the activities, offering children opportunities to practice social skills of cooperation, conflict resolution, but also pro-social behaviors.

Conflict situations were treated as situations of learning conflict management skills. Providing correct positive feedback influences the quality of the educational act. By implementing the educational program, we found the following beneficial informative influences in the process of socio-emotional development: enriching the vocabulary with words specific to socio-emotional education, understanding and expressing emotions; complying with the rules within the group; establishing concrete relationships between facts and consequences; and telling socio-emotional facts.

Regarding the formative influences of research, they are related to the competence and attitude of the teacher. He must be a motivated and motivating trainer, in order to create an affective and socially supportive framework, contributing to the development of self-esteem, stability, and inner peace. Through its own model behavior, the teacher influences the behaviors of his students.

The results obtained in this research ensure the need to apply the principles of nonformal education, but also of socio-emotional education in the daily instructive-educational activity for the preparation of children for life. This research has shown us that socio-emotional intelligence can be improved by learning and practicing its main dimensions.

References

Allport, G. (1981/1991), *Structura şi dezvoltarea personalităţii*, Editura Didactică şi Pedagogică, Bucureşti.

Balaş, E., Roman, A. (2010), *Strategii de instruire şi evaluare*, Editura Universităţii,,Aurel Vlaicu" Arad

Dughi, T., Roman, A. (2014), *Dimensiuni ale învăţării*, Editura Universităţii, Aurel Vlaicu" Arad

Goleman, D. (2001), *Inteligenţa Emoţională*, Editura Curtea Veche, Bucureşti, 2001.

Mucchielli, R. (2000), *Faţa omului şi caracterul, Iniţiere în morfopsihologie*, IRI, Bucureşti

Neagu, M., Patrovici, C. (2000), *Elemente de didactica matematicii în grădiniţă şi învăţământul primar*, Editura Polirom Iaşi

Piaget, J. Inhelder, B. (2005), *Psihologia copilului*, Editura Cartier, Chişinău

Roco, M. (2001), *Creativitate şi inteligenţă emoţională*, Editura Polirom, Iaşi

Stan, Cristian (2001), *Teoria educaţiei. Actualitate şi perspective*, Editura Presa Universitară Clujeană, Cluj-Napoca

Sonia IGNAT and Alina MICLĂUȘ

16 Methods of Managing Stress during Isolation due to Pandemic Situation

Abstract The beginning of the period of isolation due to the pandemic was marked by my participation in a workshop with the main topic, stress management. Guided by the information gathered in this online course, I wanted to apply in the current situation certain tools to measure the quality of life, the feeling of coherence and self-efficacy. This chapter aims to examine how effectively an individual manages to manage stress in a particularly stressful period. The way stress is managed can also be closely linked to an individual's sense of coherence and self-efficacy. Namely, people who are convinced that both internal and external stimuli encountered during life can be explainable and predictable, having the resources to cope with the stimuli; the involvement and investment of effort is justified because the requests have meaning and purpose to effectively manage the stressors that may occur in his life. At the same time, people who manage to mobilize the cognitive and motivational resources necessary in successfully performing tasks, and perceiving their self-efficacy in relation to a failure as not due to personal inefficiency but perceiving this failure by focusing carefully on analysis and finding solutions to its problems. This way of perceiving one's own effectiveness leads to an efficient management of stressful periods and more. In order to make this work as personal as possible, I decided to orient the testing to married people or in a form of cohabitation, who spent the period of isolation with their children, considering that in this way the stressors were increased by the constant need of negotiation during the isolation at home. This chapter aims not only to probe the elements pointed out above, but also to provide a psychological intervention plan specially adapted for families with children. It will also seek to provide increased support in optimizing the sense of self-efficacy and coherence, considering these attributes as an effective foundation in the subsequent management of stressors and disruptors in the life of each individual.

Keywords : stress, social isolation, Covid-19

1. Perceived Self-Efficacy

The concept of perceived self-efficacy was proposed by Bandura (1982, apud. Băban, 1998), and is a relevant construct for understanding the protective factors against stress and disease.

Perceived self-efficacy refers to convincing a person of his or her abilities to mobilize the cognitive and motivational resources necessary to successfully perform the given tasks.

The perception of one's own competence also changes the perception of failure or reduced performance, the failure being attributed to the reduced effort invested in the task and to a lower extent to the lack of necessary competence. Increased self-efficacy is associated with self-protective attributions of failure or success.

As a cognitive process, perceived self-efficacy generates options, motivations, emotions, ideas, and behaviors. Optimistic assessments of perceived self-efficacy are an additional impetus for action intentions and persistence in overcoming obstacles. The thought and attention processes are also affected by the beliefs about the perceived self-efficacy in the direction of enhancing or reducing their efficiency.

People who have doubts about perceived self-efficacy focus their attention on themselves, being concerned about their inability to cope with the situation, which affects the efficient use of intellectual potential, moving them away from the demands of the task to the fear of failure. On the contrary, people with perceived self-efficacy turn their attention to analysis and finding solutions to real problems.

Positive or negative emotions triggered by anticipating success or failure in turn influence the cognition and quality of taken actions. Thus anxiety is often induced by the perception of the inefficiency of coping resources and not by the stimulus or the situation itself. Pervin's (1993, Băban, 1998) research shows that the perception of one's own ineffectiveness in relation to threatening situations leads to anxiety, and the perception of the inability to achieve the proposed goals leads to depression. However, other aspects also contribute to depressive reactions: too high standards, strict goals, and excessive self-criticism. As sources of shaping the belief of perceived self-efficacy, we mention the group of affiliation, social class, the collective perception that influences to some extent the individual perceived self-efficacy. Perceived self-efficacy is a major concept in the category of self-belief with a role in maintaining health (Băban, 1998).

2. The Feeling of Coherence

Through the concept of the feeling of coherence (Antonovski, 1979; Băban, 1998), it is defined that the global cognitive orientation of the person who is convinced that both internal and external stimuli encountered during life can be explainable and predictable; has resources to cope with stimuli; and involvement and effort investment is justified as the requests have meaning and purpose. The name of the concept may lead us to the classical meaning of the feature, but the feeling of coherence is an "essentially cognitive" characteristic; it expresses the person's way of perceiving, judging, and interpreting the world and himself without referring to any emotional aspect of the personality (apud. Băban, 1998). Regardless of how we call it image, belief, or feeling, coherence synthesizes three characteristics: comprehension, control, and purpose. Comprehension refers to the fact that the person can understand the situation he is going through and can give it meaning. Through cognitive mediation, the information generated by the situation is decoded as conscious, structured, clear, not inexplicable, accidental, and chaotic. Due to the predictability of events, the person with a sense of coherence can anticipate them. It can find explanations even for untimely events and can order them (failure, war, and death). Control, in the case of a sense of coherence, refers to the perception of available resources that the person can use in dealing with stressful events. These available resources can be family, friends, colleagues, doctors, organizations, and divinity to which the person appeals in case of need. Even if the lived events have negative personal meanings, insofar as the person perceives the resources and uses them, he will not be considered the victim of destiny.

Purpose designates the perception of the necessary and desired finality of events. The importance of the person's involvement in the decision-making and modeling process of everyday situations or those that determine personal destiny is emphasized. Although some events cannot be considered exciting, the person will invite important mobilization efforts to overcome unwanted situations.

Since the feeling of coherence is a general orientation of seeing the world and oneself in relation to it, it is important to understand what the world represents for the individual. Each person establishes the boundaries of his own world, but no matter how wide or narrow it may be, it necessarily includes four spheres (Antonovski, 1987; Băban, 1998):

- inner world: own thoughts and feelings;
- sphere of interpersonal relationships: family, friends, colleagues, and organization;
- defining activity for the individual: for example, profession;
- existential problems: for example, conflicts, failure, isolation, and death.

Denying the importance of any of these spheres leads to a reduced sense of coherence.

As a relatively stable cognitive-motivational characteristic, the feeling of coherence is formed during childhood and adolescence and stabilizes around the age of 30.

Antonovski (1991, Băban, 1998) cites three major sources in the formation of the feeling of coherence: consistency of experiences, difficulty of tasks, and participation in decision.

3. Types of Thinking in Relation to Stress

"Human thinking is not uniform, it does not work the same for all people or for one and the same person at different times and situations" (Zlate, 2004).

Over time, the idea of the existence of several types or ways of thinking has been accentuated, and its classification criteria are according to orientation, type of proposed operations, finality, direction of evolution, logical approaches, development model, value, correspondence with reality, and efficiency.

In this chapter, we aim to analyze the types of thinking according to the value criterion, after which we distinguish between positive thinking and negative thinking.

4. Stress in Health and Disease

4.1 General Notions

Stress is a notion that relatively recently appeared, in 1936, and the one who introduced it is H. Selye (1978). He defined stress as a "state of the body manifested by nonspecific reactions in response to disruptive agents" (Băban, 1998). Stress is an inherent component of life.

Living organisms exist by virtue of the legitimacy of adaptation, a phenomenon historically perceived long before stress, which is often seen both as a source and as a consequence of an adaptation by defense mechanisms that remained primitive and inadequate to contemporary life. "Complete stress relief means death," said Selye (1978).

Although defined in various ways depending on the specifics of the scientific discipline from which the stress is developed, it was and remains one of the most disputed concepts in the history of science.

For new disciplines such as Health Psychology, Behavioral Medicine, and Psychoneuroimmunology, stress is a key concept in explanatory models of health and disease.

The finding of the World Health Organization is that 50 % of all causes of mortality and morbidity are due to lifestyle. Stress plays a major role in adopting inappropriate behaviors, and society's costs related to its effects are extremely high.

Due to the multiple ways of defining stress, terminological confusions have often been reached. Thus stress has been confused with anxiety or activation, reduced to the concept of coping, and assimilated to the notion of mental illness, but the person experiencing anxiety or instability is not necessarily neurotic, and anxiety or depression does not exhaust the consequences of stress (Selye, 1978). In general, stress means that state of the body characterized by a tension with different degrees of intensity, by a mobilization of the body's resources that must adapt to a problematic situation. According to the Explanatory Dictionary of the Romanian Language (DEX, 1975) stress is a name given to any factor or set of factors that causes the human body an abnormal reaction; stress is an unfavorable effect produced on the human body by an environmental factor. "A slightly simpler definition says that stress could be described as a normal response to an abnormal situation" (Selye, 1978).

4.2 Precursors of Stress Theory

Since ancient times there have been observations on the body's adaptation to the environment. Hippocrates considered disease, and the body's effort to restore balance, not just injury and suffering.

Nineteenth-century biologists and physiologists pointed to the high degree of organization of the living world that facilitates active adaptation.

The original meaning of the term stress – adversity, suffering, and difficulty – dates back to the fourteenth century. In engineering, the term was used to refer to that force/pressure that deforms bodies.

The biological sciences took over the concept of stress only in the nineteenth century. Sir William Osler equated stress with "hard work and trouble."

The most important forerunner of the stress theory is considered to be W. Cannon (1932) who demonstrated in the early twentieth century the existence of specific homeostatic mechanisms to protect the body against disruptive agents. The "emergency reaction" by which Cannon defined the body's autonomous reaction to stress is known in today's literature as the "fight or flight" reaction.

Through the theory of learning based on reflexes conditioned with anticipatory functions, I. Pavlov contributes to the problem of adaptation and indirectly to that of stress.

S. Freud in the theory of neurosis and unconscious defense mechanisms approaches the issue of adapting the individual to conflict situations in a completely new way.

The French physiologist Reilly published almost simultaneously with Selye the theory of irritation syndrome which highlighted the role of the autonomic nervous system response in the body's response to toxins.

4.3 Explanatory Models and Theories of Stress

Concerns about understanding and defining the concept of stress have led to three main directions:

a. the physiological model of explaining stress supported by physiologists and endocrinologists who experimentally claim that stress is a response of the body to external stimuli (response theory);
b. the causal model of explaining stress. This model is supported by sociologists for whom stress is due to the characteristics of the environment in which we live. The causal model of stress is concentrated in stimulus theory;
c. the interactional model that is supported by psychologists; they see in stress the result of perceiving a state of self-inefficiency. This model is presented in transactional theory.

5. Types and Forms of Stress

5.1 Classification Criteria

According to the duration of action of stressors, a distinction is made between acute stress (considered to act for minutes, hours) and chronic stress (action of days, months), for example. Psychosocial stress has a longer action, and physical stress, noise and acceleration, has a shorter duration.

As continuity and number of stressful interventions, there are stressors with continuous and discontinuous action, respectively, intermittent on the one hand and unique or repeated stressors on the other hand.

The grouping of triggers into physical and psychological or mental and social agents is highly controversial (apud. Derevenco, 1992).

Another classification based on the dichotomy systemic stress and nervous stress (neuroendocrine in fact) transposes us from the field of stressors as stimuli to that of stress reactions as a predominantly neuroendocrine and systemic response to stressors, respectively.

Also through the prism of the reaction to the stress factors and of the stimulus-response interrelation, the dichotomy "distress" with harmful effects and "eustress" with favorable effects also operates.

Derevenco (1992) also recalls the classification of stress by stimulation and overstimulation or discrimination between mandatory stressors (trauma and acute hemorrhage) and the actual stressors themselves. Among the obligatory factors are the pathological reactions from shock, collapse, burns, and shock being considered the most serious form of stress.

5.2 Forms of Stress

The main forms of stress are the predominantly physical environmental stress produced by noise, heat/cold, tremors, air pollution, and radiation; it is manifested by multiple vegetative, metabolic, and behavioral neurophysiological effects with deterioration of performance; gravitational stress caused by weightlessness or acceleration with consequences on the digestive tract central nervous system, endocrine system, blood system, and reproduction.

Physical or psychosocial urban stress is caused by congestion, pollution, and noise and is manifested by discomfort, adaptation difficulties, asthenia, and depression, especially in newly arrived population groups.

Hyperbaric, physical or psycho-emotional stress is produced by high atmospheric pressure hyperoxia and manifests itself with discordance of movements, emotionality, and nervous syndrome of high pressures.

Techno-stress is of the mental type through information excess expressed by decision-making difficulties and is related to the introduction of high technology.

Prenatal and neonatal stress is due to hypoxia; Intense prenatal stress affects the maturation of the nervous and endocrine systems and metabolic processes.

Sports stress is due to physical exertion and over training and is manifested by the emotional, anticipatory component with neuroendocrine, cardiovascular, and metabolic effects.

6. Stress Factors

Stressors are sufficiently intense or frequent environmental events or conditions that require physiological and psychosocial reactions from the individual (Elliot and Eisdotfer, 1982). Conventionally, stressors are divided into three main categories: physical, mental, and social, but in daily activity the physical aspects interact with the social and mental. Minor daily problems (losing a wallet, getting stuck in car traffic, or an argument with a colleague, neighbor, or superior) can also be felt as stressors. Major changes in the life of the individual can be a change of job, moving to another city, losing a friend, or suffering caused by a serious illness. Some events represent major changes that affect a large number of people: earthquakes, floods, nuclear accidents, and wars. But the source of stress can also be internal in the form of conflicting motives or desires. Events that are perceived as stressful usually fall into one or more of the following categories: traumatic events beyond the usual limits of human experience; controllable events; unpredictable events; events that pose a challenge to the limits of our capabilities, and internal conflicts (apud. Atkinson. 2002). Traumatic events, situations of extreme danger that are outside the realm of ordinary human experience, are the most obvious sources of stress. These include natural disasters, man-made disasters, catastrophic accidents, and physical aggression.

The common behavioral pattern in these traumatic events, beyond the extremely varied reactions, is the catastrophic syndrome. Initially the survivors are stunned, dizzy, do not realize injuries or danger being able to wander disoriented through the most dangerous areas; in the next stage the survivors are still passive, and they cannot initiate even the simplest actions, but they execute orders with ease; in the third stage, the survivors become anxious and apprehensive, and have difficulty concentrating, and repeat the story of the catastrophe indefinitely.

Most of us, fortunately, have nothing to do with traumatic events, but even more common events can lead to stress responses.

"Three characteristics of events make them perceived as stressful: controllability, predictability and the extent to which they test the limits of our capacity and self-image; of course, the level at which an event becomes stressful differs from individual to individual. (...). People differ in the level at which they evaluate the same event as predictable, controllable, and as a challenge to capacity limits and self-image; To a large extent, these evaluations influence the perception of the stress level of the event" (Lazarus and Folkman, 1984; Atkinson, 2002).

7. Ways to Adapt to Stress (Coping)

Throughout phylogeny, the human being has developed a series of mechanisms through which he copes with stressful situations.

These mechanisms act preventively (to modify or annihilate the negative effects of a presumed future situation) or adaptive (in reducing already reduced distress). In the literature these mechanisms are known as coping.

The notion of coping was introduced by Lazarus (after Miclea, 1997) and refers to all ways of managing stress.

Coping is defined as "cognitive and behavioral effort to reduce, master, or tolerate internal or external demands that exceed personal resources" (Lazarus and Folkman, 1984; Băban, 1998).

The definition highlights four essential characteristics of coping:

- the role of the cognitive process and of the action;
- as a process of transaction between person and environment, coping involves qualitative and quantitative changes of this relationship and mutual interconnection between coping, evaluation, and empathy;
- distinguishes between adjustment mechanisms and innate adaptation mechanisms;
- emphasizes the existence of efficient and less efficient coping phenomena (apud. Băban, 1998).

There are also three stages of coping:

- anticipating/warning requests, when the situation can be prevented or postponed, and the person can prepare for the confrontation, can assess the cost of the confrontation;
- confrontation/impact, in which the response takes place, redefining the situation, re-evaluating;
- post-confrontation, in which the personal significance of what happened is analyzed.

The moment of anticipation may be more intense in psychophysiological reactions than the confrontation, causing the stress of anticipation.

In the situation of untimely impact, in which there is no anticipatory moment, psychophysiological reactions can manifest after the stage of confrontation.

Coping as an adjustment effort is generally considered to be a conscious response to negative stimuli. But at the same time, as a learned adaptive form, it involves conscious effort only if it has been little practiced. The frequent use of a coping strategy leads to its automation and activation with minimal conscious control or even without conscious control.

Adjustment is a repertoire of learned behaviors. The inclusion in the coping processes of the intrapsychic phenomena called by psychoanalysis defensive mechanisms, by some authors, leads to the acceptance of the lack of voluntary and conscious effort.

A hierarchical description of the adaptive processes of the ego is provided by Hann (1985, Băban, 1998) who places coping at the higher level of adjustment. This is followed by defensive mechanisms with a relative degree of adaptability (e.g., intellectualization), and at the lower pole are located the nonadaptive, immature forms that lead to regressive, fragmentary adaptation.

Research methodology: The theoretical objective of this study is to demonstrate that a low level of sense of coherence and perceived self-efficacy leads to poor stress management and implicitly to a low level of quality of life. At the opposite pole, there is the reverse, namely, the high level of feeling of coherence, and perceived self-efficacy determines the individual to have an effective management of stress and therefore a high level of quality of life. The practical objective of this study is to probe the quality of life of the subjects through a questionnaire adapted for the eight weeks of isolation, for each week, covering ten all-encompassing areas of life. Also, in order to determine the level of coherence of the subjects, the scale of the feeling of coherence was used and in order to determine their perception on their own effectiveness, the scale of perceived self-efficacy was administered. To determine the level of stress perceived by the subjects, the stress perception scale was used. Another practical objective is to carry out an intervention plan that takes into account the deficient areas tested, namely where the scores are low. This intervention plan aims to serve the precise needs of the subjects and to be structured like a guide, easy to use by each subject. The general hypothesis of this study assumes that the level of stress is influenced by the level of self-efficacy and the feeling of coherence. Namely, an increased level of stress will be due to the low level of self-efficacy and the feeling of coherence. The ratio between them being inversely proportional.

The first specific hypothesis assumes that subjects with increased self-efficacy also have a higher level of coherence.

The second specific hypothesis assumes that the feeling of coherence contributes to maintaining a high level of quality of life.

The third specific hypothesis assumes that perceived self-efficacy contributes to maintaining a high level of quality of life.

The fourth specific hypothesis assumes that the initial stress perceived by the subjects in the first week of isolation will be higher than the final stress, the one perceived at the end of the isolation period.

The fifth specific hypothesis assumes that the average quality of life at the end of the isolation period will be higher than at the beginning of the isolation period.

The independent variable is represented by the test tools used in this study. The independent variable is unchanged in all study participants.

The dependent variable is given by the subjects' response to the received test instruments. No attempt is made to influence their responses in any way. The study only wanted to monitor the evolution of the quality of life of the subjects over a period of eight weeks of isolation at home.

Label variable: adults aged between 25 and 45, employed in a stable couple relationship.

The participants in this study are a number of 30 adults, married or in a stable relationship, aged between 25 and 45 years. Twenty-one of the adults who participated in this study are the parents of one or at most two children.

Subjects received an adapted quality of life questionnaire to monitor their isolation period more effectively. Additionally, they received the scale of the feeling of coherence and the perceived self-efficacy. To monitor the level of stress, the stress perception scale was applied at the beginning of the isolation period and at the end of it.

The method of quantitative data collection was performed online, during the isolation period due to the pandemic, between March 15, 2020 and May 10, 2020. The stress perception scale was applied twice to the subjects participating in the study. This should check the level of perceived stress during the beginning of the pandemic, March 15–22 and during the end period, May 4–10. The stress perception scales and the perceived self-efficacy scales were applied only once. The questionnaire to assess the quality of life of the subjects was also applied only once.

The questionnaires were implemented using Google Forms, and the data collected was processed using SPSS and Google Sheets. The tools used in this study are the following: – Stress perception scale (initial and final) (Annex 4) – Scale for the feeling of coherence (Annex 2) – Perceived self-efficacy scale (Annex 3) – Quality of life questionnaire – adapted (Annex 1).

7.2 Obtained Results

The results obtained in this experiment are presented in two ways, quantitatively – by analyzing the data collected using the tools used, and qualitatively – by psychological interpretation of what emerged from the experiment.

7.3 Data Presentation and Analysis

The SPSS program was used to compare the collected data. In the following, we have made a brief description of the data provided by the statistical program.

Tab. 1: Correlation between initial stress, final stress, coherence, and self-efficacy

Correlations					
		Stress Initial	**Coherence**	**Self-efficacy**	**StresFinal**
StresInitial	Pearson Correlation	1	−.641**	−.567**	.644**
	Sig. (2-tailed)		.000	.001	.000
	N	30	30	30	30
Coherence	Pearson Correlation	−.641**	1	.809**	−.678**
	Sig. (2-tailed)	.000		.000	.000
	N	30	30	30	30
Autoeficacitate	Pearson Correlation	−.567**	.809**	1	−.541**
	Sig. (2-tailed)	.001	.000		.002
	N	30	30	30	30
StresFinal	Pearson Correlation	.644**	−.678**	−.541**	1
	Sig. (2-tailed)	.000	.000	.002	
	N	30	30	30	30
TotalLifeQuality	Pearson Correlation	−.737**	.455*	.505**	−.590**
	Sig. (2-tailed)	.000	.012	.004	.001
	N	30	30	30	30

**. Correlation is significant at the 0.01 level (2-tailed).
*. Correlation is significant at the 0.05 level (2-tailed).

This study started from the general hypothesis that assumes that the level of stress is influenced by the level of self-efficacy and the feeling of coherence.

Correlation between the initial stress, perceived by the subjects at the beginning of the isolation period, the final stress, perceived by the subjects at the end of the isolation period, and the feeling of self-efficacy and coherence.

As can be seen, all correlations are significant. Especially the correlations between stress, coherence, and self-efficacy. Tab. 1 shows that stress values remain high when perceived self-efficacy and a sense of consistency are low.

Tab. 2: Correlation between initial stress, coherence, self-efficacy, final stress and total quality of life. This table is a separate part of Tab. 1. Also, the quality of life is correlated with the values of perceived stress, and when the latter is high and the quality of life is low.

Correlations		
		TotalLifeQuality
StresInitial	Pearson Correlation	–.737
	Sig. (2-tailed)	.000
	N	30
Coherence	Pearson Correlation	.455**
	Sig. (2-tailed)	.012
	N	30
Self-efficacy	Pearson Correlation	.505**
	Sig. (2-tailed)	.004
	N	30
StresFinal	Pearson Correlation	–.590**
	Sig. (2-tailed)	.001
	N	30
TotalLifeQuality	Pearson Correlation	1**
	Sig. (2-tailed)	
	N	30

**. Correlation is significant at the 0.01 level (2-tailed).
*. Correlation is significant at the 0.05 level (2-tailed).

7.4 Psychological Interpretation Data

This study started from the general hypothesis that assumes that the level of stress is influenced by the level of self-efficacy and the feeling of coherence. Namely, an increased level of stress will be due to the low level of self-efficacy and the feeling of coherence. The ratio between them being inversely proportional.

The results obtained in this study validate the general hypothesis. It is confirmed that the level of stress is influenced by the level of perceived self-efficacy and that of the feeling of coherence. Moreover, the relationship between them is inversely proportional. Perceived stress values increase in people with low values of self-efficacy and consistency.

Therefore, subjects who are convinced of their abilities to mobilize the cognitive and motivational resources necessary to successfully meet the obstacles encountered (perceived self-efficacy) will have a lower level of stress.

And subjects with a global cognitive orientation toward the belief that both internal and external stimuli encountered throughout life can be explainable and predictable, that they have the resources to cope with stimuli, and that their involvement and effort are justified because the demands make sense and purpose (sense of coherence), and they have low values of perceived stress.

The first secondary hypothesis assumes that subjects with increased self-efficacy also have a higher level of coherence. This hypothesis is confirmed, and subjects who have moderate and high values of perceived self-efficacy also have average and high values of the feeling of coherence, which indicates a possible connection between these two features. Namely, a subject with a high level of self-efficacy is more likely to have a medium to high level of coherence.

The second specific hypothesis assumes that the feeling of coherence contributes to maintaining a high level of quality of life. This hypothesis is confirmed, this aspect can be observed in the correlations in Tab. 2 and in graph 5. When the values of coherence are low, the quality of life level is low. The relationship between these two variables is directly proportional. Subjects who obtained medium to low values of coherence also had low values in the quality of life questionnaire.

The third specific hypothesis assumes that perceived self-efficacy contributes to maintaining a high level of quality of life. This hypothesis is confirmed, subjects who have a high level of perceived self-efficacy also have a medium to high level of quality of life. From this relationship we can conclude that perceived self-efficacy contributes to maintaining the quality of life.

The fourth specific hypothesis assumes that the initial stress perceived by the subjects in the first week of isolation will be higher than the final stress, the one perceived at the end of the isolation period. This hypothesis is partially confirmed, the values of perceived stress were higher in the first period of isolation, normalizing after the middle of this period and following a partially downward path towards the end of the isolation period. Through the graph with number 4, it is possible to observe the evolution of the values of the initially perceived stress, in the first week of isolation and the perception of the final stress, in the last week of isolation.

The fifth specific hypothesis assumes that the average quality of life at the end of the isolation period will be higher than at the beginning of the isolation period. This specific hypothesis is confirmed, and the quality of life is higher at the end of the isolation period.

8. Conclusions

The aim of this chapter was to investigate certain features of the subjects participating in the study, namely perceived self-efficacy and sense of coherence, and to determine whether their values will influence the level of perceived stress and quality of life. The period in which this study took place was one with stress potential. The subjects have never encountered such a situation in their lifetime so far. Therefore, the interval between March 15 and May 10 was a good time to test the effectiveness of certain coping traits. The results obtained by processing the data collected using testing tools, confirm that the level of stress is influenced by perceived self-efficacy and sense of coherence of the subjects. Moreover, the quality of life perceived by the subjects varied depending on the values obtained at the scales specified above. Subjects with low levels of perceived stress had high values of self-efficacy, consistency, and quality of life. And those who had high values of perceived stress had low values of consistency, self-efficacy, and quality of life. In most subjects, the relationship between coherence and self-efficacy was directly proportional.

The importance of the results obtained through this study is somewhat high, because this information can be used in developing a more effective psychological counseling plan. Specifically, knowing exactly what traits can help individuals cope optimally with stress we can create precise steps to raise the values of these traits. By creating a plan that aims to increase these traits, we are confident that subjects will have a better chance of coping with stress much better and raising their quality of life.

This study was limited by the inability to interact directly with the subjects. Although the subjects (declaratively) carefully completed the battery of tests, an improvement could have been achieved by applying the test tools face to face, making it easier to answer any questions that may arise. However, in the online environment, there were some subjects who wanted to be assisted at certain points of the tests. Another possible limitation of this study is given by the small number of subjects. An increase in the number of participants could reveal new correlations.

As a possible direction for the future of this study, I would also carry out a subsequent test to apply the psychological intervention plan and the observance, by the subjects, of the steps recommended in the guide to increase the feeling of coherence and perceived self-efficacy. In this phase of the study, I would apply the same battery of tests with a single change – the stress perception scale will be applied only once.

In conclusion, the results of this small study were satisfactory for me as a master student. Based on these, I will try to create in the following chapter a psychological counseling plan addressed to people with a high level of stress. In the last part of the chapter, I will present a guide to improve the feeling of coherence and perceived self-efficacy. This guide is intended to be an easy-to-follow document and will present methods of relaxation, mainly in the field of occupational therapies. The orientation toward this type of therapies occurs as a result of discussions with some subjects who participated in this study. Some of them stated that during the isolation period, they turned to different means of occupational therapies to cope with stress.

References

1. Antonovsky, A., *Health, stress and coping*, Editura Jossey-Bass, San Francisco, 1979.
2. Antonovsky, A., *Unraveling the mystery of health: How people manage stress and stay well,* Editura Jossey-Bass, San Francisco, 1987.
3. Antonovsky, A., *The structural sources of salutogenic strengths*, Editura John Wiby, Chichester, 1991.
4. Atkinson, L., Rita, Atkinson, C. Richard, Smith, E., Edward, Bem, J., Daryl, *Introducere în psihologie,* Ediția a XI-a, Editura Tehnică, Bucureşti, 2002, p. 675, 679.
5. Bandura, A., *Self-Efficacy mechanism in human agency,* Revista American Psychologist, nr. 37, 1982, pp. 122–147;
6. Băban, A., *Stres şi personalitate*, Editura Presa Universitară Clujeană, Cluj-Napoca, 1998, p. 17, p. 49.
7. Cohen, S., *After Shock*, Editura Paladin Books, Londra, 1991.
8. Coteanu, I., Seche, L., Seche, M., *Dicţionarul explicativ al limbii române*, Editura Academiei R.S.R, Bucureşti, 1975, p. 898.
9. Cannon, W., *The wisdom of the body,* Edutura Norton, New York, 1932.
10. Derevenco, P., Anghiel, I., Băban, A., *Stresul în sănătate şi boală*, Editura Dacia, Cluj-Napoca, 1992.
11. Elliot, G., Eisdotfer, C., *Stress and human health*, Editura Springer, New York, 1982.
12. Frankenhaeuser, M., *Dynamics of stress*, Editura Prenum, New York, 1988, pp. 101–116.
13. Hann, N., *Conceptualizations of ego: Processes, functions, regulations, stress and coping: An anthology*, Editura Univ. Columbia, New York, 1985.

14. Henry, J. P., Stephens, P. M., *Stress, health and the social environment*, Editura Springer Verlag, New York, 1977.
15. Hobfoll, S., Lilly, R., *Resource conservation as a strategy for community psychology*, Journal of Community Psychology, nr. 21, 1993, pp. 128–148.
16. Lazarus, R. S., Folkman, S., *Stress, appraisal and coping*, Editura Springer, New York, 1984.
17. Leahy, R. L., Holland, S. J., Planuri de tratament şi intervenţii pentru depresie şi anxietate, Editura Asociaţia de ştiinţe Cognitive din România, Bucureşti, 2012.
18. Lundberg, U., *Psychophysiological aspects of performance and adjustment to stress*, Editura Hemisphere, Washington, 1980.
19. Marian, M., *Psihoterapii*, Editura Universităţii din Oradea, Oradea, 2004.
20. Miclea, M., *Stres şi apărare psihică*, Editura Presa Universitară Clujeană, Cluj-Napoca, 1997, p. 19.
21. Mosey Cronin, A., *Occupational therapy: Configuration of a profession*, Editura Raven, New York, 1981.
22. Rapaport, A., *Culture and the subjective effects of stress*, Revista Urban Ecology, nr. 3, 1978, pp. 241–261.
23. Toffler, A., *Şocul viitorului*, Editura Politică, Bucureşti, 1973.
24. Selye, H., *The stress of life*, Editura Mc-Graw Hill, California, 1978.
25. Zlate, Mielu, *Psihologia mecanismelor cognitive*, Ediţia a II-a, Editura Polirom, Bucureşti, 2004, p. 273, p. 291.

Webografie

1. Borindel, R., https://www.cdt-babes.ro/articole/igiena-somnului.php, 2020.
2. Dragomir, C., https://doc.ro/lifestyle/tehnica-de-respiratie-care-te-calmeaza-instantaneu, 2020.
3. https://evolutiepersonala.ro/2017/07/22/cum-sa-faci-meditatie-daca-esti-incepator/, 2017.
4. https://color-mind.ro/terapia-ocupationala/, 2016.
5. Selhub, E., https://www.health.harvard.edu/blog/nutritional-psychiatry-your-brain-on-food-201511168626, 2015.

Gabriela KELEMEN

17 Children's Well-Being in Early Childhood Education and Care (ECEC)

Abstract: There are constant discussions about educating children at an early age as a priority for education policies in all countries. In Europe, particular emphasis is placed on the implementation of directions towards stepping up efforts to create an economic and legislative financial base to facilitate the development of the education system from the earliest ages, with a view to create an educational and social context that achieves a state of well-being for all children. By providing children with the necessary conditions for natural development from birth, they will develop their innate potential at maximum levels (Virgovski). In this chapter, we want to specify what is that state of well-being for children as it is talked about and presented in all research related to early childhood education and care and also to mark the main directions towards which we must move our efforts in creating the best living and development conditions for children at early age. We will focus on some ideas found in the literature that promote early age education as an undeniable need to grow a generation that is ready for social integration and that brings prosperity and added value to the future society. Focusing on increasing the chances of development for all children in the early years of life, giving them optimal conditions for education, health and safety services will give them the chance to develop optimally and the chance to continue the same throughout their life. In this study, we want to highlight the importance of introducing early education from the earliest ages and the need to carry out activities and games according to an age-appropriate curriculum, implemented by teachers specialised in early education. A quality education is based on a specific curriculum implemented by competent specialists.

Keywords: Early education, well-being, children, quality of education, care, curriculum

Introduction

In order to understand better what quality education at early age means, we need to explain some of the concepts commonly used in literature when talking about early, inclusive and quality education. The notion of education, social well-being, quality growth is discussed in all social and economic fields, as well as in the educational field. Social progress is determined by the level of education of the population of that society. A society that emphasises the quality of education will have short- and long-term benefits in all areas. Education provides undeniable opportunities in shaping a society full of prosperity and with a quality of life that manifests itself in all sectors of activity. In practice, it is shown that nations that focus on education by assigning means of development of educational infrastructure have remarkable social, cultural and economic results. Let us think only of the Scandinavian countries where a particular emphasis is placed on the education system, on supporting all young people to train, through substantial material efforts in support of everyone's access to education, thus training and shaping the future generation. The social and economic results are obvious, and the best results in international evaluation tests are achieved by educators from Scandinavian countries (PISA test) (ecd.org/pisa/pisaproducts/pisa2009).

So how can we support children in the early years of life so that they have high-quality educational influences? Why do children need in the first years of life to develop harmoniously, healthy, to their maximum capacity according to innate abilities. If we take into account studies on constructivist orientation with regard to the psychophysical evolution of the child, we should have a child-focused educational approach, focusing on those educational resources and learning activities that arouse the interest, motivation and satisfaction of the child (Melhuish, E., Quinn, L., Sylva, K., Sammons, P., Siraj-Blatchford, I., & Taggart, B. 2013). Focusing all educational and childcare actions will induce a chance for each child to physical mental development according to its nature and progress in its future school activity (Sammons, P., Sylva, K., Melhuish, E., Siraj-Blatchford, I., Taggart, B., Toth, K., Draghici, D., & Smees, R. 2012).

Recent studies conducted mainly on twins have shown substantial differences in the psychophysical development of humans. The educational context identifies the idea of well-being with the process that facilitates the full development of the child according to its nativeness, through access to education and care from early age, in empowered institutions, which provide opportunities for care and education to all children without discrimination, in an appropriate development and educational environment. It is known that in the development of human personality three factors are defining: heredity, environment and education. Studies in the field of neuroscience confirm once again the idea that the development of psychic processes is determined by quality educational influences started early (Reynolds, A. J., Temple, J. A., Ou, S., Arteaga, I.A., & White, B. A. B. 2011). Children from culturally deprived social backgrounds will have a poor start compared to children who benefit from a socio-cultural environment that offers opportunities for normal education and development. Neuroscience confirms once again the fact that the development of psychic processes is determined by quality educational influences started at early ages (Bernard, 2012; Dominguez et al., 2010).

These children will be less developed in all respects, that is, health, physical and cognitive development. Children's behaviour is influenced by the social and cultural environment in which they grow up; they tend to learn through imitation, and thus influenced by a precarious cultural environment, they will develop inappropriate social behaviours. A life lived in poverty, deprived of affection, education and adequate care will lead to problems that will manifest themselves in the child's subsequent social behaviour. We cannot deny the fact that the social origin of the child has major influences on its development. Unfortunately, social, economic inequities exist for a certain category of population, even in economically developed countries. What to do to eradicate these inequities!? There is growing discussion of integrated education, equal opportunities for education and socially economically disadvantaged children, as well as access to education for all children without discrimination. It is a moral but also social imperative. Again we emphasise the fact that education in early years shapes the child's future. The social capital invested in the child's early years of care and education is a capital with valuable future results (Eriksson, U., Apllund, K., & Sellstroøm, E. 2010).

1. Curriculum for Early Education

The attention of researchers has been increasingly focusing on developing a curriculum to guide the work of early education specialists towards those actions that really contribute to stimulating early age learning (Havnes, T., & Mogstad, M. 2009). The Ministry of Education also supervises preschool education, which must aim at the general, harmonious development of the child, from birth (according to some specialists even from the intrauterine period) in order to ensure a normal start in life. The age-specific preschool curriculum aims to respect the child's developmental areas, starting with physical development, alongside health and personal hygiene, continuing with cognitive development: language and communication, thinking, attention, memory, imagination, but with particular emphasis on socio-emotional development, an essential part in establishing the child's well-being (Bernard, M. 2012). All these curricular directions are essential for achieving an authentic education and involve adapting educational requirements to the child, customising and centering educational interventions on the child, in accordance with the psychophysical peculiarities of the child, with its innate potential, as well as by an early identification of the difficulties/deficiencies of each child. Childhood is the age of the game, play, therefore the whole educational approach for the early age must have as its fundamental activity the game with all its facets, and the toy as the main object of stimulating knowledge.

1.1. Correlation between Curriculum and Children Needs

The early age curriculum stipulates the need to put emphasis on:

- Play as a natural activity, specific to childhood, combining all categories of games according to the age of the children, but with a focus on free, unguided playing;
- Plastic artistic activities: drawing, painting, modeling, collages combined with practical/household activities;
- Eurythmic activities, music and music games, combined with motion games;
- Activities that stimulate the children's creativity through stories, fairy tales, memorisations and communication based on intuitive support;
- exploratory activities of environmental discovery through exploration, experimentation, observation and application;
- outdoor activities: free games, rule games; fun games; motion games; device games; sand games; walks; visits.(https://eacea.ec.europa.eu/national-policies/eurydice/content/teaching-and-learning-early-childhood-education-and-care-8_ro; accessed 11.09.2020)

It is also noted that there are great distances and differences between educational policies at a declarative level, which appear to be fair and reasonable, and those at the applicative level (Kallery & Psilos, 2002; Kavalari & Kakaka, 2004).

Accusations against educational policies relate to:

- inadequate curriculum to the interests of the child (Lawrenz, 1986; Kruger & Summers, 1988; Kruger, 1990; Kallery & Psilos, 2001; Kallery, 2004);
- poor professional training of early education personnel (Harlen & Holroyd, 1997; Yoon & Onchwari, 2006);
- subject-based approach of learning situations to the detriment of a holistic approach (see Eurybase Network, 2009);
- insufficient relationship between educational partners for a unified education (Dafermou, Koulouri, & Mpasagianni, 2006).

Quality education in educational institutions empowered to achieve early age education: nurseries, kindergartens, centres in association with parents will provide real opportunities for child development.

1.2. The Family Environment

The family living environment contributes substantially to the development of the child's well-being and promotes his/her natural development. When the child is offered various learning opportunities, they will fully contribute to its cognitive, emotional and social development (Camilli, G., Vargas, S., Ryan, S., & Barnett, W. S. 2010). A partnership between educational institutions and families is an asset to the full development of the child. If parents participate in lectures or at round tables along with other parents, the focus group will provide information and the ways of effective educational intervention thus favouring the development of parenting skills.

1.3. The Educational Environment

It has also been proven that the environment is the third teacher in the child's education. The child has the chance to compensate for an inappropriate family environment when attending appropriate educational institutions with a favorable environment, emotionally saturated, with many means of stimulating and promoting learning. Educators can contribute to the development of an appropriate educational environment in the child's family if, in addition to meetings, lectureships within educational institutions, private meetings will be held with parents. Educators should visit the children's home and build partnerships with other social partners: social workers, doctors, etc. This partnership has the possibility to identify the child`s early problems, to provide the necessary help and to support parents to cope successfully with the given situation. It has been noticed that the integration of early education along with efficient care has led to remarkable results in the psycho-physical development of children as well as remarkable results in school activity (Gormley, W., Phillips, D., & Gayer, T. 2008). A good start in life leads to social success, the development of social and cultural competences, normal development of cognitive abilities, especially language and thinking and also the prevention of inappropriate social manifestations. Studies have shown that children who received early quality education with parental involvement had good results in their future school activity (Reynolds, A. J., Temple, J. A., Ou, S., Arteaga, I. A., & White, B. A. B. 2011 Vandell, D. L., Belsky, J., Burchinall, M., Steinberg, L., & Vandergrift, N. 2010).

2. The Research Study

In this study, we have focused on analysing the answers given by teachers who teach in preschool education with the aim to improve the curriculum for early education of children between 1 and 3 years of age. Thus we have examined the information provided by the teachers and the directions of action so as to find the best directions of action, to form a rich child-focused educational environment.

2.1. Aim of Research

The aim of our research is to find out the best solutions given by professionals in education for the development of a child-centred curriculum that aims the child's well-being.

2.2. Hypothesis

Our hypothesis is based on the presumption that educators can contribute to the improvement of early education curriculum based on their classroom experience. If we presume that educators are specialists in early education, then they can identify the directions that have to be taken for the improvement of early education curriculum.

2.3. Method of Research

2.3.1 Investigation

The selection criteria of the subjects took into account both the quality of tenured teacher in preschool education with the first teaching degree in education, and the experience assimilated throughout the teaching career. The eligibility of the study relies on the teachers` competencies in identifying the strengths and weaknesses of preschool children in order to find the best solutions to improve the process of education and childcare services.

For data collection we used the interview applied to a number of 30 educators with experience in teaching (10 years experience with preschool work) for a period of 30 minutes. They were asked 10 questions referring to the usefulness of implementing a differentiated curriculum for early education for children 1 to 3 years of age.

Tab. 1. The question asked by the full-time teaching staff, with the didactic degree I

No.	Questions	1	2	3	4	5
1	To what extent do you consider important a formal curriculum for early education?					
2	Do you consider that education from 1 to 3 years must be carried out by teachers specialized in early education?					
3	To what extent do you think educational environment can improve child development?					
4	Play and toys which combine movement and sound may be the most user-friendly and educationally appropriate for early education					
5	To what extent do you consider early education is important for a better start in school and life?					
6	Integrated activities conducted in Early Childhood Education do help children recreate knowledge, canonic practices and relationships?					
7	To what extent must teachers know basic parenting skills?					
8	Developing emotional intelligence, self-esteem, positive identity in individuals is as important as basic care					
9	How important is the relationship between early education institution, family and community?					
10	Early education institution must be under the umbrella of Educational Ministry instead of Health Ministry?					

3. The Results

3.1. Data Collection and Analysis

All participants in the interview consider that the existence of a preschool-age adapted curriculum is necessary for joint requirements and equal opportunities for children, within which an integrative, holistic learning is approached, and learning situations are stimulated and motivated. Respondents stressed out the need to start education from birth for a good start in school, presenting examples from everyday life that confirm the statement (Fig. 1). As far as the teaching staff is concerned, it is considered that for the educational activities it is necessary to employ specialized persons in early education, with childcare studies with skills in early education. It is considered that only competences in the field offer a quality professional training, which includes elements of pedagogy, psychology, sociology and parenting. There have been a lot of discussions

Tab. 2. Sample size per each step in the methodological process

Sample Size	Step
Interviews	30
Response option evaluation	300
Item development per criteration	10
Validation	10

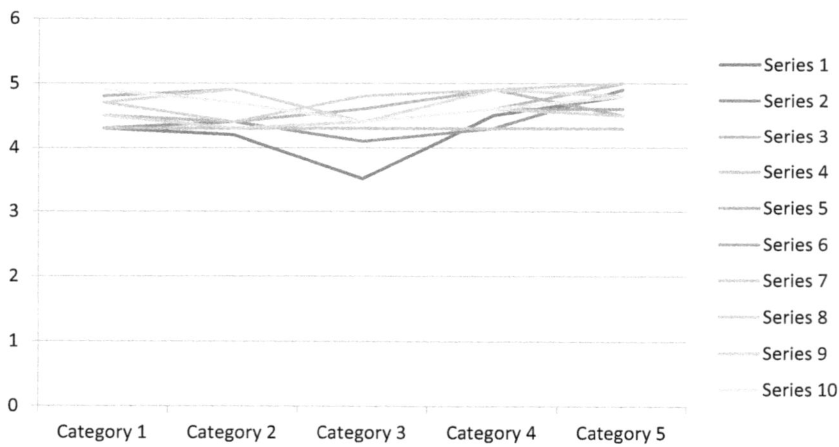

Fig. 1. Hystograme responding questionnaire

about a fair and close relationship with educational partners, especially with the children's families, in order to develop the children's autonomy and independence skills, with an emphasis on parental involvement for better knowledge of their own children and support for their development.

In Romania, the nursery system is organized by the Ministry of Health, fact considered unnatural by the respondents. The emphasis is shifting from care and education to education and care, so it is recommended a takeover of all nurseries by the Ministry of Education.

3.2. Discussion

The relationship between the training level of the responding educators and the results of the interview shows a statistically positive correlation ($\rho = .88$ ($r = 0.198$), confidence limits 0.133, 0.263), without identifying any significant differences between the results and the statistic of the result. The statistical coefficient *Q* is calculated for the relevance of the factor τ^2 (Higgins & Thompson, 2002). For a more appropriate accuracy and homogeneity of results, we have also introduced the statistical factor I^2 (cf.Higgins & Thompson, 2002). Our research hypotheses support the idea that field-related training of teaching staff and their teaching experience *determine* the appropriate directions of action for the education of preschool children, for the construction of well-being states and the development according to their capabilities. For this, I evaluated the Pearson correlation coefficient. Below we present the results regarding the correlation of the coefficients with the 10 questions:

- positive correlation between teachers' competencies and elements for improving the curriculum at an early age (r = 0.214, 95 % confidence limits 0.414);
- positive correlation between teachers' skills and practical experience and the need for specialised qualifications for early education (r = 0.204, 95 % confidence limits 0.140);
- positive correlation between teachers' competencies and practical experience and the role of the educational environment required for early education (r = 0.203, 95 % confidence limits 0.282);
- positive correlation between teachers' skills and practical experience and age-specific activities based on games and toys (r = 0.189, 95 % confidence limits 0.321);
- positive correlation between the competencies and the practical experience of the teachers and the conditions necessary for a good start in life (r = 0.199, 95 % confidence limits 0.280);
- positive correlation between teachers' skills and practical experience and the introduction of integrated activities as methods of stimulating and developing children in all areas of knowledge (r = 0.122, 95 % confidence limits 0.253);
- positive correlation between teachers' skills and practical experience and parenting skills (r = 0.127, 95 % confidence limits 0.189);
- positive correlation between teachers' competencies and the role of volitional and affective emotional development for the child's well-being (r = 0.095, 95 % confidence limits 0.239);
- positive correlation between teachers' skills and practical experience and educational partnerships and their role in early education; ρ = .80 (r = 0.173, confidence limits 0.399);

- positive correlation between the competencies and the practical experience of the teachers and the need to transfer preschool education from the Ministry of Health to the Ministry of Education.

Based on the results in Tab. 3, we find that there is a significantly negative correlation between the *competencies* and *the experience of the teaching staff with the first degree in teaching* and the answers for the entire questionnaire, which means that the directions are viable.

We find that the ideas supported by the professionals positively correlate with those confirmed by studies in the specialised literature regarding the main directions of action for the development of a quality educational system at preschool level. Such educational system should be child-centred, developed according to its interests and appropriate for education and childcare.

Tab. 3. Pearson correlation of coefficient

Corelația coeficienților	**r**	**p**	**confidence limits**
Q1	*r*=0.214,	p=0.003	0.414
Q2	*r*=0.204	p=0.001	0.140
Q3	*r*=0.203	p=0.002	0.282
Q4	*r*=0.189	p=0.003	0.321
Q5	*r*=0.199	p=0.005	0.280
Q6	*r*=0.122	p=0.004	0.253
Q7	*r*=0.127	p=0.003	0.189
Q8	*r*=0.095	p=0.001	0.239
Q9	*r*=0.173	p=0.003	0.399
Q10	*r*=0.242	p=0.005	0.189

4. Conclusions

We can draw significant conclusions by discussing with practitioners specialised in preschool education. The earlier the children's education starts, the better will be their start in life and the smoother their fulfilment path. Investments in early education, demonstrated by good practices in the countries that have invested in this segment, produce significant qualitative changes in the economic sphere of society. Studies confirm that investing in early education will bring benefits over time that will triple the initial investment. The research emphasises the need to reform educational policies in the education system so that the Ministry of Education provides more logistical support by creating a nursery infrastructure where children receive high quality care and education. If belonging to the Ministry of education, the nurseries can offer a specialised and quality education to the children. We emphasise once again the importance of children's interaction in learning activities led by educators specialising in early education, as a mechanism with a positive effect in the development of preschool children. The entire educational design must be based on a curriculum adapted to the children's age but also to individual needs, which aims at a holistic development, integrated through various learning situations, motivating incentives and leading children to free and creative development. The proposed activities will follow a bio-ecological model that will combine stimulating learning sequences for the development of mental processes, activities that will satisfy the need for movement and outdoor play of children. The quality of education provided to children is closely dependent on the teachers' quality and skills. Having professionals in the preschool segment leads to a quality education and has a positive impact on the level of children's development assuring a good start in life with long-term effects for both family and society.

5. Acknowledgements

We would like to thank all the teaching staff, preschool teachers from Arad, Timiş, Caraş-Severin counties involved in the research for their valuable contribution.

References

Bauchmüller, R., Gørtz, M., & Rasmussen, A. W. (2011). *Long-run benefits from universal high quality pre-schooling*, AKF Working Paper, 2011(2), AKF. www.cser.dk/fileadmin/www.cser.dk/wp_008_rbmgawr.pdf

Berlinski, S., Galiani, S., & Gertler, P. (2009). *The effect of pre-primary education on primary school performance*. J. Pub. Econ. 93, 219.

Bernard, M. (2012). *The Importance of social and emotional learning dispositions to the achievement and well-being of young children*. Melbourne: University of Melbourne.

Camilli, G., Vargas, S., Ryan, S., & Barnett, W. S. (2010). *Meta-analysis of the effects of early education interventions on cognitive and social development*. Teachers College Record, 112, 579–620.

Dominguez, X., Vitiello, V. E., Maier, M. F., & Greenfield, D. B. (2010). *A longitudinal examination of young children's learning behavior: Child-level and classroom-level predictors of change throughout the preschool year.* School Psychology Review, 39(1), 29–47.

Dumas, A., & Lefranc, A. (2010). *Early schooling and later outcomes: Evidence from pre-school extension in France*, Thema Working Paper n°2010–07, Université de Cergy Pontoise: France. http:// thema.u-cergy.fr/IMG/documents/2010-07.pdf

Eriksson, U., Asplund, K., & Sellstrom, E. (2010). *Growing up in rural community – children's experiences of social capital from perspectives of wellbeing.* Rural and Remote Health, 10(1322), 1–12.

Gormley, W., Phillips, D., & Gayer, T. (2008). *Preschool programmes can boost school readiness.* Science, 320, 1723–1724. 42 If you could do one thing..." Nine local actions to reduce health inequalities

Havnes, T., & Mogstad, M. (2009). *No Child Left Behind: Universal Child care and Children's LongRun Outcomes, Discussion Papers* No. 582, Statistics Norway: Oslo. www.ssb.no/publikasjoner/pdf/dp582.pdf

Julian P. T. Higgins, & Simon G. Thompson, (2002). *Quantifying heterogeneity in a meta-analysis,* Volume21, Issue11, Special Issue: 3rd Symposium on Systematic Review Methodology, doi:10.1002/sim.1186, https://onlinelibrary.wiley.com/doi/10.1002/sim.1186 (accessed 1.06.2020).

Kelemen Gabriela, *Developing early childhood education competences (early childhood education and care, ECEC),* Educaţia Plus, Volumul XXVII, Nr. 2, 2020, pp. 304–312, ISSN: 1842–077X, E- ISSN (online) 2068 – 1151, Editura Universităţii „Aurel Vlaicu", Arad, 10.24250/JPE/2/2020/GK.

Melhuish, E., Quinn, L., Sylva, K., Sammons, P., Siraj-Blatchford, I. & Taggart, B. (2013). *Preschool affects longer term literacy and numeracy: Results from a general population longitudinal study in Northern Ireland, School Effectiveness and School Improvement.* An International Journal of Research, Policy and Practice, 24(2), 234–250, doi:10.1080/09243453.2012.749796.

OECD (2010). PISA 2009 Results: Overcoming Social Background: Equity in Learning Opportunities and Outcomes (Volume II), Paris: OECD. www.o Melhuish, E., Quinn, L., Sylva, K., Sammons, P., Siraj-Blatchford, I. & Taggart, B. (2013). ecd.org/pisa/pisaproducts/pisa2009 resultsovercomingsocialbackgroundequityinlearningopportunitiesandoutcomesvolumeii.htm OECD (2010), PISA 2009 Results: What Makes a School Successful? (Volume IV), Paris: OECD.

Reynolds, A. J., Temple, J. A., Ou, S., Arteaga, I. A., & White, B. A. B. (2011). *School-based early childhood education and age-28 wellbeing: Effects by timing, dosage and subgroups*, Science, 9 June 2011, DOI: 10.1126/science.1203618.

Sammons, P., Sylva, K., Melhuish, E., Siraj-Blatchford, I., Taggart, B., Toth, K., Draghici, D., & Smees, R. (2012). *Effective Pre-School, Primary and Secondary Education Project (EPPSE 3–14) – Influences on students' attainment and progress in Key Stage 3: Academic outcomes in English, maths and science in Year 9*. London: DfE. www.education.gov.uk/publications/RSG/NewRsgPublications/Pagel/ DFE-RB184A

UNICEF, The Convention on the Rights of the Child: The children's version, https://www.unicef.org/child-rights-convention/convention-text-childrens-version (Accesed on 3.11.2020) https://eacea.ec.europa.eu/national-policies/eurydice/content/organisation-early-childhood-education-and-care-8_ro

Vandell, D. L., Belsky, J., Burchinall, M., Steinberg, L., & Vandergrift, N. (2010). *Do effects of early child care extend to age 15 years? Results from the NICHD study of early child care and youth development*, Child Development, 81, 737–756. https://eacea.ec.europa.eu/national-policies/eurydice/content/teaching-and-learning-early-childhood-education-and-care-8_ro

www.ingramcontent.com/pod-product-compliance
Ingram Content Group UK Ltd.
Pitfield, Milton Keynes, MK11 3LW, UK
UKHW020153290926
15471UKWH00005B/852

9 783631 852781